Dealing with Deities

Dealing with Deities
The Ritual Vow in South Asia

EDITED BY

SELVA J. RAJ

AND

WILLIAM P. HARMAN

STATE UNIVERSITY OF NEW YORK PRESS

Published by
State University of New York Press, Albany

©2006 State University of New York

All rights reserved

Printed in the United States of America

No part of this book may be used or reproduced in any manner whatsoever
without written permission. No part of this book may be stored in a retrieval system
or transmitted in any form or by any means including electronic, electrostatic,
magnetic tape, mechanical, photocopying, recording, or otherwise
without the prior permission in writing of the publisher.

For information, contact State University of New York Press, Albany, NY
www.sunypress.edu

Production by Kelli Williams
Marketing by Anne M. Valentine

Library of Congress Cataloging-in-Publication Data

Dealing with deities : the ritual vow in South Asia ; edited by Selva J. Raj, William P. Harman.
    p. cm.
  Includes bibliographical references and index.
  ISBN 0-7914-6707-4 (hardcover : alk. paper) — ISBN-13: 978-0-7914-6708-4 (pbk. alk. paper)
  1. South Asia—Religious life and customs. 2. Vows. I. Raj, Selva J. II. Harman, William P.

BL1055.D44 2006
204'.46—dc22
                                                                2005014625

ISBN-13: 978-0-7914-6707-7 (hardcover : alk. paper)

10 9 8 7 6 5 4 3 2 1

For
*J. Charles Amalathas, Bindu Madhok, George Strander,
Richard Good, and Lilan Laishley*

Contents

Maps and Illustrations — ix

Acknowledgments — xiii

Sites Associated with Vow Rituals — xvii

1. Introduction: The Deal with Deities—Ways Vows Work in South Asia
   Selva J. Raj and William P. Harman — 1

2. "The Vow": A Short Story
   Shankarrao Kharat — 15

I. Getting What You Want

3. Negotiating Relationships with the Goddess
   William P. Harman — 25

4. Shared Vows, Shared Space, and Shared Deities: Vow Rituals among Tamil Catholics in South India
   Selva J. Raj — 43

5. Religious Vows at the Shrine of Shahul Hamid
   Vasudha Narayanan — 65

6. In the Company of *Pirs*: Making Vows, Receiving Favors at Bangladeshi Sufi Shrines
   Sufia Uddin — 87

7. *Bara*: Buddhist Vows at Kataragama
   Sunil Goonasekera — 107

8. Performing Vows in Diasporic Contexts: Tamil Hindus,
   Temples, and Goddesses in Germany
   Martin Baumann   129

II. Getting What You Need

9. Singing a Vow: Devoting Oneself to Shiva through Song
   Karen Pechilis   147

10. Monastic Vows and the Ramananda Sampraday
    Ramdas Lamb   165

11. Negotiating Karma, Merit, and Liberation: Vow-taking
    in the Jain Tradition
    M. Whitney Kelting   187

12. Vows in the Sikh Tradition
    Louis E. Fenech and Pashaura Singh   201

III. Getting Nothing At All

13. When Vows Fail to Deliver What They Promise:
    The Case of Shyamavati
    Tracy Pintchman   219

14. Two Critiques of Women's Vows
    Jack E. Llewellyn   235

IV. Conclusion: Some Promising Possibilities

15. Toward a Typology of South Asian Lay Vows
    Selva J. Raj and William P. Harman   249

Glossary   257

Contributors   269

Appendix: Essays Arranged According to Tradition   273

Index   275

Maps and Illustrations

Map 1 Sites associated with ritual vows	xix
Figure 3:1 Small roadside Mariyamman shrine in Tirunelveli district	26
Figure 3.2 A woman performing the rice-flour healing ritual on a man in Samayapuram	30
Figure 3.3 A renouncer at the Mariyamman Samayapuram temple	31
Figure 3.4 A female in ecstatic trance carrying a firepot inside the Mariyamman Samayapuram temple	34
Figure 3.5 Christian husband and wife carrying a firepot at the Samayapuram Mariyamman temple	35
Figure 3.6 Mother and son (who was healed of paralysis) carrying firepot to Mariyamman temple; the mother vowed her son would carry a firepot every year for the rest of his life in gratitude for the healing	37
Figure 3.7 Ecstatic dancing in front of Mariyamman temple by worshippers who have been healed by the goddess	38
Figure 4.1 Shrine of St. John de Britto, Oriyur	46
Figure 4.2 A young boy has his head shaved as a sign of dedication to St. John de Britto	50
Figure 4.3 A young girl has her hair shaved in fulfillment of a vow her parents had taken	51

Figure 4.4   A pilgrim mother and son at the shrine of
St. Anthony, Uvari in June 2000. The mother fulfilled a
dedication vow by having her son's hair tonsured to resemble
St. Anthony's hair style, locally known as *anthoniar pattam* — 52

Figure 4.5   A young girl offers a coconut sapling to
Britto and prays for health — 53

Figure 4.6   The parish catechist auctions a baby in
fulfillment of the parents' vow to St. Anne of Arulanandapuram,
Tamil Nadu, as the baby's mother looks on — 54

Figure 4.7   The baby's parents proudly show off the baby
to the villagers after redeeming her in the ceremonial auction — 55

Figure 4.8   Asanam meal served to female ritual surrogates
of St. Anthony — 58

Figure 4.9   A young possessed woman rolls on the ground
at the shrine of St. Anthony, Uvari — 60

Figure 5.1   Water pond behind Shahul Hamid's tomb;
the tallest minaret was built by a Hindu devotee — 70

Figure 5.2   Offering box outside the tomb — 74

Figure 5.3   Hindu women devotees in line inside the *dargah* — 75

Figure 5.4   Muslim women praying at the shrine of Shahul Hamid — 76

Figure 5.5   Women and men worship together at the *dargah* — 78

Figure 5.6   Descendants of Shahul Hamid say prayers
for Hindu devotees — 79

Figure 5.7   The sacred well inside the *dargah;* the waters of
the Zam Zam (the spring in Mecca) are said to flow inside
this well. Hindu women bathe here to acquire "merit" — 84

Figure 6.1   Women feeding giant turtles at the *mazar*
of Bayazid Bistami — 89

Figure 6.2   Poor and hungry visitors await a hot meal
prepared by *mazar* workers — 96

Figure 6.3   Husband and wife with son fulfilling a vow
at the *mazar* of Shah Jalal — 98

Figure 7.1   Kanda Kumara — 109

Figure 7.2	Wrap a coin in a strip of cloth and tie it on a lime bush	113
Figure 7.3	*Puja vattiya*—a tray of offerings	115
Figure 7.4	Making a vow elaborately by holding a coconut	120
Figure 7.5	Smashing a coconut on the rock inside the metal	121
Map 8.1	Tamil Hindu Temples in Germany, December 2002	133
Figure 8.2	Five men perform the rolling ritual around the Vinayakar temple in Hamm, Germany during the 2005 festival	135
Figure 8.3	*Kavati* dancers fulfilling vows during the Sri Kamakshi Ampal temple festival in Hamm, Germany, 2000	137
Figure 8.4	A young man performs a rare and highly demanding vow ritual during the annual festival in 2003 at Sri Kamakshi Ampal temple in Hamm, Germany	138
Figure 10.1	A Ramanandi family, consisting of both Tyagi and Mahatyagi members	171
Figure 10.2	Munjiya Baba	175
Figure 10.3	A young Tyagi, about to begin the practice of *dhuni tap*	179
Figure 10.4	Several Tyagis performing *dhuni tap;* the various arrangements of dried cow dung piles to be burnt reveal the number of years each has performed the *dhuni tap*	179
Figure 10.5	Several of the *mahants* or heads of the various Ramanandi subgroups joined together in procession to the Ganga during a Kumbha Mela festival in Prayag	181
Figure 13.1	The Ganges River flowing at the edge of Benares	221
Figure 13.2	Shyamavati using Ganges mud to make icons for use in Kartik *puja*	222
Figure 13.3	Women gathered in a circle ready to perform Kartik *puja*	223
Figure 13.4	Kartik votaries listening to a Ganesh story and offering dub grass	224

Acknowledgments

This book is our modest attempt to share with a wider public the richness and vibrancy of lay religious life in South Asia. A chance meeting at the Midwest American Academy of Religion in St. Louis began our collaboration, one in which we discovered a sense of intellectual kinship and an affinity for religion in southern India. Since then, we have sought for several years to identify what variables might consitute a central characteristic of South Asian lay religion, variables that, we suspected, might transcend religious, cultural, ethnic, and geographic boundaries. Eventually, we found ourselves focusing on the phenomenon of lay vows. We settled on a plan to investigate the practice of vow-taking in the six major religious traditions of South Asia (Hinduism, Islam, Christianity, Jainism, Buddhism, and Sikhism).

In conversations with colleagues specializing in various South Asian religious traditions, we discovered a common concern for vows as ritual anchors in the lives of the faithful throughout much of South Asia. We organized a panel entitled "Dealing with the Deity: Religious Vows in South Asian Hindu, Muslim, and Christian Places of Worship" for the annual meeting of the American Academy of Religion in 1998 in Orlando as a prelude to an edited volume. With Paul Courtright presiding, Tracy Pintchman, Vasudha Narayanan, William Harman, and Selva Raj presented papers on Hindu, Muslim, and Christian vows. Mary McGee served as respondent at this panel. We thank the participants for enthusiastically signing onto the project long before we were certain of its eventual outcome. Several members in the audience—too many to mention by name—offered constructive feedback and helpful suggestions for which we are grateful. Encouraged by colleagues' interest and support, we organized two panels for the 18th Quinquennial Congress of the International Association for the History of Religions in Durban, South Africa, where a new team of scholars, including Martin Baumann, Jack Llewellyn, and Karen Pechilis, presented their research on the subject of lay vows. The feedback and support we received after these panels provided further stimulus to forge ahead with our project. We owe a huge debt of gratitude to each of our contributors for their intellectual generosity, collegiality, patience, and understanding as this volume took shape. Their collective expertise has been a source of constant reinvigoration for us.

We offer our thanks to the many scholars who first isolated the vow as a basic element in the lives of South Asian women. Their studies provided sensitive and sensible models for our own research on lay vows in South Asia. Notable among these author–investigators are Susan Wadley, Anne Pearson, Mary McGee, Ann Gold, and June McDaniel. Our special thanks to Ann Gold, who recognized before we did that "dealing with deities" is an appropriate way to talk about South Asian religious activity. Corinne Dempsey, Rachel McDermott, and Paul Watt supported our work in various ways. They deserve special thanks. We wish to express our sincere gratitude to the anonymous reviewers of our initial manuscript. They provided insightful and constructive comments that greatly aided in revising the essays. On the home fronts, we are indebted to Albion College for the Stanley S. Kresge endowed professorship and two Hewlett-Mellon grants that supported Selva Raj's field research. Our thanks are also due to Albion College's Instructional Technology staff, especially Cathy Saville, Melinda Kraft, Robin Miller, and Ralph Haughton for providing valuable technical support. The Martha Rieth Faculty Research Fellowship awarded by DePauw University to William Harman provided both time and funds for much of the preliminary research and writing that led to the book we now have. We are grateful for that assistance as well as for the assistance of the University Honors program and Professor Greg O'Dea of the University of Tennessee at Chattanooga. The Honors program made available Derek Gosma, who patiently and cheerfully assembled parts of the index. We are deeply indebted to Nancy Ellegate, Senior Acquisitions Editor at the State University of New York Press, for her remarkable patience, uncommon practical wisdom, and exemplary humanity in the preparation of this manuscript. We thank Kelli Williams, Senior Production Editor at the State University of New York Press, for her assistance and counsel, and Dana Foote for her careful copyediting of the manuscript. Our thanks also to the State University of New York Press for permission to reprint " 'The Vow': A Short Story," by Shankarrao Kharat and to use four photographs (Figures 13.1, 13.2, 13.3, and 13.4) that appear in Tracy Pintchman's recent book *Guests at God's Wedding: Celebrating Kartik among the Women of Benares* (2005).

The contributors and the editors express their deep appreciation and gratitude to the countless South Asian devotees who generously and willingly shared their lives and cherished stories with us. We have been abundantly enriched by this contact. During the summer of 2002, together we visited several of the sites mentioned in the essays in this volume. We shall never forget the remarkable receptions we received at St. John de Britto Shrine in Oriyur, at Kabaleeshwarar

Temple in Chennai, at the Samayapuram Mariyamman Temple, at the Bangla Saheb Gurdwara in New Delhi, and at the dargah of Shahul Hamid in Nagore. Whitney Kelting was our hostess when we visited the Jain community in Pune where our welcome was as touching as it was informative. Kamal Mustafa took us under his wing in Chittagong and helped us to visit every Muslim Sufi shrine in the region. His gracious enthusiasm was infectious and inspiring. A finer source of information on Islam in Chittagong would be almost impossible to find.

Selva J. Raj
William P. Harman
Albion and Chattanooga

Sites Associated with Ritual Vows

Arulanandapuram: A tiny Catholic village near Madurai, Tamil Nadu, where the shrine of St. Anne is located.

Ayodhya: An ancient north Indian city sacred to Hindus and Buddhists, and home to many Ramananda Sampraday ascetics.

Benares: Hindu holy city and pilgrimage site on the banks of the Ganges River, where millions of Hindus bathe to gain earthly blessings and ultimate liberation. Hindu women's communities studied by Pintchman regularly undertake domestic vows here.

Chennai: Formerly known as Madras, Chennai is the capital of the state of Tamil Nadu and a major city for Shaiva devotion. The famed Kabaleeshwarar temple is located in Chennai.

Chittagong: A major port town in Bangladesh that has scores of Sufi Muslim shrines (*mazars*).

Kataragama: Major center in Sri Lanka for vow rituals and for the worship of Kanda Kumara. Here Buddhists, Hindus, and Christians dedicate vow rituals to a popular Hindu deity.

Nagore: Location of the tomb of Shahul Hamid where vow rituals are offered in Tamil Nadu by Hindus and Muslims.

New Delhi: Capital city of India and location of a major Sikh temple (*gurdwara*).

Oriyur: Martyrdom site of St. John de Britto and a major pilgrimage center for various vow rituals in rural southeastern Tamil Nadu.

Pune: A major city in western India and home to a large concentration of Svetembra Jains.

Samayapuram: Village location of a major temple near Tiruchirapalli dedicated to Mariyamman, the Tamil goddess of disease and healing.

Uvari: A coastal village in Tamil Nadu and location of a major Catholic pilgrimage center dedicated to St. Anthony.

Sites Associated with Ritual Vows xix

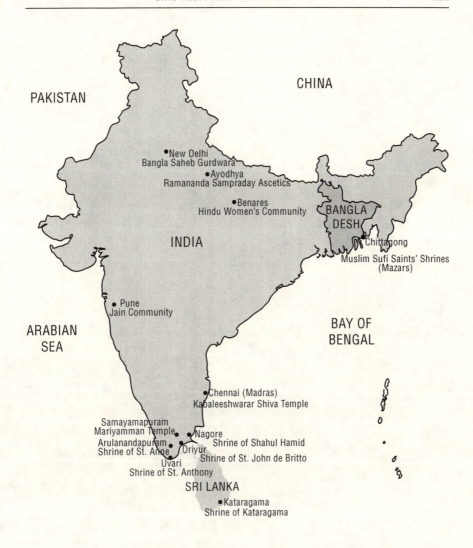

1

Introduction
The Deal with Deities—Ways Vows Work in South Asia

SELVA J. RAJ AND WILLIAM P. HARMAN

Setting out to find common threads among the major religious traditions of South Asia— Hinduism, Islam, Christianity, Buddhism, Sikhism, and Jainism— had better be a daunting task. Our resolve here is to propose a few modest but significant generalizations about six major religious traditions as they are understood by specialist scholars who offer here their collective expertise. The ambitious abstraction of our task may be, we hope, balanced by the fact that we are offering specific studies of particular religious practices in specific locations involving particular groups of devotees. Still, the sacred places studied vary enormously. They include the Muslim shrine of Shahul Hamid in Nagore; the Hindu Mariyamman temple at Samayapuram in Tamil Nadu; newly constructed Hindu temples for Sri Lankan immigrants in Germany; the majestic Sikh Bangla Saheb Gurdwara in New Delhi; Sufi Muslim shrines (*mazars*) in Chittagong, Bangladesh; Christian shrines in southern India, including those dedicated to St. Anne, St. Anthony, and St. John de Britto; and the Buddhist Kanda Kumara Shrine in Kataragama, Sri Lanka. Culturally, historically, and geographically we propose to cut across a wide swath of spiritually significant locations and traditions.

Well before undertaking this project we were aware that scholars have quibbled—and continue to quibble, almost ad nauseam—in their attempts to isolate the defining features of religiosity in South Asia. One ominous instance: Hinduism, one of the most dominant traditions of this region, seems to defy all attempts to define its essential or unique characteristics (Smith 1988: 32–55).

Recently, in a public forum that was later published, specialists in Hinduism brought a bewildering series of perspectives to bear on attempts to determine who is best equipped to speak authoritatively for that tradition.[1] No one perspective received enthusiastic acclaim.

In the context of such disagreement about identifying the distinguishing features in just one tradition among the six we are considering, skepticism about finding common features among them all seems wise. If it is so complicated to agree about the common defining features of a single South Asian tradition, how much more complicated must it be to deal with common elements in all six? Our determination to proceed with this project emerged slowly and only after we discovered in conversations with fellow authors in this volume that there seem to be basic common motifs, and that those motifs are possible to isolate and to analyze. In what we do here, we take refuge in the advice attributed to Alfred North Whitehead: "Seek simplicity and distrust it." At the least, our efforts may encourage our more cautious and specialized colleagues to ask larger, comparative questions about religion in South Asia. Perhaps, too, it will become obvious that elements of these traditions have been selectively dissolved in a historically, culturally, and geographically saturated solution, a solution that in turn seeps into and leaves its cumulative residue in unpredictable patterns on the traditions of which it is composed.

Our efforts to achieve a bigger picture might be regarded as premature or even foolhardy. Within and among these six traditions there is much that is dynamic and still changing. As readers will soon see, the "imported" traditions of Christianity, Islam, and Buddhism as described here respectively by Raj, Narayanan, and Goonasekera have had to accommodate to South Asian apprehensions of the supernatural in India and Sri Lanka. If it is true that travel changes people, the same can be said of religious traditions: when religious traditions travel, they must adapt to new contexts if they are to survive. Whether that adaptation achieves official opprobrium among authorities of that tradition is often an issue, and in all three of these described cases the official perspective taken toward certain kinds of religious vows is one of disapproval.

In short, culture and geography inevitably modify what traditions become and how they are practiced. From our perspective, the theme that emerges time after time in these essays is how a tradition learns to accommodate itself to changing circumstances, demands, and requirements. But more to the point, it is how faithful lay members of traditions will take steps to make a tradition meet and fit their own needs, often despite officially sanctioned instructions by the professional guardians of that tradition. Lay people will improvise on the traditions in many ways, but most spontaneously and effectively they do it by formulating and acting out religious vows.

Fenech and Singh discuss how vows have evolved into basic forms of ritual activity, even though there was no clear place for vows in the early Sikh tradition or in the scripture. The same is true of Islam in Bangladesh, where Uddin remarks that at important Muslim shrines we can even find officially sanctioned signs posted that forbid the taking of vows, an alleged form of idolatry. And yet, undeterred, religious devotees proceed with their vows, taking little notice. Even in the Roman Catholic context of St. John de Britto's shrine, Raj notes that priests will have nothing to do with many specific ritual vows. Yet, the vows grow in importance at this shrine, attracting Hindu and Muslim worshippers as well. Processes acting upon these religions have been called many things: "indigenization," "acculturation," "accommodation," even "corruption." But they are real, and in many ways they account for the primacy of vows we see today in South Asia.

Generally speaking, the impetus and energy for changes, and particularly for the changes we describe here, do not come from the top down, from the professional religious leadership directing lay people to conform to institutional expectations. Most studies of vows in this volume concentrate on vows initiated by and taken by ordinary worshippers, the laity. These people take vows because they need to seize control of their own perceived spiritual and existential fates. Depending upon others—and especially upon the professional guardians of a tradition—is something they may have neither the time, the patience, nor the confidence to do. Going directly, without mediation, to what they believe to be the source and solution to their concerns is an act both of faith and of devoted daring.

Lay vows, then, are "unmediated and personal" (Christian 1981: 31–32).[2] They are "made inside oneself'" and—like birthday cake wishes made before blowing out the candles—they are often not revealed to others until their fulfillment (Dubisch 1990: 126). But vows are more than this: they frequently involve an outward element that expresses, ritualizes, and sustains the interior dimension. Taking a ritual vow formally in the presence of your guru in which you declare your determination and intentions (see Lamb's chapter in this volume), offering a "down payment" in the temple to signify publicly a person's entering into a vow with Mariyamman (see Harman's chapter), and offering a written document (a *muri* or promissory note—see Raj's chapter) to a priest or the formal representative of a Catholic saint in order to receive a boon—all these are examples of the public dimensions of vows. In fact, some vows emphasize the public over the private, such as vows described by Fenech and Singh in the Khalsa Sikh community.

Public displays are basic to the vitality of the vow as a religious phenomenon, particularly in traditional and small-scale societies, where religion is "more outward than inward looking, more concerned with external images, with the public and communal than with the interior or the mystic." This is the realm where "morality is defined not so much by what one does as by whether others know about it" (Dubisch 1990: 129). Dubisch suggests that the emphasis on public manifestation and display of vows may "serve to mask the discrepancies that exist between popular and official interpretations" (131; see also Behar

1990: 103–6). In the South Asian context, vows reveal the tension between popular and official religions. The public displays of extreme physical hardship and spiritual endurance prominent in some South Asian vow performances seem even to strengthen participants' faith in the power and efficacy of the vow ritual. Spectacular fire-walking, tongue-piercing, hook-swinging, and baby auction rituals documented in this volume provide compelling and concrete South Asian examples. Conventional wisdom suggests that people do not willingly endure such physically and emotionally demanding tests unless reliable evidence—and traditional knowledge—confirms the efficacy and utility of such behavior.

As unmediated acts freely embraced and self-monitored by the laity, vows generally do not require or involve the participation of official ritual specialists either in their declaration or their execution. Nor do ritual specialists generally supervise or contribute to the efficacy of South Asian vows. Occasionally, and for ceremonial reasons, certain ritual specialists may be called upon to lend additional authority to the proceedings. This tends to be especially true when vow fulfillment assumes dramatic forms.[3] In certain situations, the presence of an official ritual specialist can be manipulated. In such cases the priest acts as a buffer providing official sanction and validation for an otherwise officially embarrassing ritual practice. This may help neutralize or nullify potential perceptions of deviation from orthodoxy. The blessing of a goat by a Catholic priest before its slaughter at Catholic shrines in south India is a common event and a case in point. The priest is no more than a silent and reluctant—frequently helpless and disapproving—spectator rather than an active participant since ritual leadership fully rests with the laity. This serves to reverse the structural hierarchy and traditional power relations (Bretell 1990: 68–73; Behar 1990: 96–106; Raj 2002: 50–55).[4]

A related feature of lay vows, particularly in South Asia, is their intrinsic informality, spontaneity, and flexibility. Institutional vows are usually solemn, public, and formal, but lay vows are informal and private. Lay vows couch in secrecy the intention of the person taking the vow. The nature of the informal vow, its stipulations, modality, locus, and execution are determined almost exclusively by the vow-taker and by her or his grasp of what local or family traditions demand. As such, lay vows are self-initiated and self-monitored. The devotee functions both as the agent taking the vow and as the authenticator of its having been suitably executed.

For the religiously and socially marginalized groups of South Asia—such as ascetics (see Lamb), women (see Kelting), and prostitutes (see Uddin)—vows can be undertaken without any official sanction and so act as the primary—if not the sole—means of access to supernatural powers. For others seeking not just divine gifts, but also official or popular approval, vows afford a public platform where the dramatic display of presumed personal piety and religious commitment heightens a person's prestige. As attested in McDaniel's recent study of Bengali women's vows in folk Hinduism, lay vows and vow stories serve as a religious index and a barometer offering valuable clues to grassroots folk traditions, ethics, and worldview. McDaniel writes: "The *brata* [Bengali term for 'vow'] stories provide models for ethics, compassion, and caring for others, making virtuous daughters and wives who fulfill the ideals of Hindu female behavior" (McDaniel 2003: xii).

The religious lives of devotees in much of South Asia are marked by a long series of seasonal and life-cycle rituals presumed appropriate for all people. Their timing and structure are determined by a person's age, life stage, astrological charts, or the calendar. But the practice of taking and fulfilling vows is quite different. It is not bound by this cycle. In this sense vows become the most important way an individual takes charge of her or his religious life and so moves beyond this standard, impersonal, traditionally based ritual round onto which an individual's spiritual journey is appended without any necessary reference to what the individual wants.

Given the variety and diffuse quality of this thing we call "the vow", and for which there are hundreds of different words in the different language areas this volume represents, we once again emphasize that the sum total of what we are able to uncover about vows comes out of particular contexts. The rituals described here encompass a wide array of forms ranging from the repetition of simple prayers, to the offerings of money, hair, coconuts, silver and gold representations of body parts, as well as more arresting performance/offerings, such as demanding pilgrimages, animal sacrifices, fire-walking, hook-swinging, and tongue-piercing rituals. And some vows—none we will ever know about—are drenched in silence and secrecy made in the form of a private resolution, communicated with no one, and acted out in utter privacy. What provides coherence and unity to this rich panoply of ritual expressions is an indigenous South Asian strategy concerning human collaborations and interactions with sacred figures. These collaborations and interactions are intended to bring about either profit in this world or improved soteriological status vis-à-vis the sphere of the supernatural. Whether deities are helping folk in this world or whether folk are achieving enhanced status in the world of the deities, people are dealing with deities, and vice versa. This, then, is the essence of what we call "the deal with deities."

This book would not exist if we did not believe that, in some measure, we have succeeded in finding some crucial commonalities among the traditions studied. In this effort, we want to concentrate on a single issue that appears consistently, indeed almost stubbornly. We have isolated the ritual activity of the vow as a basic aspect of how devotees in each of these traditions participate in religious activity. The practice of taking and acting on vows will not, of course, wholly circumscribe or define any single South Asian tradition. And yet, for a remarkable number of South Asian adherents, vows tend to be the primary and most accessible form of entry into a relationship with divine or, in some cases, demonic, powers. Immediate and unmediated access to the supernatural seems to be most readily available to those willing to take vows to those powers. This theme appears time and time again in the essays included here. Some authors suggest more, in fact. Lamb, for example, asserts that among the Hindu ascetics of the Ramananda Sampraday, vows literally define the renunciant: they are, as he puts it, "what gives life meaning." To be an ascetic, a person must take and perform specific monastic vows. Pechilis focuses on the vow as the very heart and soul of *bhakti*, or loving devotion, in Tamil Hinduism. She describes how the vow of dedication to a particular deity determines thenceforth the tenor and intensity of devotion in the life of a "god-lover" (*bhakta*). And in her moving description of the Hindu woman Shyamavati, whose faithful life of regular and devoted participation in specific cycles of women's seasonal vows was shattered by a series of familial misfortunes, Pintchman indicates how severe disappointments can bring a woman to the brink of losing her faith. A loss of faith for Shyamavati meant ceasing to perform religious vows. Being religious for her is defined almost entirely by performing women's religious vows.

If forsaking vows can be a visible indicator of moving away from a tradition, we can find a very different dynamic in Baumann's description of how immigrant Sri Lankan Tamils reconstruct their identities as Hindus when they migrate to Germany. There, vows taken and observed during festival rituals are—aside from the construction of Hindu temples—one of the most assertive and visible ways these immigrant Hindus can claim and affirm their commitment to a tradition that risks being lost or forgotten in a new world. Taking vows to Hindu deities on German soil demonstrates and reinforces who these immigrants are—Tamil, Hindu, Sri Lankan, and yet German.

Vows in South Asia can, for selected devotees, constitute the core—and sometimes even the entirety—of how the nonprofessionally religious (the lay people) participate in their tradition. In other words, what makes them devoted and religious within a chosen tradition is the vows they take. They are religious because they take vows. Women in Hinduism (see Pintchman's chapter), in Jainism (see Kelting's chapter), and in Islam (see both Narayanan's and Uddin's chapters) gain access to the ritual activity and spiritual benefits of their respective traditions through the vows they take. Taking vows is their way of entering into a tradition where there are fewer ritual opportunities available to women to participate in their religion. So true is this of Hinduism that the major studies of vows in Hinduism have focused on the religious activities of women.

But if vows can provide a means of affirming a person's membership and devotion to her own tradition, they can almost as easily act to do the opposite. They can, and do offer options to devotees to participate in religious traditions other than their own, formally outside their own. Vows not only reinforce your connections to your own tradition; they provide avenues for seeking assistance in other religious traditions, especially if you find that your own tradition is inadequate in certain circumstances.

Western sensibilities find this sometimes difficult to understand. Western monotheistic traditions are accustomed to the idea—and the practice—of mutually exclusive boundaries between religions; to the idea that a person must participate in only one religious tradition at a time. Normally, a bona fide Jew will not seek spiritual assistance in the formal activities of, say, Christianity, and vice versa. We have treated religious affiliation as a form of monogamy: being faithful to your tradition is as morally important as being faithful to your spouse. But the common folk among South Asian Hindus, Buddhists, Muslims, Jains, and Christians don't understand religious adherence in such exclusive terms. They are willing on occasion to step outside their own traditions and to take vows in traditions and in sacred spaces to which they do not formally have an allegiance. Here we have what may be the most extraordinary feature of commonly practiced South Asian vow-taking. With a vow, a person can affirm her own official and traditional religious commitment and yet, on another day and in another circumstance, she can move entirely outside that commitment momentarily to marshal assistance from supernatural sources normally worshipped by members of another, different tradition.

The South Asian "investor" in the performance of vows understands spiritual capital a bit like an investor in the financial markets regards financial capital—diversifying your portfolio increases the probability of success and often minimizes the risks involved in depending on any single source for propitious results.[5] Taking vows to deities of a different tradition becomes a bit like investing spiritually in a hedge fund. It becomes a quick and easy way to supplement the resources—possibly the limited resources—that characterize your own religious tradition. Several authors in this volume note this dynamic: Raj, in particular, describes how Christians and Hindus share an ease and freedom in taking vows at each others' shrines and to each others' deities. Because specific shrines are specialized, some concentrating on fertility, others on specific kinds of healing, and still others on such matters as passing examinations or getting jobs, each particular shrine will attract takers of vows according to their needs rather than according to their traditionally religious affiliations. Harman notes that Christians, Muslims, and Hindus find in Mariyamman a powerful source of healing not readily available within the Christian and Islamic traditions. Hindus turn to the shrine of a great Muslim saint, as described so vividly in Narayanan's chapter. Similarly, Christians and Hindus turn to a Muslim dargah, or place of worship, in the religious context described by Uddin in Bangladesh. Goonasekera's chapter treats the compelling attraction the Buddhist shrine of Kataragama exerts on Buddhists, Hindus, and Christians, all of whom take vows there. And Kelting describes the ease of interplay between Jain and Hindu traditions. Since the great Jinas no longer respond to human requests, vows directed toward Hindu deities make ever more sense for Jain women.

In selecting the vow as a distinctive quality of religiosity in South Asian religions, we are not claiming that vows are inoperative in Western religious traditions. In their chapters, Harman and Pechilis both acknowledge that vows are found in several Western traditions. In fact, significant studies on Catholic vows in Spain, Portugal, France, and Ireland have recently appeared. In her study of popular religion in Europe, Ellen Badone has convincingly argued that the notions of equity, exchange, and reciprocity act as the governing principles of popular religion and the vow or promise serves as the "the primary means whereby individuals can establish a reciprocal relationship with divine figures" (1990: 16). Badone argues that devotees bind themselves to particular patron saints/deities with whom they seek to establish a special, reciprocal spiritual relationship and whose aid they seek in times of need and crisis. Scholars like Christian (1972, 1981) and Boissevain (1977) link this phenomenon of supernatural patronage to the patron–client relationships found in normal social interaction. Based on his study of Marian devotions in northern Spain, Christian maintains that "the human modes of exchange with divine figures (and ultimately, with God) parallel their modes of exchange with each other. The shrines are the major exchange centers where debts to the divine are paid" (Christian, 1972: xiii). "The different ways of communicating with the divine," he continues, "and making bargains with the divine are related to the ways people arrange transactions with each other. Secular transactions of exchange can be arranged on a continuum from strict reciprocity to a kind of family communism"(168). In brief, when relating to the divine, humans replicate the norms and mechanics of social relations. These European studies parallel the religious dynamics and ritual patterns we detect in South Asian lay religion. Integral to the making and execution of vows is the sense of personal obligation, commitment, and indebtedness devotees express and manifest toward the deity. As Harman points out, the South Asian religious vocabulary, especially in Tamil, captures the notion that financial metaphors referring to "loans," "debts," and interest paid on a "loan" from a deity are quite common. The devotee pledges to undertake specific self-selected obligations until the request, or "loan," is granted.[6] Once the request is fulfilled, the devotee is indebted to the deity according to the stipulations of the original agreement, or vow.

What we find less frequently in the West is South Asia's remarkably widespread, short-term, practical, and utilitarian dependence on vows as a basic strategy for gaining temporary access to the supernatural for specific purposes. Still, other sorts of South Asian vows can be found. For example, the vows Pechilis attributes to bhaktas tend to be more like those found in the mainline Western traditions. The classical models for bhaktas (such as Manikkavacakar) become "god-lovers" for life. Their vows take on the gravity of a functional ordination. Similarly, Lamb's ascetics take a vow to become Ramananda monks, but follow that vow with a series of very specific vows that define the parameters of the life to which they are devoted—a combination of both the very diffuse and the very specific. And among the Khalsa Sikhs, vows focus less on an individual's supernatural needs and more on how a person seeks to become identified with the community, setting himself or herself apart from the non-Sikh population. There is a diffuse quality to the vow that presumes spiritual benefits for being inside rather than outside the Khalsa community.

For many devotees in South Asia, taking vows constitutes the full extent of religious belonging, though it is also true that those who opt for vows are likely to do so liberally, that is, to take concurrent or even serial vows in other traditions. At moments of need, South Asians may well regard distinctions between religious boundaries as fungible, arbitrary, often irrelevant. As Poincare is credited with saying, "It is the scale that makes the phenomenon." The sheer numbers of South Asians who take vows reveal that the vow is enormously influential and important to an understanding of South Asian religiosity. And it is this prodigious prevalence that leads us to propose that in its South Asian context—more so than anywhere else—the vow provides a comprehensible and comprehensive way to begin looking at religion in this part of the world.

Though we believe that the religious vow in South Asia is likely to have a more utilitarian and goal-directed focus, we need also to indicate that taking vows—especially vows to deities outside of your own tradition—involves a certain amount of time, dedication, concentration, and even spiritual preparation. No matter from which tradition a person approaches a supernatural figure, that supernatural figure is commonly portrayed as having a unique "personality." Each will have distinctive iconographic forms, specific narrative histories—whether written or oral—and traditionally transmitted preferences for certain kinds of gifts or offerings. Deities tend to be offended by specific kinds of conduct, and they have the ability to grant a range of boons. They have their unique abilities and talents and are understood to be able to grant only specific kinds of requests. It therefore follows that it pays for a devotee to know well the deity with whom she or he is dealing. Before assuming a vow, preparations are usually necessary. A person must become informed about habits and characteristics of the supernatural power involved. To perform the attendant rituals properly, the devotee must learn what offerings and rituals are appropriate. For some supernaturals, the offering of sacrificial meat is quite appropriate; for others it would constitute a severe offense. Performing a vow often involves prescribed preparatory periods of ritual fasting, sexual abstinence, and ascetic exercises.

All well and good: having suggested the prevalence, flexibility, appeal, and utilitarian character of the vow in South Asia, we will likely be expected to address the question, What is a "vow," exactly? Because no definition of "vow" was imposed on our authors when we made plans for this volume, readers will discover that several scholars here have offered their own conceptions of what a vow is and what it does. We object to none, but endorse none exclusively. A word's meaning can be deduced only after a scrutiny of the variety of contexts in which it is used. With this in mind, we want initially to direct your attention to the remarkable essays in this volume. These essays emerge out of the community and context each author studies. Harman, for example, emphasizes the process of negotiation in vow-taking, showing how vows can be utilitarian instruments to which people resort in requesting a boon from the Goddess. They do so by offering the Goddess something they have—money, ritual activity, devotion, service, a willingness to undergo pain—in return for assistance from the Goddess. It is a business deal and, once concluded or "paid off," potentially finishes the relationship between Goddess and worshipper.

Whitney Kelting's study of vows among Jains suggests that the sort of vows about which Harman writes are only half the story. Like the vows to Mariyamman, certain vows taken by Jain women are intended for familial well-being, prosperity, and protection. These vows are frequently directed to Hindu deities or to guardian deities. But vows directed to the Jinas, those enlightened beings who have transcended this world of rebirth, are nontransactional vows. No negotiation is involved. Vows do not effect the Jinas and no response is expected. Rather, the vows are more diffuse and are intended for "karma reduction," that is, for liberating the soul from attachment to this life of rebirth and passion.

In her treatment of bhakti, Pechilis adds another dimension to how vows might be understood: she emphasizes the unpredictability of human life and the importance of making commitments in the face of that unpredictability. A vow becomes a defiant affirmation, a declaration of assertion and confidence in the face of chaos, a commitment to structure in a world that to the faithless eye seems all too unstructured. She notes further that vows can be short-term or long-term; or they can be vows of acquisition (the utilitarian sort) or vows of maintenance. And finally, vows can set a person apart from the social world or place a person squarely in it as a result of specific commitments.

Possibly the best illustration of the long-term maintenance vows can be found in the chapter by Lamb. Ascetics should begin taking vows within a few months after their initiation, and their vows are generally not for the acquisition of worldly things such as health or wealth, but rather for more abstract, diffuse gifts such as liberation from the cycle of death and rebirth or unwavering devotion to their deity. The vows of this sort tend to impose some sort of discipline or sensory deprivation, including food restrictions. The determined pursuit of monastic vows and the spectacular nature of certain disciplines chosen constitute for these monk–ascetics both a reverence and an identity quite set apart in the Hindu tradition.

The maintenance vows of the Jain and Hindu traditions are, it seems, quite foreign to vows found in Christianity and Islam. The soteriology of neither of these Western-originated traditions is predicated on notions of rebirth and release from the round of rebirth. Like the brand of vow-taking we find in the worship of the village goddess, the vows Raj describes in the Christian context are vows intended to help people prosper and do well in this life. They are very much utilitarian. There seem to be certain unique features to the Christian Catholic vows described by Raj. First, there is a legal superstructure that takes ritual form in the writing and signing of a specific document that designates a vow's contents: a promissory note, in effect, signed by the person taking the vow and by an official representing the deity. Second, there are clearly designated distinctions between devotional and nondevotional vows. Devotional vows are more familiar and are treated in the chapters by Harman, Pechilis, Uddin, and Narayanan. In these, the deity is known, indeed often beloved, to the vow-taking supplicant. Nondevotional vows differ. They are intended to appease a supernatural power not particularly well-known or not particularly pleasing to the person taking the vow. Both kinds of vows are concerned with specific goals, and, in Raj's view, at least half of them are directed toward achieving fertility—human, agricultural, animal.

Muslim vows tend also to be more concerned with a supernatural power whose characteristics and history are well-known to supplicants. Requests described in both Narayanan's and Uddin's chapters are directed toward specific saints, or *pir*s, who once lived and whose hagiographies the supplicants know reasonably well. As with most devotional vows in Hinduism, vows to Muslim *pir*s are goal-directed and usually request concrete results according to the needs of the petitioner.

Defining vows becomes more and more difficult the longer we study them. They have a protean quality that makes them fascinating to study but frustrating to isolate. At this point, then, we can say that vows have much to do with entering into relationships with supernatural powers; with promises made, obligations incurred, and hopes that these obligations or promises, once taken on, will result in divine blessings or supernatural gifts. Having said that, we invite you to listen to some very accomplished voices that range from an Indian fiction writer's attempt to capture the power of vows in the lives of simple people; to Llewellyn's presentation of critical voices in Hinduism that wish to consign the vow to an instrument of superstitious female oppression; to a series of remarkable scholarly essays that locate themselves somewhere in between these two extremes.

Notes

1. For a detailed discussion of this debate, see "Who Speaks for Hinduism?" *Journal of the American Academy of Religion* 68, 4 (December 2000): 705–835.

2. Christian (1981) maintains that the "unmediated and personal" character of vows in part accounts for the lack of attention to the study of vows as an important religious phenomenon.

3. In her study of Greek Orthodox Christians' religious practice, Dubisch provides a compelling cross-cultural example for this phenomenon. She writes: "These vows are not overseen by a priest, either in their making or their execution, though they may be recorded by the church, especially if they involve the presentation of a gift to the church, or are especially dramatic in form. As examples of such gifts one may observe in the church a gold and silver orange tree ... a silver ship with a fish stuck in a hole in its side (representing the rescue of a sinking ship at sea), and a marble fountain in the inner courtyard" (1990: 126–27).

4. In her study of village Catholicism in Spain, Behar alludes to the disjunctive relationship between ordinary devotees and the religious elite who maintain an intellectual distance from folk religious practices based on mutual devaluation of each other's religious perspectives and practices and the ensuing power struggle between the two groups (Behar 1990: 77, 106).

5. Here, the word "investor" is used deliberately, since taking a vow involves devoting time, energy, and money for proper performance. Buying specific ritual objects and using them at an auspicious time determined by custom or astrology are important parts of the vow-taking process.

6. Pearson sees parallels between the vows *promesa* (a kind of conditional vow) made by Catholic women in rural Spain documented by William Christian (1972) and the *vrats* practiced by Hindu women in India. Pearson notes that in both cases "something is given up in order to secure something else, redemption or aid. In a *promesa*, a pledge is made involving some sacrifice of resources such as money or time, sacrifice of pride, denial of pleasures or the undertaking of hardships (e.g., making a pilgrimage on bare feet). These forms of self-imposed hardship may occur in a *vrat*. For both *promesas* and *vrats*, a specified proxy may be used. ... but the vow must be fulfilled or dire consequences are believed to ensue" (Pearson 1996: 3).

References

Badone, Ellen, ed. 1990. *Religious Orthodoxy and Popular Faith in European Society.* Princeton: Princeton University Press.

———. 1990. "Introduction." In *Religious Orthodoxy and Popular Faith in European Society,* ed. Ellen Badone, 3–23. Princeton: Princeton University Press.

Behar, Ruth. 1990. "The Struggle for the Church: The Popular Anticlericalism and Religiosity in Post-Franco Spain." In *Religious Orthodoxy and Popular Faith in European Society,* ed. Ellen Badone, 76–112. Princeton: Princeton University Press.

Boissevain, Jeremy. 1977. "When the Saints Go Marching Out: Reflections on the Decline of Patronage in Malta." In *Patrons and Clients in Mediterranean Societies,* eds. E. Gellner and J. Waterbury, 81–96. London: Duckworth.

Bretell, Caroline, B. 1990. "The Priest and His People: The Contractual Basis for Religious Practice in Rural Portugal." In *Religious Orthodoxy and Popular Faith in European Society,* ed. Ellen Badone, 55–75. Princeton: Princeton University Press.

Christian, William A., Jr. 1981. *Local Religion in Sixteenth-century Spain*. Princeton: Princeton University Press.

———. 1972. *Person and God in a Spanish Valley*. New York: Seminar Press.

Dubisch, Jill. 1990. "Pilgrimage and Popular Religion at a Greek Holy Shrine." *In Religious Orthodoxy and Popular Faith in European Society,* ed. Ellen Badone, 113–39. Princeton: Princeton University Press.

McDaniel, June. 2003. *Making Virtuous Daughters and Wives: An Introduction to Women's Brata Rituals in Bengali Folk Religion*. Albany: State University of New York Press.

McGee, Mary. 1987. *Feasting and Fasting: The Vrata Tradition and Its Significance for Hindu Women,* Th.D. dissertation, Harvard University.

Pearson, Anne Mackenzie. 1996. *"Because It Gives Me Peace of Mind": Ritual Fasts in the Religious Lives of Hindu Women*. Albany: State University of New York Press.

Raj, Selva, J. 2002. "The Jordan, the Ganges, and the Mountain: The Three Strands of Santal Popular Catholicism." In *Popular Christianity in India: Riting Between the Lines,* eds. Selva J. Raj and Corinne G. Dempsey, 39–60. Albany: State University of New York Press.

Smith, Brian. 1988. "Exorcising the Transcendent: Strategies for Defining Hinduism and Religion." *History of Religions* 27: 32–55.

2

"The Vow": A Short Story

Shankarrao Kharat
Translated by Maxine Berntsen

Full-moon day, the day to keep the vow to the goddess. Midnight had passed, the night was almost over. Under its basket, the rooster crowed. And Tatya Nailk sat up with a start. His wife Sarji sat up too. Tatya got up and walked to the corner of the room. He leaned down and felt with his hand under the basket, listening to the muffled *krr krr* of the chicken inside. He rose again, took the board leaning against the door and put it on top of the basket. Then with a sense of relief he sat looking at the door. Without getting up, he turned his head and spat in the corner. He called softly, "Sarji, are you awake?"

Sarji immediately awoke from her doze. "What do you mean? Of course I'm awake! Look here, it is almost morning. Didn't you hear the rooster crow?"

"Of course, that's what woke me up." "Well then it's better to get started early making the food offerings."

"Yes, but it's still night. That's the first time the rooster has crowed and everybody is still asleep."

"Are you sure?"

"Why, I haven't slept all night, I've been half awake. Look it's not quite dawn yet."

This short story was originally written by Shankarrao Kharat and appeared as "Navas" in the Marathi short story collection Sangawa. It was translated by Maxine Berntsen as "The Vow: A Short Story." See Bernsten, Maxine and Eleanor Zelliott, eds., *The Experience of Hinduism* (Albany: State University of New York Press, 1988), 7–17. It is reprinted in this volume with permission from SUNY Press.

Though Sarji had tried to reassure him, Tatya was still worried. "But the sooner we get started for the temple the better."

Sarji answered quickly, "Yes, yes, that's true, but there is not a drop of water in the house, and this is the full-moon day of the goddess. How can I start without taking a bath?"

"Are you going to follow all those rules and waste time and not be ready to leave for the fair till everybody else has gone?"

"It won't take any time. You put a little water in the jar and I'll get my work done in a hurry."

So husband and wife talked in the early hours of the morning.

Then Tatya got up, opened the door, and went out; he stretched and cracked his joints; he walked behind the house and looked up at the moon. It was still high in the sky. Tatya looked around at Naikwada.[1] The whole neighborhood was still fast asleep. There was no movement anywhere, no sound of voices. The trees by the doorway were silent. Somewhere in the distance the bark of a dog fractured the silent moonlight. Tatya looked around again. Seeing that everything was still quiet he said to himself, "Hey, it's still the middle of the night." He went back inside the house.

Today was the fair of the goddess Mariai[2] at Deagon, six or seven miles from Tatya's village. It was held once a year on the full moon of Chaitra. Huge crowds always gathered. People came like thousands of ants. In bullock carts or on horseback they came from miles around. A rich man might bring a goat as offering to the goddess, a poor one might offer a cock to keep his vow. Some would bring food-offerings, along with a green blouse and a coconut for the goddess. Others would come prostrating themselves at each step or rolling their bodies through the dust; and when they arrived they would bathe the image in curds and milk. Some came to keep the vow they made the previous year.

Throughout the area the goddess of Deagon was known as a harsh and powerful deity. If a man did not keep his vow, it is said, the goddess would raze his house or cast thorny branches at his door. So on the full moon of Chaitra people would go with fear and devotion and would try at any cost to keep their vows. Last year Sarji had made a vow, "Mother goddess, let the crops grow well and watch over my children. And next year I will offer a cock and give a feast at your door."

Sarji kept firmly in her mind that she had to keep her vow. So when the full moon of Chaitra drew near she set about making preparations. Begging a little from this farmer and that, she had managed to collect a *payli* [measure] of *jawar* [flour] and a few measures of wheat. The spices of curry were ground and ready, and she brought a measure of rice and a little jaggery from the grocer's shop.

Sarji had taken care of getting all the little things they needed, while Tatya had promised to bring the cock. He had kept his word and now they had no anxiety on that account.

She lay down again, keeping an ear open for the next crowing of the cock. Tatya opened the door, and hearing the sound of Sarji, called without getting up, "Are the neighbors up yet?"

"No it looks like it's still night. The whole place is still quiet. Even the birds are quiet. The moon is still up."

"Then why don't you lie down for awhile? Why are you staying up?"

"Do you think I could sleep? I'm worried about today."

"What are you worried about?"

"Well, there is nothing really, but I was wondering who all we'll find at the fair. We'll have to round up people for the feast. Every now and then they've invited us for meals, and now we'll have to pay them back."

"You don't have to worry about that! They'll all come flocking like crows."

"But it's a big fair. And everyone is involved in their own business."

"Don't worry, two weeks ago I sent a message to everyone —Maushi's daughter in Charegon, your nephew in Limbuda, and there'll be someone from my family. And we'll meet people from Itlapur and Ranjangaon there."

"Why, you've lined up so many! And how are you going to feed them all with one chicken?"

"So what if there are a lot of people? I'll make a big stack of *bhakris* [griddled cakes]. You put some water to boil in a big pot. The chicken is nice and fat. We can let the kids eat their fill. They never get a chance to eat meat otherwise; at least let them get a taste in the name of the goddess!"

"But all those people, besides you and me."

"Don't you worry. I'll take care of everything."

"All right, do as you please."

Their conversation was suddenly interrupted by a loud, long crow from the rooster. Tatya started. Sarji was shaken. Immediately Tatya called to his wife, "Sarji, get up, the rooster has crowed again."

"I'm up. That rooster must have been sent by the goddess. It wakes us up just in time." She looked at the white moonlight and said to her husband, "Now get up. Go to the stream and have your bath, then bring me some water from the spring before there's a whole line of people there."

"You look after your work and I'll take care of mine," Tatya said, taking a dhoti from the clothesline. He went outside. Putting a water pot on his shoulder, he went down to the stream. He washed himself clean in the water, while reciting the name of the goddess. Then making rapid trips from the stream to the house, he filled the water jar in the house.

By then the day had dawned, the sky became bright. Naikwada awakened. The birds began to twitter. Doors on the surrounding houses opened and people came out. The dogs that had been sleeping in the doorways came out in the yards. They stretched and ran about. In some houses the cooking fires were lit. Smoke started coming out of the roofs. The men and women from the wada [village] filed down the stream. A crowd gathered at the spring. Everyone was in a hurry to go to the fair.

Sarji plastered the earthen stove with cow dung, lit the fire, and put an iron pot on to boil. In the shed at the back of the house she sat on a stone and poured water over herself. Then she quickly scoured the pots and pans until they shone, put some sticks in the fire, and sat down to make *bhakris*. She worked rapidly. *Bhakris* after *bhakris* fell onto the griddle. A stack of puffed *bhakris* grew on the piece of cloth at her side.

Full-moon day had dawned. Tatya looked at the light and folded his hands in worship. As Sarji saw the mild rays of the morning sun cross the threshold, she called to her husband, "Say, you'd better get the kids up." She looked angrily at the children, muttering, "Brats, they run around all over the place chasing birds, then they sleep like the dead." She raised her voice again, "Did you hear me?"

"I can hear you. What do you want?"

"Get those kids up and wash them. It's full-moon day." Again she muttered to herself, "Damn kids, look at their hands and feet. You'd think a dog peed on them."[3]

"Why don't *you* give them a bath? There is a whole jar full of water."

"Just listen to him! I've got to make a whole *payli* of *bhakris* and I have offerings for the goddess to get ready. And besides, these sticks won't stay lit. I'm half dead from blowing on them."

"Take your time, and when you're done with everything else, wash the kids."

"Here I've already got my hands full and you just go on without even paying attention to what I'm saying. Now take some water in a pan and wash those kids!"

As the sun grew warm, Sarji's hands worked faster. The *bhakris* were more than half done. Tatya got the boys up and gave them a bath. He took their new clothes from the bundle in which they were tied.

Delighted with their new clothes, the kids frisked about like lambs, then sat down by the stove watching their mother with avid interest.

Just then the rooster crowed and began to call *ko ko*. The wily youngsters were suddenly alert. They immediately spotted the basket. They ran toward it and started to lift it up. Sarji raised her flour-covered hand and shouted, "Why are you looking under that basket? Are you going to go outside or should I give you both a good whack?"

The older boy, six-years-old, answered, "Mother there is a chicken under the basket. When did Baba bring it?"

At this Sarji got wild, "Damn you to hell! Why are you getting after that rooster? Are you going outside or shall I call your father?"

At that moment the rooster screamed again and began to cackle. The youngsters wheeled around from the door and dashed up to the basket. With their ears to the basket, they listened intently. They began beating on the basket.

Out of her mind with their antics, Sarji picked up a brass pot full of water and poured it on one child's back. He let out a yell and ran outside. Tatya came in and asked angrily, "What's going on here? Here it is full-moon day and you're making the kid cry!"

"Let both of them go to hell! They're getting after the rooster!"

"They're just kids you know."

"I know, I know. But you better throw a gunny sack on top of the basket. The rooster keeps crowing and people are passing by our house all the time. Can't you imagine what will happen?"

Tatya tried to reassure her, "What is there to worry about? We're practically ready to go. Once we're on our way we are as good as there."

Sarji retorted, "Have you forgotten that we still have the cooking and everything to do?"

"It won't take long," he answered.

Suddenly Sarji thought of something, "Oh go to the store and bring a coconut, incense, and camphor. Otherwise we'll forget it in the rush."

"Now you're ordering me around. And how am I supposed to pay the shopkeeper—knock out my teeth?

"Ask him just this once to let us buy it on credit. And don't say unlucky things!"

"But we still owe him some money."

"So what? Tell him we'll pay him back everything at harvest time."

"You mean he's going to take my word for it?"

"Instead of talking back, why don't you at least go and see?"

"You always bring something up at the last minute!" Tatya grumbled and got up to go to the store. Just at that moment Pandu Naik walked in, and hearing Tatya's angry voice said, "Sounds like a fight going on."

"You said it! Half the people in the *wada* have already left and we don't even have the offerings or the camphor, incense, and coconut yet."

Pandu casually poked his head inside the door and saw Sarji at the stove. "Vahini,[4] you're making a lot of *bhakris*," he said. "Looks like there's chicken or mutton for the fair."

Sarji laughed easily and answered, "No chicken or mutton, Dajiba—we're just getting ready a coconut and food offerings for the goddess."

"Just thought I'd ask." Hardly had Pandu gotten the words out than the rooster crowed loudly and began to cackle in fright. Hearing the crowing, Pandu said, "Well, Tatya, so there *is* a chicken for your fair. Hope I'm included."

"That's right, ol' friend, it's the rooster we promised the goddess."

"Whatever it may be, don't leave me out."

"Of course not, you know we wouldn't do that!" Tatya answered and left hurriedly for the store in town. By then Sarji had finished everything. She sprinkled water on the stove and leaned the griddle against it. She took a dhoti and started tying up the food, putting the stack of *bhakris* at one end and the offering at the other. For cooking the chicken, she took a big nickel-plated pot. Into it she put two brass plates and a water pot and tied them all together in a big cloth. She cleared everything up. And then, because she was going to the fair, she put on her best sari, the one with tiny checks. After she put on her new blouse with an embossed design, she stood at the door looking toward the town and waiting for Tatya's return. Keyed-up with excitement, the kids kept jumping around, running to the basket to listen to the bird, and slapping the basket with a stalk of fodder. "Mother, show us the rooster," they kept begging, while Sarji in her turn kept scolding them.

Meanwhile Tatya had climbed the bank of the stream and was hurrying toward the house. When Sarji saw him she went inside. Tatya handed her the incense, camphor, and coconut. She took them and tied them in the bundle with the food offering. Everything was set. Just then Tatya said, "Sarji, bring the stuff out to the door. I'll go and say a prayer before our Khandoba and be right back."

"Don't take too long. We'd better get started before the sun gets too hot."

"I told you I'd be right back," Tatya answered and hurried off to the temple at the western side of the Naikwada to take *darshan* [religious viewing] of Khandoba.

Sarji quickly picked up the bundles one by one and carried them out to the door.

Meanwhile, three men coming from the town left the main path and headed toward Tatya's house. They walked straight to his door. By then Tatya had returned from the Khandoba temple. His face fell when he saw Nana, owner of the big farm down below. He started to sweat. When Sarji saw the men, she hung her head. She recognized the *patil*[5] and the policeman and was scared.

As soon as he saw Tatya, Nana demanded loudly, "Tell us, Tatya, did you come to my farm last night?" Nana raised his voice even more, "It's all right to ask for grain, that we'll give. But that doesn't mean you can steal a rooster right out of my pen."

At the mention of the rooster Tatya quaked inwardly. His eyes turned toward the house. Still he answered calmly, "How would I know, Nana? After all, it's open land. It only takes a split second for a fox to run away with a chicken!"

"True enough! But how could he manage to get a chicken in the pen? Come on now, admit it!"

"Nana, I swear on my child I'm telling you the truth! If you say so, I'll place my hand on my son's head and swear before the *patil* here."

At that moment, the cock crowed loud and long. The cramped and frightened bird cackled noisily. Tatya was speechless. He sat down heavily, as if all the strength had drained out of him.

Hearing the crowing, both kids jumped with glee and ran to the basket, saying, "Mother, show us the chicken!" Meanwhile the policeman and the *patil* had taken custody of Tatya and set off for the police station. Nana went along taking his rooster as evidence. Both kids went dancing behind him.

Watching this whole performance, Sarji was struck dumb. She was at a loss as to what to say or do. Finally she picked up a bundle of *bhakris* and started after her husband. As she set off, she made a silent vow, "Goddess Mariai, get my husband out of this! And next year I'll give you a cock!" She put the end of her sari to her eyes to dry her tears.

Notes

1. Naikwada indicates the section of a village in which Naiks predominate. The term Naik is usually used for the low but not untouchable castes of this area, but the author does not make the caste clear.

2. The goddess Mariai is found in every village and usually is served by Mahars, although as the goddess of pestilence she is worshipped by all.

3. The author, himself an ex-untouchable brought up in a village, delights in the detail of village life, making the harshness of existence in rural Maharashtra clear through description and dialog.

4. Vahini, lit. brother's wife, is used here in the way that neighbors would use family terms to indicate a respectful familiarity with each other.

5. The patil is the village headman.

I

Getting What You Want

3

Negotiating Relationships with the Goddess

William P. Harman

Further on in this chapter I shall draw some generalized conclusions about vows that devotees take to the Indian Tamil goddess Mariyamman. But for the moment, I prefer to begin by emphasizing the specific and local nature of my topic. I shall be speaking here about a particular goddess in a particular temple in a particular town. I shall also be concerned with the people who worship her—her devotees—whose understandings of the dynamics of vows to the goddess are shaped by a partly localized and a partly South Asian approach to devotion.

Samayapuram is a sleepy village in Tamil Nadu that lies on a major highway 15 kilometers northeast of Tiruchirapalli and 275 kilometers southwest of Chennai (formerly Madras), Tamil Nadu's largest city and its administrative capitol. Samayapuram has minimal tourist facilities for overnight accommodations, in terms of both quality and quantity, but it is served eighteen hours a day by hundreds of buses running both to and from Tiruchirapalli as well as to and from Chennai. In addition, tourist vans arrive in droves. Nearly everyone coming and going to the town is making a trip to the temple of Samayapuram Mariyamman. This fact is remarkable, in part because the temple of the goddess is so surprisingly unremarkable. It has a relatively recent history and was probably remodeled as a major temple around the middle of the eighteenth century. I have found no literary references to a shrine to the goddess in Samayapuram earlier than the seventeenth century. Moreover, it is small and architecturally undistinguished, but during the 17 hours it is open it is thronged in normal periods and unbearably packed during festivals. Several thousands of people visit and depart this

Figure 3.1 Small roadside Mariyamman shrine in Tirunelveli District

temple every day. What does distinguish the temple, from the point of view of its administrator and the government-appointed manager, is its income. They claim, and offer government records to back that claim, that this small temple has the third largest income of all temples in India, behind the shrines of Venkatesvarar at Tirupati and of Murugan at Palani. Enormous, locked steel contribution boxes (*untiyal*) are available throughout the temple complex, and by the time for evening retrieval of offerings, they are brimming with gifts in coin, paper, gold, and silver. Because it constitutes a part of a temple network in the same region that includes the enormous and imposing temple of the famous deity Ranganatan at nearby Sri Rangam, a portion of the Samayapuram Mariyamman Temple income is used to support this much larger (probably by a factor of 20), much older, more famous, and more beautiful counterpart. But every day thousands of Mariyamman's devotees/pilgrims cruise by the great Sri Rangam temple in buses, cars, vans, auto-rickshaws, and on foot proffering barely a nod to this massive temple and its famous but generally otiose form of the deity Vishnu. They have more pressing business as they make their way to visit the Samayapuram shrine and the goddess whose involvement in the most intimate of life's issues, healing and surviving, is legendary. All are bent on becoming a part of the throng that fills the goddess's temple, coffers, and consciousness.

Strangely, however, during the six weeks I spent poking around the temple and chatting with pilgrims in Samayapuram, I saw not a single distinguishable foreign tourist face, though there were many Indians who spoke no Tamil and who came from the North.

There are thousands of temples to Mariyamman in southern India, but none is more famous or more recognized than Samayapuram. This Samayapuram Mariyamman is especially powerful when it comes to matters of health and illness. Traditionally, Mariyamman is associated with fevers and disease, and with the protection of health. This may be one reason why the temple is so unappealing to casual tourists and therefore goes unmentioned in tourist brochures written in English. It is a haven for the ill and the infirm, many of whom suffer obvious pain and discomfort, in addition to being quite needy and dependent on handouts either from the temple or from worshippers. Most goal-directed visitors enter and leave quickly to discharge obligations contracted by vows. Indeed, it is best to have a task to perform, a vow to discharge: tarrying among the constant throngs of thousands of afflicted and suffering people who go there to live, and to await the healing of the goddess, is not easy. I found I couldn't return more than five consecutive days at a time to do research, lest a low-grade depression once more set in. The sights of human suffering are both moving and off-putting: open wounds, running sores, misshapen limbs, and festering eye ailments are common, for the goddess is associated with smallpox, cholera, rashes, skin diseases, blindness, and infirmity. Cripples with disfigured limbs struggle after anyone who they feel might be moved to offer them alms.

For those who are very seriously ill and who have taken a vow to remain in the precincts of the temple until they are healed, there is a spartan, common dormitory area attached to the southwest end of the temple. And while I was encouraged by all concerned to enter into the inner sanctum of the temple to watch the puja activities and to follow certain people with whom I had spoken, I was aggressively forbidden to enter this dormitory for the seriously ill. I was told that there were several cases of smallpox inside, but I also know that tradition about Mariyamman commonly asserts that the goddess, when she possesses a person with her fevers, recoils at the presence of anything strange or foreign. Whether the residents of this convalescent dormitory represented a danger to me—or I a danger to them—was not clear. What did become clear was, simply, I couldn't go in, and I could find no sympathetic support for suspending this commonly taken-for-granted but unexplained and unposted rule. The matter was not simply an issue of impropriety. The prospect of my presence inside the dormitory horrified everyone, and, to tell the truth, my exclusion gradually became a relief for me when I was able to glimpse the disfiguring pustules, rashes, and fevers the more ambulatory residents suffered as they occasionally entered or departed. Doing responsible research would require that I enter and investigate; doing what I felt like doing meant avoiding the place like . . . the plague.

Vows to Mariyamman

With very few exceptions, people with whom I spoke arrived at Samayapuram because they understood themselves to be under the requirements of a vow. Some excellent and constructive studies of vows in South Asia have proliferated in recent years, most frequently focusing on the roles vows play in the lives of women.[1] My perspective is both more diffuse and more specific. Here I am concerned with vows taken both by men and women, but they are vows taken in the context of worship of one particular goddess in one particular temple. What, then, can we say in general and specifically about vows in Samayapuram? First, I would want to say—and this conclusion contradicts the occasional claims even of people I interviewed—that vows are not disinterested acts of spontaneous worship and praise. My questioning of devotees at the Samaypuram temple leads me to assert that vows to this goddess constitute an approach to the divine that is highly interactive and instrumental and that they suggest activities much akin to cutting deals, striking bargains, and entering into covenants, that is, being or becoming involved in relationships characterized by varying and variable obligations between humans and perceived supernatural powers.[2] Individuals or groups often accept certain obligations and responsibilities to the supernatural in return for a benefit either 1) assumed, 2) expected, or 3) requested and therefore anticipated. This interaction also symbolizes obligation on the part of supernatural powers involved.[3] The act of stipulating consciously, though not necessarily publicly, the terms of these obligations I understand to be the act of entering into a religious vow. Specifically, the religious vows made to Mariyamman reflect an understood (and sometimes publicly expressed) relationship of obligation between humans and the supernatural. Because the intensity of the relationship varies, it can involve what we perceive as a deal or a bargain. It normally involves a mortal and a perceived supernatural power, either of which can be reported as having initiated the vow. It also involves a specific, articulated desire or a diffuse sense of appropriateness on the part of the one initiating it. This diffuse sense of appropriateness, often reappearing in domestic vows performed by women, tends to be reflected in the title of Anne Pearson's book, *"Because It Gives Me Peace of Mind": Ritual Fasts in the Religious Lives of Hindu Women.* Also in women's practice of domestic vows can be found a diffuse desire to keep marriage and family life intact, as reflected in the title of Holly Baker Reynold's monograph, *"To Keep the [Marriage] Tali Strong": Womens' Rituals in Tamilnad, India.*[4] Whatever it takes to keep family intact is what women request: good health, prosperity, children who behave, harmony, the sudden disappearance of a husband's concubine. Whatever it takes.

These kinds of vows, however, are rarely associated with Samayapuram Mariyamman.[5] For one thing, all iconography and mythology are quite specific that Mariyamman is not the name to invoke for the sake of domestic tranquility and happiness. Mariyamman, everywhere I have encountered her, is unmarried.[6] Indeed, several variants of her mythology assert that she is a widow because she murdered her own husband, who either deceived her or defiled her. She is neither the model of nor the model for the good wife and mother.[7] Nor is she the benevolent and loving goddess to whom a diffuse sense of devotion tends to be appropriate. Her efficacy, power, and strength seem to derive from the fact that she is exacting and demanding. She does not gratuitously or even reliably protect from disease. She protects whom she will and, occasionally, she sends afflications to her followers to test them and to punish their failure to live according to her preferences.

Some vows are inappropriate for some people. Brahmins would hesitate to vow to offer sacrifices of blood, though they might commission someone of a lower caste to take a proxy vow to make blood offerings in their stead. And there are certain vows that tend to be gender specific, though many more are performed both by men and women. One particular sort of healing ritual I have seen in Mariyamman temples, and in Samayapuram, involves rice-flour lamps. Women exclusively are the ones who fashion these small lamps with rice dough, place oil and a wick into them, and then place them lighted on the body parts of those afflicted with pain or disease. Both men and women can be treated in this way, but only women make the lamps, light them, place them on the ailing body parts, and recite prayers as the wicks burn. Women tend also to be the only ones who perform the ritual of pouring numerous pots of water around the outer perimeter

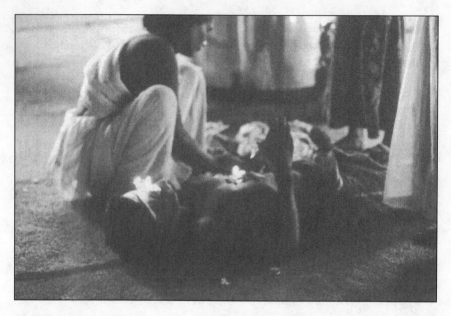

Figure 3.2 A woman performing the rice-flour healing ritual on a man in Samayapuram

of the goddess shrine, ostensibly to cool the anger of the goddess. Men have their own, usually exclusive vows. Men are more likely to honor the goddess by shedding their own blood with piercings and cuts. I would speculate that this pattern generally holds in much of Tamil Nadu because the myths about Mariyamman's origins tend to emphasize how the goddess originated as a result of being unjustly treated by the male of the species: some stories describe her rape, others her being forced into marriage with a man far inferior, and others discuss her as a woman who has to bear the unjust judgment of an impulsively cruel husband. To offer blood is considered a severe form of atonement. But it could not be said that men alone enact severe or demanding vows. The vast majority of vows are taken and performed by men and women and some are physically quite demanding: carrying firepots, long periods of fasting, disciplined periods of prayer and temple visits, body rolling, to name a few.

Crucial to my understanding the vow in the context of the worship of Samayapuram Mariyamman is its specificity and its dialogical quality. Both parties (the devotee and the supernatural power addressed) have an interest in profiting from the transaction, though almost always these transactions are salubrious for the devotee: he, or she, will always end up better off from the successfully completed transaction. There are two caveats here, however: to take a vow to the goddess and to fail in its performance is to place yourself in great jeopardy. Similarly, in taking a vow to a deity, it is important to know what particular actions that deity appreciates. You must become familiar with the preferences and characteristics of that deity. You must, in short, spend time getting to know her. There are times and places for offering Mariyamman blood sacrifices, for example. Doing this at the wrong times or places is offensive to the goddess.[8]

Though I have tried to indicate generally the way I use the term "vow," the English word is not so rich nor so nuanced as, for example, the widely used Sanskrit *vrata* or the variety of more general Tamil terms, such as *poruttanai, pirarttanai,* and *nerttikkatan.* In speaking of the Sanskrit usage, Mary McGee concludes, "I have found vrata translated as fast, feast, festival, vow, ceremony, calendrical rite, and a woman's rite. . . . I have chosen to render vrata as votive rite, or votive observance.[9]

This emphasis on "votive observance" gives prominence to the intentionality of vows, as I have concluded must be done in my consideration of vows to Mariyamman.

If *vrata* is the generic term associated in Sanskrit with vows—albeit, these days, primarily with womens' vows—the Tamil language seems to have a wider

Figure 3.3   A female renouncer at the Mariyamman Samayapuram temple.

range of terms to connote vows. I have tracked down at least 104 Tamil terms referring to vows, many of them very specific, descriptive words that indicate what kind of activity a devotee is willing to perform for the deity in return for a boon either requested or granted. Many involve a severe discipline, such as walking on a pit of glowing coals (*tikkulipayatal; teemiti*), thrusting steel rods through one's sides to draw blood while circumambulating a shrine (*kuttiyaattam*), or allowing oneself to be hoisted in the air by hooks imbedded in the flesh (*pakkacedil*). But there are much less severe disciplines. They include the shaving of one's head (*kutumivankutal*), or simply giving fruits to the temple (*katampattal*). Several vows involve the early morning performances of rituals and the singing of songs, particularly by women (*nonpu*). Others are actions performed in such a way as to keep that vow constantly in mind, such as the *kappukkattutal,* an act of tying a yellow string or an amulet on the arm as a reminder and pledge to fulfill the vow, or the *kankanankattutal,* the act of tying a cord around the wrist as a visible reminder of a vow taken. I have seen examples of each one of these performed in the context of the temple at Samayapuram. In performing such vows, usually devotees will do so with a particular goal in mind. The most generic of the Tamil terms for "vow" tends to be *nerttikkatan.* The word refers to vows taken by anyone: male, female, Hindu, Christian, Muslim.[10] The term is a combination of the words *katan,* meaning "debt," "obligation," or "borrowed article" and *ner,* meaning "that which is fit, appropriate, or complete." Though a single word, the term *nerttikkatan* may be used to refer to two distinct acts as well as to the content of the agreement. The first act is that of worship, during which a person makes a request of a deity. The second refers to the act of paying off the "debt" once the request is granted (*Tamil Lexicon*, 2,357; Diehl 1956: 256ff; Reiniche 1979: 162ff; Moreno-Arcas 1984: 19ff). In some cases, a gift may be presented at the time of the request. In some, it may be presented after a specific amount of time, to "remind" the deity of the request. However, the more pragmatic devotees, or those interested in a largely instrumental relationship with the deity, will pay only for divine services rendered, and after they are rendered.[11] The process constitutes a classic quid pro quo agreement: once the devotee has received what she or he asks of the deity she or he must repay the loan by living up to her or his side of the bargain. Manuel Moreno-Arcas, an anthropologist, has been concerned with the financial metaphors that surround this process in issues of healing. As he writes,

> Once the affliction is removed, the devotee will again worshipfully approach the god to repay the debt (*nerttikatan*) contracted with the deity, thus restoring part of the god's depleted power. The fulfillment of debts ("vows" in more traditional parlance) is a crucial dimension of worship. Although eminently generous, gods are always seen as

concerned with repayment to them by humans of gifts given away in the past. The more universal a god is, that is, the more actively he engages in substantial transactions with all kinds of humans, the more concerned he appears with repayment. The two most popular south Indian gods, Venkateswarar of the Tirupati Hills and Murugan of the Palani Hills, are often depicted with metaphors suggestive of banking and loans. The god of Tirupati is often addressed by devotees as "Vaddikkasula Vada," "The Collector of Interest," while the god of Palani concludes his daily routine with "the reading of accounts" (*annata Kanakku*), the daily statement of temple income presented to him by his priests. While failure to repay is thought to be accompanied by dire consequences for the worshipper, the immediate repayment of a debt to the god is equally considered to be distasteful and ungrateful. A suitable period of time must pass wherein the worshipper is bound to the god by obligation.[12]

What deities wish to be offered in a vow transaction will differ enormously. Mariyamman, judging by the worship at Samayapuram, receives enthusiastically money (including gold and silver models of body parts that require healing), blood, and intense ascetic heat generated by demanding, harsh devotional acts that testify publicly to sacrifices her devotees are willing to make.

One of the more common visible vows people take to the goddess is what is called *ankappiratatcinam,* a term derived from the Sanskrit meaning "body circumambulation." It involves lying prone on the hard stone ground in the courtyard directly outside the temple complex, and rolling one's body clockwise around the shrine, always keeping the head toward the image of the goddess. This entails covering a distance of about a quarter mile for each circuit around, and frequently people will vow to make the circuit 108 times. It is physically very demanding, very disorienting, resulting often in extreme dizziness, passing out, illness, and constant humiliation at having to roll over ground where people walk, discard their trash, and break green coconuts, thus creating pools of coconut water and filth. The temple elephant also roams this corridor, fettered only loosely, thus posing a serious physical danger as well as dropping occasional solid or liquid excrement through which devotees must roll. This sort of vow is clearly a demonstration that 1) you really want what you've asked the goddess for or 2) you've taken a negotiated deal seriously and have returned to repay your debt. This particular vow, like so many others, puts the devotee in what can only be described as a compromising position in relation to the goddess. The act forces a devotee into a position of humble vulnerability, in which a person becomes deliberately weakened, even humiliated, for the sake of the relationship that is being established with the goddess.

Figure 3.4 A female in ecstatic trance carrying a firepot inside the Mariyamman Samayapuram temple

Another very common vow at Samayapuram is the carrying of firepots (*ticetti*). These are large clay pots into which have been placed neem wood chips soaked in oil. The wood is then ignited and the pots are carried in procession by individuals who have contracted, by taking a vow, to carry in their bare hands a threatening serving of leaping flames that brush their faces and singe their hair. Frequently the firepots will have been transported on foot from many miles away, and individuals doing this tend to combine it with a special regimen of fasting, prayer, and worship for weeks or months before the event. Normally, they wear saffron clothing and are accompanied by relatives. Mariyamman is understood to be the goddess of fevers, and in assuming this vow, devotees share the heat attributed to the goddess. It is a natural way of approaching her, of

Figure 3.5 Christian husband and wife carrying a firepot at the Samayapuram Mariyamman temple

becoming like her, of imitating her. Many who carry firepots are seized by glossolalia, and are thereby understood to become the mouthpiece of the goddess. Worshippers and bystanders often take this moment to enter into dialogue with Mariyamman's temporarily possessed representative. Some firepot carriers will pierce themselves through the tongues, cheeks, or back: an added measure of sacrifice for a goddess said to appreciate blood offerings. A day at Samayapuram is not particularly easy on the average Western bystander. Nor is it easy on certain worshippers who have taken physically demanding vows. But one impression it leaves is that the devotion centered on vows is quite palpable, specifiable, even measurable. By entering into vows, devotees are negotiating what they are willing to give up, what they are willing to suffer, in order to achieve the healing or assistance they need. It is as though the goddess poses a rather stark question: "You want to be healed? What's it worth to you? What are you willing to give up or to suffer to get it?" In answering the goddess's implied question people are forced to invest themselves in their own requests. They must take responsibility for what they want. They no longer become helpless bystanders, but active participants in a communal effort to bring about transformation in their lives. Simply standing near the flagpole of the temple, about halfway between the entrance to the shrine and the inner sanctum, a person begins to realize that the negotiation process must start with getting the mother's attention. People will often enter and burst out in the most shrill, blood-curdling screams, "Mother, help me!" they shriek. And then, with the Mother's attention, they proceed to make a verbal offer describing the exchange they propose, such as: "Mother, my son has been ill for five months now. If he is healed both he and I will walk from our home to your temple carrying firepots in a procession, observing all the ritual abstinences during the preceding month." Whether, in fact, petitioners receive what they want and need is not a matter I have been able to investigate with follow-up interviews after people return to their homes. But taking these vows to the goddess had some clear and immediate effects, I noticed. It created a sense of community among those suffering similar problems, bringing them together at a particular place for the reason of seeking out healing. It also gave these petitioners a reassurance that they are not helpless victims—they find comfort in knowing that there is something they can actually do about their illnesses, a place they can go and a process into which they can tap in order to deal with their problems. That consequent sense of confidence and resolve, combined with a creation of temporary community among like-minded devotees also seeking assistance, seems to be, at the very least, a credible beginning for the process of healing based on vows.

  This healing is not a process unique to worshippers of Mariyamman. The culture of vows in Tamil Hinduism presupposes that many deities, though

Figure 3.6 Mother and son (who was healed of paralysis) carrying firepot to Mariyamman temple; the mother vowed her son would carry a firepot every year for the rest of his life in gratitude for the healing

not all, are capable of assisting the ill and the afflicted. Some deities have a wider array of talents; still they cannot accomplish all things. The bottom line is that deities with specialized talents, such as, apparently, Mariyamman of Samayapuram, can be located and consulted by virtue of community attestation to their powers. There are active, healed witnesses who will and do testify that healing is available in a particular shrine from a particular deity. I return, then, to emphasize the particularity of taking vows to Mariyamman. Particular vows taken by particular persons to particular deities become manifestations of the more generalized and widespread culture of taking vows in South Asia.

Figure 3.7 Ecstatic dancing in front of Mariyamman shrine by worshippers who have been healed by the goddess

Notes

1. General discussions of the dynamics of these vows can be found in Diehl (1956: 256ff), Reiniche (1979: 162ff), Moreno-Arcas (1984: 19ff). More specifically elaborate material can be found in Reynolds (1978), Cutler (1979), McGee (1987), and Pearson (1996), especially Appendix 1, "History of Scholarship on Vrata," 223–27.

2. In contrast, negotiations with supernatural powers in Western monotheism are sometimes viewed with less enthusiasm and more suspicion: vows, bargains, or deals with the supernatural are more often associated with interactions with malevolent forces. Seventeenth-century European witch trials were often predicated on the notion that individuals had entered into compacts with the devil to gain unusual powers. Goethe's *Faust* is perhaps the classic example of the appeals and dangers involved in such deals. Still, other vows or "deals" are held in high regard in Western monotheistic traditions. The Decalogue in the Hebrew scriptures might be seen as one of the more prominent examples, for it is cast in the form of a formal agreement between a sovereign and that sovereign's subjects. In return for adherence to specific requirements, subjects receive protection, security, and a unique identity. In later Western traditions, entrance into religious life—that of priest, nun, monk, for example—often involves taking solemn vows of chastity and obedience in return for admission into an order and all which that admission implies. In middle-class North America, one form of religious vow is implicitly a part of the North American male Christian movement called "Promise Keepers."

3. Monotheistic traditions tend less to dwell on the failures of the supernatural to adhere to expected standards. In the Hebraic tradition, Job did not exactly indict Yahweh, but he did not accept that justice had been done in his whimsically inflicted suffering. That was the original deal as he and his friends understood it. In polytheistic contexts, by contrast, it is not unusual to find devotees making subtle, implied threats that they will seek assistance from other deities—indeed, from deities in very different religious traditions—if their requests are not honored and their vows are not respected by the deity in question.

4. The symbolism of the marriage vow has often been used as an analogy or a metaphor to elaborate on the dynamic of vows between humans and deities. Indeed, there are frequent instances in which deities marry humans in order to establish a kinship relationship (with its attendant obligations and privileges) between transcendent and human parties. See my *The Sacred Marriage of a Hindu Goddess*, especially chapter 5, and my article (1985).

5. There are, no doubt, exceptions to this rule. In the past fifty years or so, Mariyamman has become much more diffuse in her functions, and her specific powers associated with disease and health have been less emphasized, often in favor of an image of a more "middle-class," respectable, and beneficent goddess who brings general welfare and well-being. As this occurs, especially in the larger urban areas, women have begun to practice vows in her name that include fasting, worship, and special preparations of puja foods. See my article (2004: 2–16) and Waghorne's unpublished essay (2000).

6. Nevertheless—and much to my surprise—this particular Mariyamman temple has a "marriage hall" for the celebration of marriages, the only one I have seen attached to a Mariyamman temple. It was constructed in 1982, and I conclude that it reflects the move toward gentrification of the goddess, and away from the more violent mythologies associated with her widowhood and single status.

7. Moreno-Arcas (1984a).

8. Another indication of Mariyamman's moving toward middle-class acceptability is the growing distance from the temple at which officials will permit blood sacrifices of goats and cocks. Older priests told me that fifty years ago, blood sacrifices were permitted inside the temple. But this is no longer the case. Today, animals are given to the temple to be resold to devotees; or they are slaughtered at some significant distance from the temple in a designated area. The same is true of offerings of hair: once it was done in the temple, but it is a ritually polluting activity and as the goddess makes new claims to respectability, the activity has moved to a special hall outside the temple where many hundreds line up each day to fulfill this vow. Humans may still shed their blood within the temple, but the flow must be initiated outside the temple.

9. McGee (1987: 12).

10. I did encounter both Muslims and Christians at Samayapuram, but none of them were interested in talking to me about what they were doing there.

11. This latter option seems to be the norm in the worship of Murugan at Palani. See Fuller's comments on this process in the Madurai temple (1984: 21, note 33). Moreno-Arcas (1984b: 19) makes the fascinating observation that "[t]he more universal a god is, that is the more actively he engages in substantial transactions with all kinds of humans, the more concerned he appears with repayment." If we play with the metaphor a bit, we discover that this seems to make some financial sense: a banking operation that serves the larger public is more likely to observe stricter rules in its transactions. In contrast, a loan to a "relative," someone to whom the debtor is in some sense personally related, is less likely to involve a strict, principled arrangement, in part because the loan is secured by other connections and relationships. Possibly, devotion in the Madurai Temple (where locals understand themselves to be in a kinship relationship with the deities) is, to a greater extent, predicated on kinship metaphors, while devotion in Palani more often evokes financial metaphors. At the least, I am suggesting that financial metaphors and kinship metaphors are not mutually exclusive ways of thinking about and acting out responsibilities and obligations generated by vows, either personal or group, as would be the marriage ceremony of Madurai.

12. See Moreno-Arcas (1984: 9).

References

Cutler, Norman. 1979. *Consider Our Vow: An English Translation of Tiruppavai and Tiruvempavai.* Madurai: Muttu Patippakam.

Diehl, Carl Gustav. 1956. *Instrument and Purpose: Studies on Rites and Rituals in South India.* Lund: C. W. K. Gleerup.

Fuller, C. J. 1984. *Servants of the Goddess: The Priests of a South Indian Temple.* Cambridge: Cambridge University Press.

Harman, William. 2004."Transmitting a Tradition Means Changing a Tradition: The Fever Goddess of Southern India." *Manushi: A Journal of Women's Studies,* 140: 2–16.

———. 1989. *The Sacred Marriage of a Hindu Goddess.* Bloomington: Indiana University Press.

———. 1985. "Kinship Metaphors in the Hindu Pantheon: Siva as Brother-in-Law and Son-in-Law." *Journal of the American Academy of Religion,* 53, 3: 411–30.

McGee, Mary. 1987. "Feasting and Fasting: The Vrata Tradition and Its Significance for Hindu Women." Th.d. dissertation, Harvard University.

Moreno-Arcas, Manuel. 1984. "Murugan, A God of Healing Poisons: The Physics of Worship in a South Indian Center For Pilgrimage." Ph.D. dissertation, University of Chicago.

———. 1984a. "Virgin, Wife, and Widow: Complementary Performances and Perceptions in the Mariyamman Festival of a Tamil Town." Unpublished paper presented at the 13th Annual Conference on South Asia, Madison, Wisconsin, November 2.

Pearson, Anne Mackenzie. 1996. *"Because It Gives Me Peace of Mind": Ritual Fasts in the Religious Lives of Hindu Women.* Albany: State University of New York Press.

Reiniche, Marie-Louise. 1979. *Les dieux et les hommes: Études des cultes d'un village du Tirunelveli, Inde du Sud.* Paris: Mouton.

Reynolds, Holly Baker. 1978. *"To Keep the* Tali *Strong:" Womens' Rituals in Tamilnad, India.* Ph.D. dissertation, University of Wisconsin-Madison.

Waghorne, Joanne Punzo. 2000. "Reinventing the 'Village Goddess'/Revisioning the Urban Middle Class." Paper presented at the panel Reinventing Tradition: Contemporary Trends in Religious Practice in India. Annual Meeting of the Association for Asian Studies. San Diego, Saturday, March 11.

4

Shared Vows, Shared Space, and Shared Deities: Vow Rituals among Tamil Catholics in South India

Selva J. Raj

Introduction

Taking vows is a popular religious activity among Tamil Catholics in rural south India. Collectively known as *nerccai* or *nerttikkatan*, vows are particularly prominent during religious festivals, pilgrimages, life-cycle celebrations, and crisis interventions. Though some scholars of Hinduism consider vows in South Asia primarily, if not exclusively, as a female devotional exercise, the *nerccai* rituals are gender neutral. These rituals assume a variety of forms ranging from the simple offering of money, prayer, and votive offerings such as the silver shoe, gold cradle, flour lamps, and silver or gold facsimile of body parts to the more spectacular expressions like goat or fowl sacrifices and the ceremonial "baby auction." These various expressions serve as effective mechanisms for entering into or reaffirming a relationship with a powerful supernatural figure, such as a Catholic saint or Hindu deity. In this relationship humans can request such things as protection, fertility, healing, and general well-being. Based on field research conducted between 1990 and 2003 at three rural Catholic shrines in southeast Tamil Nadu, this chapter examines the nature and types of Tamil Catholic *nerccai* rituals and proposes a typology of Catholic vows. In light of this analysis, I examine the phenomenon of shared vows, shared deities, and shared space as illustrated in a select number of *nerccai* rituals.

The Catholic *Nerccai* System

The Meaning and Nature of Nerccai

In Tamil, the term *nerccai* denotes an offering made as part of a contractual agreement between a devotee and a saint or a sacred figure.[1] It may be performed either before the boon is granted and therefore as a promise or as a thanksgiving ritual after the boon is granted, in gratitude for the fulfillment of a vow. The Catholic *nerccai* ritual structure is founded on a system of faith in and fidelity to a particular supernatural figure who evokes personal devotion, and is affectionately called a *kula teiyvam*. Individual families, villages, and even clans may share a single patron saint as their *kula teiyvam* whose assistance and protection are considered crucial for general well-being.

Nerccai rites are thus a contractual agreement, a "deal" made between the devotee and the deity believed to be *legally* binding on both parties. The use of a legal promissory note (*muri*) to record the terms of the agreement and the ceremonial signing of the document by the devotee and the deity's proxy in the presence of eyewitnesses emphasize this fact. While some devotees offer the promissory note to the saint, others take it home and keep it in a safe place until the vow has been granted. Then it is destroyed. *Nerccai* vows are thus promises made and promises kept. Until the promises are kept, the devotee feels "in-debted" to the deity. Feelings of guilt, uneasiness, anxiety, and even fear are manifest among those who either fail or postpone the repayment of the agreement. Devotees and their extended families take great pains to ensure the proper "payment" of the debt since any violation of the terms of the contract would have negative consequences not only for the individual devotee but for the entire extended family, including the village. Thus the notion of "debt," conveyed by the popular Tamil term *nerttikkatan* (*katan* = debt), serves as the foundational basis for the *nerccai* system. In most instances, however, this contractual aspect is buffered by a certain personal affection for the deity or saint.

A wide variety of practical needs sustain the *kula teiyvam* phenomenon and the *nerccai* ritual system. They include agricultural success, marital stability, family unity, freedom from specific illness, and the health and general well-being of the family including cattle, fertility of the land and family members. Each *nerccai* is offered in the hope of maintaining conditions of health and prosperity or in the hope of gaining a remedy for a specific problem. To an extent, the *nerccai* system is essentially a crisis-solving religious strategy. Belief in the power and efficacy of *nerccai* rituals is based on the proven experience of elders and past success.

Types of Nerccai Rituals

Nerccai rites of Tamil Catholics may be classified as either devotional or nondevotional. In each of these divisions, there are rituals that involve the shedding of blood and rituals that do not. Though both types of *nerccais* are prompted by specific individual or collective needs, devotional *nerccais* are characterized by a certain personalism, faith, affection, and loyalty to a Catholic or Hindu saint/deity, whereas nondevotional *nerccais* are primarily induced by a desire to appease a sacred figure whose religious identity might not be well known to the worshipper, and in some cases totally unknown. Tamil Catholics perform both types of *nerccais* in Catholic or Hindu sacred sites to Catholic or Hindu figures. Conversely, Hindu devotees execute *nerccai* rituals at Catholic centers to Catholic saints as well as to Hindu deities. In most cases, Hindus offer vow rituals to Catholic saints instead of—and occasionally to supplement—those offered to Hindu deities. These facts are well borne out in the ritual life and popular practices associated with all three south Indian Catholic shrines discussed in this essay. A brief word about each of these three shrines will foreground the discussion on three popular devotional *nerccai* rituals.

The Shrines

Shrine of St. John de Britto

Situated near Tondy along the Coromandel coast in southeast India, the shrine of St. John de Britto at Oriyur is a popular regional center for a wide array of *nerccai* rituals including animal sacrifice.[2] The history and popularity of the shrine are related to the events surrounding the martyrdom in 1693 of John de Britto—affectionately called Arulanandasamy—a Portuguese Jesuit missionary—who in the late seventeenth century spearheaded a mass conversion movement in southeast Tamil Nadu, known as the Marava country (Sauliere 1947). Tradition holds that Britto soon came to be perceived as a holy man of great power and accordingly a threat to Setupathi, the Raja of Ramnad. Setupathi eventually had Britto beheaded and impaled on a stake after decapitation (Bayly 1989: 399–404).

The development of the Britto cult and the popularity of the Oriyur shrine are closely linked to his martyrdom and his assumed sacral powers, especially his fertility powers. A rich collection of legends and folk songs celebrates his fertility and healing powers. A special power attributed to the shrine derives from the color of the soil surrounding the shrine. Miracle stories attribute the red soil surrounding the shrine to the sacral powers of the martyr's blood. The shrine festival attracts thousands of pilgrims from far and near who regard it as an auspicious site for various vow rituals including animal sacrifices. Some estimate that an average of over six hundred goats are sacrificed during the annual festival.

The vast majority of Britto's devotees belong to the three Marava caste groups of the region, namely, Pallars, Udayars, and Kallars. The cult of Britto is centered around caste identities rather than religious affiliation.

Figure 4.1 Shrine of St. John de Britto, Oriyur.

Thus, regardless of their individual religious loyalties, all members of these caste groups, Catholics and Hindus alike, regard him as their favorite clan or family deity (*kula teiyvam*), to whom special honor and affection are accorded during the festival season. So extensive is Britto's patronage among the Marava Catholics that he is affectionately called the Marava saint. In addition to these groups, Britto also commands the devotion of the Vellala Catholics in the village and in the vicinity. In terms of Tamil caste hierarchy, Vellalas are ranked higher than Nadars, Udayars, Kallars, and Pallars.

At the time I conducted my third field research, the total population of Oriyur numbered 120 Catholic families. Pallars and Vellalas are the two major caste groups in the village with the former accounting for 75 percent of the population. Occupationally, Pallars are farmers and unskilled laborers whereas the Vellalas, who have had more formal education than the Pallars, serve as parish catechists and teachers in the parochial elementary and high schools. Though Udayar and Kallar Catholics do not reside in Oriyur, there is a heavy concentration of them in the neighboring villages.

The Shrine of St. Anne

Ten miles south of the city of Madurai, the shrine of St. Anne at Arulanandapuram—a tiny, nondescript village of 150 households on the banks of the Vaigai River—is another popular rural Catholic center in southern Tamil Nadu. Renowned for her fertility and healing powers, St. Anne, mother of the Virgin Mary and patron saint of the village, is the revered recipient of various *nerccai* vow rituals. Whereas Kallars and Pallars form the dominant caste groups at Oriyur, Arulanandapuram is a Vellala Catholic village whose residents are agriculturalists by occuption, working in sugarcane, rice, and betel-leaf fields. In addition, unlike the Oriyur shrine, which enjoys regional fame, the shrine of St. Anne has the limited patronage of the local village, its diaspora community settled in larger cities like Madurai and Tiruchirapalli and the neighboring villages. The village name "Arulanandapuram," ("the village of St. Britto") indicates its special religious significance. By virtue of its association with two powerful saints (Britto and Anne), the village shrine is believed to contain the combined sacral powers of two distinct sacred figures. The annual festival, when the statues of Britto and Anne, enthroned in colorfully decorated chariots are drawn through the village streets, is a public declaration of their dual patronage and protection. Though sponsored by the dominant Vellala Catholic group, the festival attracts many Marava Catholics and Hindus living in the vicinity.

The Shrine of St. Anthony

Popularly known as the "Padua of the East," the shrine of St. Anthony at Uvari on the Pearl Fishery coast—thirty miles north of Kanya Kumari at the tip of the Indian peninsula—is another popular Catholic shrine in south India.[3] According to the 1995 village Panchayat census, the total population of the village numbers 1,600 Catholic families of the Parava (fishing) caste group.[4] The Catholic community of Uvari proudly traces its Christian heritage to the missionary efforts of such notable Portuguese Jesuits as St. Francis Xavier. Among the four Catholic churches that dominate the local landscape, the recently renovated shrine of St. Anthony is undoubtedly the most prominent when measured by the extraordinary sacred powers attributed to it and the number of pilgrims it attracts.[5] Once a simple wayside shrine (*kurusadi*) cared for by a Hindu family, this shrine is now under the jurisdiction of the local Catholic diocese. Local residents never tire of telling pilgrims and visitors the Uvari legend that recounts the shrine's humble yet wondrous beginnings.[6] Marion—an eighty-year-old retired catechist—enthusiastically recounted this legend to me. Long, long ago, nearly three or four hundred years ago—so goes the legend—Uvari had a small harbor town known as "Obeer" where local villagers traded with incoming ships. The crew of a Portuguese ship approaching Uvari contracted cholera and the crew lost some of its members to this deadly disease. Upon seeing this misfortune, a sculptor on board the ship began chipping a block of wood and carved the image of St. Anthony. As soon as he completed the sculpture the entire crew was miraculously healed from cholera. The ship then was docked at Uvari for some days. In gratitude for the miracle, the sculptor and the sailors installed the miraculous wooden statue on the shores of Uvari against the backdrop of a huge rock instructing the natives to pray to him in times of trouble. That is how St. Anthony made Uvari his home, according to Marion. Around the eighteenth century a modest hut made of coconut leaves was built to house the saint's wooden statue under the care of a Hindu family that looked after the hut for several generations until the Catholic Church took it over from its descendents. A full-fledged shrine dedicated to St. Anthony was built in 1940 and remodeled in 2003. Uvari residents claim that the wooden statue of St. Anthony enshrined on the altar is the same wooden statue installed by the Portuguese sailors. From its modest beginnings in a humble village, the shrine has grown into a famed regional pilgrim center attracting tens of thousands of devotees of all castes and creeds. Although the shrine is a one-stop complex for various spiritual and human needs, the Uvari shrine is reputed for healing.[7]

Its patron saint, St. Anthony of Padua—a native of Lisbon, Portugal but commonly referred to as the saint of Padua since he spent his mature years in the Italian city of Padua—is well-known throughout the Catholic world as the "finder of lost articles" and the bestower of fertility. However, this European saint gains new powers and attributes from his indigenous clientele, so that Uvari St. Anthony is known for his ability to ward off the negative effects of black magic and sorcery. He is also reputed for his powers over demonic spirits, particularly malevolent local Hindu deities and spirits like Isakki Amman and Chutalaimadan, who command the religious attention of a vast number of his local Hindu and Catholic devotees (Raj 2004: 33–44). "Million Miracle Worker," "Wonder-worker," and "Superdoctor" are some of Anthony's affectionate, indigenous titles. Uvari residents also regard St. Anthony as the guardian of their village. The spectacular annual chariot procession of St. Anthony's statue through village streets powerfully reveals the saint's protective role and function.[8]

Though located in the caste-conscious Parava Catholic village, the shrine's appeal extends beyond its geographical, religious, and caste boundaries as its patron saint draws devotees from all socioeconomic, caste, and religious groups. Many regard him as their chosen family, clan, or village deity (*kula teiyvam*). During my field research in 2000 and 2003, I met several Hindu devotees who claimed to have co-opted Anthony as their "new" *kula teiyvam*. According to some unofficial estimates, nearly 40 percent of Anthony's loyal devotees are Hindus. Throughout the year, pilgrims flock to the shrine to perform vow rituals. Their number escalates during the two shrine festivals—observed in February and mid-June—that attract tens of thousands of pilgrims of all religious affiliations. According to a conservative estimate, the February festival draws over 100,000 pilgrims from far and near. During the annual festival, Parava Catholics of the village extend generous hospitality, offering their homes and food to visiting pilgrims of diverse religious and caste groups with whom they otherwise do not maintain social relationships.

Renowned for their powers of fertility and healing, the shrines profiled above are three of the more popular rural sites for *nerccai* rituals in southeast Tamil Nadu. Their patron saints—all foreigners, two European and one Mediterranean—enjoy the principal patronage of three distinct caste groups. Though these shrines share many performance features, each has its distinctive character and reputation largely defined by the personal identity and special sacral powers of its patron saint, its ritual tradition, and, more importantly, by the caste identities of its principal clientele that together reflect the role social realities play in the indigenous construction of the saint's persona, powers, the shrine, and its ritual tradition. Let us take a close look at three specific examples of devotional *nerccai* rituals—one from each of these three shrines.

Three Examples of Devotional *Nerccais*

Hair-shaving Rite

Among the various *nerccai* rituals, hair-shaving is perhaps the simplest and most popular devotional exercise. Though hair-shaving may be done throughout the year, the festival season is considered especially auspicious. Devotees perform hair-shaving for four different purposes. First, as a petitionary or promissory rite where the devotee offers hair as a token offering for favors sought. In this case, the hair serves as a form of "down-payment" to the saint. Second, it is performed as a fulfillment or thanksgiving rite for favors already received. Here the hair serves as the full payment of debt. Third, as a dedication rite where the first crop of hair of a newborn child is offered to the patron saint to insure his special protection and assistance for the child. Here, hair takes the form of an insurance premium. Finally, as a pilgrimage devotional rite through which the devotee affirms his or her continued faith in and loyalty to the patron saint. In this instance, the hair functions as an annual payment or tribute owed to the patron in return for his continued protection for the devotee and his extended family. Depending on the context, hair-shaving may function either as an autonomous or as a preliminary, ancillary rite. In some *nerccai* performances, like the animal sacrificial rites and fertility rites, hair-shaving acts as an ancillary rite. In other instances, it functions as an autonomous rite since it is the sole contractual item. For example, an individual devotee may promise to offer his or her hair, either as a promissory or payment gesture, in return for a specific favor like freedom from a specific illness.

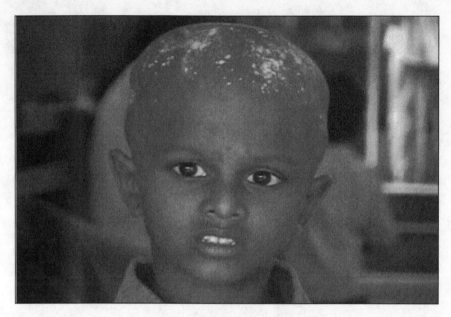

Figure 4.2 A young boy has his hair shaved as a sign of dedication to St. John de Britto

The prevalence of hair-shaving has led to the development of church-sponsored tonsure houses in such well-known Catholic centers as the shrines of Our Lady of Good Health in Velankanni and John de Britto at Oriyur. In these institutionalized shrines, only church authorized barbers are licensed to perform hair-shaving, most of whom are Hindus. These Hindu barbers pay a small percentage of their earnings to the shrine as certification fee. This suggests that the move to institutionalize and streamline the ritual is inspired more by economic realities than religious considerations. In lesser-known local shrines like the shrine of St. Anne at Arulanandapuram, hair-shaving is less formal and less structured where freelancing Hindu barbers serve as ritual specialists.

During the annual festival at the shrine of St. John de Britto, a steady stream of devotees flocks to church-sponsored tonsure houses for hair-shaving where dozens of barbers are pressed into service. On the last day, an average of six hundred devotees have their hair shaved. The rite itself is simple, devoid of any official liturgical elements. Conspicuous by his absence is the shrine priest who has no part or function in this rite. According to an elderly parish catechist, in the past, the shrine priest at Oriyur used to cut a few plaits of hair prior to the actual hair-shaving. Today however the shrine priests have no such symbolic roles, although occasionally devotees may seek the priest's blessing before proceeding

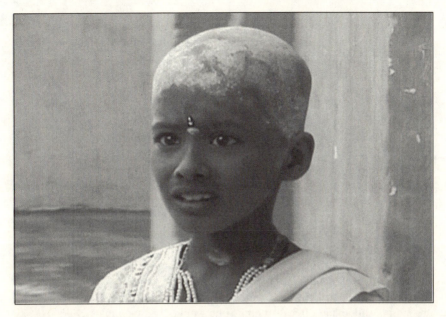

Figure 4.3 A young girl has her hair shaved in fulfillment of a vow that her parents had taken

to the tonsure house. Similarly, some devotees may request the shrine priest to bless the goat before it is slaughtered. Most priests perform these duties rather unwillingly and reluctantly because, they say, these lay practices are at odds with their own theological training and beliefs. Ironically, however, many of these priests, who are disdainful and indifferent to such popular practices as tonsure or goat sacrifice in their professional context, become deeply invested and involved when their own family members undertake such practices. Following the hair removal, the devotees bathe, apply sandal paste on the head, circumambulate the shrine and offer prayers, candles, and cereal offerings to the patron saint. Depending on the context, the promissory note is either submitted along with other votive offerings or destroyed to signal the fulfillment of the vow.

Fertility Nerccais

Fertility rites constitute another important strand of the *nerccai* ritual scheme. Indeed, no human need so commands the religiosity of the Catholics in rural Tamil Nadu as much as the need for fertility—the fertility of women, land, cattle, and crops. So dominant is this need that the fertility motif—in my view— forms the nerve center of the *nerccai* ritual system. According to some estimates, about 50 percent of all *nerccai* rites are inspired by fertility concerns. In this section I focus on two specific fertility rites—the colorful coconut sapling rite and the baby auction ritual.

The Coconut Sapling Rite

A popular *nerccai* ritual at the shrine of St. John de Britto is the presentation of coconut saplings to the patron saint. Women praying for progeny write a promissory note documenting the terms of the contract, have their hair shaved at the church tonsure house, take a ritual bath, circumambulate the shrine three times with a coconut sapling in hand, and place the promissory note (*muri*) and coconut sapling at Britto's altar. The use of the coconut sapling has much symbolic significance. In Tamil folk tradition, the coconut sapling is a popular fertility symbol. The Tamil word for coconut sapling (*tennam pillai*) has phonetic resonance to the Tamil word for child (*pillai*). As with hair-shaving, devotees perform the coconut sapling rite either as a promissory or fulfillment gesture. The following testimonial by a devotee captures its essential spirit. "Last year I offered a *nerccai* to Britto and promised that I would carry a coconut sapling around his shrine and offer it to him, if he would give me a male child. Thanks

Figure 4.4 A pilgrim mother and son at the shrine of St. Anthony, Uvari in June 2000. The mother fulfilled a dedication vow by having her son's hair tonsured to resemble St. Anthony's hair style, locally known as *anthoniar pattam*.

Shared Vows, Shared Space, and Shared Dieties 53

Figure 4.5 A young girl offers a coconut sapling to Britto and prays for health

to Britto, now I have a son." Pointing to the child in her arms she said: "This child is Britto's gift to my family. As promised, I shaved off my hair and carried a coconut sapling in thanksgiving for the favor."[9] Though formerly the coconut sapling rite was observed only when praying for children, nowadays the coconut sapling serves as a generic symbol for various fertility needs including the fertility of land, crops, and cattle.[10]

The "Baby Auction" Rite

Another expression of the "debt payment" motif is the ceremonial auctioning of babies that is unique to the shrine of St. Anne. Couples seeking children indicate in a promissory note that, if their prayer is granted, they will return the child to the saint. Signed by two witnesses and notarized by the parish catechist, the promissory note is kept in the shrine until its fulfillment. If and when the prayer is answered, couples pay off their debt by returning the child to the saint in a carefully orchestrated ceremonial auction. One such auction that I witnessed at this shrine in July 1990 well illustrates the salient features of this vow ritual.

Joseph, a police officer in the city of Madurai, and his wife Mary, an elementary school teacher, got married in 1982 but were childless for seven years. After persistent admonition and prompting from family and friends, they went on pilgrimage to several shrines—Catholic and Hindu—including the popular shrine of Our Lady of Good Health at Velankanni and offered numerous *nerccai* rites praying for a child, but to no avail. In early July 1988, they met a native of Arulanandapuram who testified to the special sacral powers of the shrine of St. Anne and persuaded the young couple to offer *nerccai* rites during the annual festival in the month of July. Desperate to have a child, Joseph and Mary went on a pilgrimage to the shrine of St. Anne in July 1988 and submitted a prom-

Figure 4.6 The parish catechist auctions a baby in fulfillment of the parents' vow to St. Anne of Arulanandapuram, Tamil Nadu, as the baby's mother looks on

issory note (*muri*) pledging to return the child to St. Anne if she would grant their prayer. Later that year Mary conceived and gave birth to a baby girl in 1989. The following year, the couple returned to the shrine with the ten-month-old baby during the annual festival to pay off their debt. At the couple's express request, the village catechist rang the church bell announcing the couple's intention to fulfill their vow and inviting the entire village to witness the ritual. After placing various votive offerings at the altar of St. Anne as thanksgiving for favors received, the couple entered the vestibule and handed over the infant to the village catechist. Conspicuous by his absence was the shrine priest who stayed back in his residence that is just 100 yards away. With the whole village now in attendance, the catechist received the baby, called for bids on the baby, and proceeded to auction off the baby. All members of the assembly—men and women, young and old, local villagers and visiting pilgrims—enthusiastically participated in the auction by making bids. Joseph and Mary stood on the side and watched as the ceremonial auction gained momentum. When the bidding reached 100 rupees, the child's father made a bid for 101 rupees (a paltry sum even by local economic

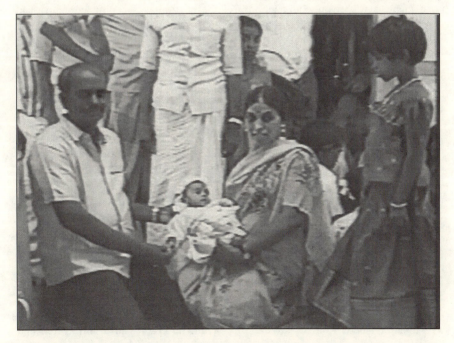

Figure 4.7 The baby's parents proudly show off the baby to the villagers after redeeming her in the ceremonial auction

standards), and the auctioneer quickly concluded the auction and handed over the baby to the highest bidder—the child's natural father!

During my interview with the couple soon after the auction, I learned that prior to the ceremony they had made a private deal with the auctioneer so that when the father bid 101 rupees, the auctioneer would quickly conclude the auction. Thus the auction was conducted as scripted with everyone taking active part. All participants in this ritual drama knew and played their part diligently—some by their presence and others by making bids—knowing full well that there were no real losers and winners in this game and that everyone would come out as winners. The auctioneer knew well that he was presiding over a pretend auction that has serious implications. Members of the assembly were serious about making bids on the child knowing that they would never make the final bidding. Yet they played a crucial role insofar as they helped the parents fulfill their promise to pay off the debt. The parents initiated the auction confident in the knowledge that they would not in fact lose the baby even if the ritual caused some internal anxiety. According to devotees, the saint also knew that she would not get the baby, as did the priests and church officials. With the exception of the screaming baby—the central character in this ritual drama who was blissfully innocent of the multiple and multilayered negotiations and deals—everyone knew it was a pretend auction. Yet the auction was conducted with dead seriousness. By participating in this ritual drama, devotees fulfill their part of the deal and signal to the saint, the church officials, and the village community that the transaction is complete. While devotees acknowledge the ritual maneuvering and manipulation implicit in this transaction, they do not think that they are short changing the saint. What matters to the saint, they say, is not the child per se, but devotees' commitment to fulfill their part of the deal in some form. This ceremonial auction benefits all concerned; parents have the satisfaction of living up to their part of the contractual agreement; the shrine gains additional revenue; the villagers gain renewed faith in the efficacy of their rituals and the sacred powers of their local shrine; the saint's sacral powers are authenticated, enhancing her spiritual prestige and gaining her some new devotees. I learned that an average of six such ceremonial auctions take place every year during the annual festival.

A minor variation of the baby auctioning ritual is the "cradle rite" popular at the shrine of John Britto. Couples who had promised to return the child to Britto fulfill their promise by carrying the child in a cradle—made of cloth and sugarcane trees—and circumambulating the shrine three times, after which flowers, candles, money, and cereal items are offered as votive offerings. In this case, the child is not surrendered but instead dedicated to the saint. Another version of the cradle rite is common at the shrine of Our Lady of Good Health in Velankanni where women praying for a child tie cradles to a shrine tree and promise to offer a silver cradle in lieu of the child. When their prayer is granted, devotees pay off their debt by offering a silver cradle to the Virgin Mary.

Healing Rituals

Whereas Oriyur and Arulanandapuram are noted for fertility, Uvari, as noted earlier, is reputed for healing. Many regard the shrine of St. Anthony at Uvari as the preeminent site for healing from demonic possession and various forms of black magic and sorcery. Devotees bring those who are said to suffer from the effects of demonic possession to the shrine—often bound in chains—to pray for healing. In return for favors and boons hoped for, they promise to carry out a series of ritual obligations known locally as *asanam*.

Centerpiece of Uvari ritual life, *asanam* is a collective term for a series of ritual actions that include, but are not limited to, fasting, ritual sacrifice of a goat or chicken, hair-shaving, and feeding thirteen poor persons. It is especially meritorious and auspicious to offer *asanam* on a Tuesday since St. Anthony died on a Tuesday. Church officials state that an average of about thirty-five to forty *asanams* take place every Tuesday. Many arrive early in the morning by bus, rented vans, or private cars, spend the day at the shrine to complete the rituals, and return by dusk while others stay in the church guest house for an extended period that can be anywhere from two days to three weeks. Devotees take special care to ensure the proper execution of their promises and payment of the debt owed to the saint lest they incur the saint's wrath. Uvari Anthony has a reputation to be vengeful and wreak havoc on those who break their promise. An elderly villager commented: "If we don't fulfill our promises, St. Anthony will beat us to death. Every night he goes around the village on a white horse wielding a silver stick. He chases the delinquents and causes misfortune for them. He does not spare even the priests who occasionally become greedy for church funds."[11]

The general pattern for *asanam* rites is as follows. Preliminary ceremonies begin with a purificatory bath with thirteen buckets of water drawn from the miracle well at the shrine.[12] Although this is mandatory only for the principal petitioner or beneficiary, other family members also take this purificatory bath. Then the sacrificial animal—usually a male goat—is similarly bathed with thirteen buckets of water and garlanded. Accompanied by family members carrying rice, vegetables, and other items, the petitioner and the goat—both drenched in water—circumambulate the shrine thirteen times. When this is concluded, the whole group assembles in front of Anthony's altar to offer thanks for favor(s) received and to signal its resolve to fulfill the vow promised to the saint. Family members then guide the goat to the slaughterhouse located behind the shrine where it is ritually slaughtered and skinned. Whereas the skin is usually donated to the church, the meat is used in preparing an elaborate meal in the community kitchen.[13] The preparation of the ritual meal is a collaborative exercise where all family members take part. Cooking in a communal space also produces spontaneous interaction—even commensality—with fellow pilgrims of diverse castes and creeds.

Meanwhile, each pilgrim family sponsoring the *asanam* is assigned thirteen beggars and destitutes of different gender, caste, and religions to whom the ritual meal is to be served. Family members take special care to treat them with utmost respect and special honor since they are believed to be the saint's ritual surrogates at the meal.[14] Devotees stress that religious identities and caste considerations do not play any role in who gets selected especially since the vow-taker does not make the selection. A popular story recounted by pilgrims and villagers alike has the basic ingredients of a religious parable: "Many decades ago a poor man had cooked a meal and offered it to others. Nobody was willing to eat it. He cried before the Lord. He then dug a pit in front of the church, spread some leaves in it, put the food in and covered it with leaves. He then covered up the pit and left." The village elder's eyes lit up and his voice broke as he related, "Six months later they were digging a pit to hoist the flag for the festival. Vapour rose from the food which was still fresh. Devotees scrambled to eat it. After that incident people accept food here from everybody irrespective of caste, creed, colour or riches" (http://www.rediff.com/travel/1998/dec/19chris.htm).[15] Those selected for the ritual honor may be Hindus, Muslims, or Catholics. Thus, Hindus may partake of the *asanam* meal hosted by a Catholic family, and vice versa. During my recent field research in January 2003, I attended several *asanams* where Catholics were fed by Hindu sponsors. Though

Figure 4.8 Asanam meal served to female ritual surrogates of St. Anthony

asanam may be offered for any number of human and/or spiritual needs, including fertility, it is particularly efficacious in obtaining a cure for various physical diseases and mental disorders including possession.

While *asanam* is the final payment promised to the saint, devotees also promise and execute a series of ritual observances when they are at the shrine that may be—depending on the patient's psychophysical condition and the family's financial situation—anywhere from three to six months.[16] Their daily routine consists of a number of rituals that demonstrate to the saint and fellow-pilgrims their faith in the saint's special sacred powers as well as the urgency and sincerity of their petition. An early morning purificatory bath at the "miracle well" in the shrine premises, circumambulating the shrine thirteen times in wet clothes, fasting, eating balls of neem paste (locally called "*puthumai* paste" or wondrous paste), attending Mass, reciting rosary, and participating in mid-day and evening Catholic prayer services are the most common daily rituals. These on-site rituals serve as spiritual down-payments or premium for healing. If one observes these rituals faithfully and regularly, devotees say, they would begin to be healed. The six possessed women and their relatives I interviewed at the shrine endorsed this view. Subha, a twenty-three-year-old Hindu woman, said:

> When I was nine-years-old I first became possessed by a woman who had committed suicide. Later when I turned sixteen Isakki Amman took hold of me. Now I am tormented by two spirits. My family took me to several Hindu *pujaris,* magicians and sorcerers who performed numerous pujas to our devatas but there was no improvement. We spent 20000 rupees in the process. Then we heard about Uvari St. Anthony and came here three months ago. Since then I have been diligently performing all the rituals my mother and relatives have instructed me to do. After I began following these instructions, I began to feel better. Earlier, I used to run naked and do all sorts of crazy things. But I do not act that way anymore. The demon has not left me as yet. She still tortures me and sometimes my head is ready to explode when she taunts me. Once a day I go into possession frenzy and dance. Otherwise, I am feeling better now. I want to be free and only Anthony can drive this demon away. I know he will. We have renounced our former *kula teiyvams.* Now St. Anthony is our *kula teiyvam.* My mother and I have promised Anthony to offer a goat and observe *asanam* when I am fully cured.[17]

Subha is not an isolated or exceptional case but typifies the bulk of Anthony's devotees seeking healing from possession. According to church authorities, nearly 80 percent of these are Hindus; more precisely, they are Hindu women. What is

Figure 4.9 A young possessed woman rolls on the ground at the shrine of St. Anthony

noteworthy about this particular cultic constituency is that almost all of them claim to be possessed by one or more of the malevolent Hindu village deities like Isakki Amman and Chutalaimadan whose notoriety is well known in the region. Many say that first they seek relief through familiar Hindu and secular sources such as medicine men, magicians, sorcerers, doctors, and Hindu *pujaris*. When these fail, as a last recourse they turn to St. Anthony whom they come to revere as their "new" *kula teiyvam*. Young Subha's religious odyssey not only serves as a textbook case for the possessed but vividly illustrates the dynamic of multileveled sharing that occurs in Uvari where Hindus apparently possessed by malevolent Hindu deities seek relief from a European Catholic saint enshrined in an Indian Catholic shrine through locally constructed Catholic rituals that are profoundly influenced by Hindu religious imagination. This necessitates a close look at this phenomenon of shared rituals, shared space, and shared deities.

Shared Vows, Shared Space, and Shared Deities

Derived from Tamil popular Hinduism, evidently the Catholic *nerccai* system bears a strong family resemblance to the Hindu *nerttikkatan* rituals. The data furnished previously suggest that the Catholic system retains the basic principles, idiom, vocabulary, content, and rubric of the Hindu system. The notions of *kula teiyvam* and debt payment are central to both systems. Some devout Catholic *nerccai* performers also wear *kavi* clothes traditionally associated with Hindu ascetics and renunciants. With the exception of certain obvious Catholic items like the candle, cross, saints, and scapulars that serve as identity markers there is very little difference between Catholic and Hindu *nerccai* ritual performance. This suggests that, with some minor variations, Catholics and Hindus share a common ritual system.

This system of sharing extends beyond the realm of rituals to include shrines and deities as well. In other words, Catholics dedicate vows not only to Catholic saints but also to non-Catholic deities—often Hindu deities—in alien sacred space. The testimonial of a Catholic devotee of Oriyur is worth noting. "Just three miles away from the shrine of St. John Britto is the Karuppannasami temple. Many of us Catholics go there to offer goat sacrifice, perform the hair-shaving rite, and garland the Hindu deity. We also partake in the communal meal following the goat sacrifice."[18] Sometimes, Catholics also take vows in order to appease a powerful Hindu deity like Mariyamman, the Tamil goddess of disease and healing (see chapter 3 in this volume). It is also not uncommon among some Tamil Catholics to offer *nerccai* rituals to a Catholic saint and a Hindu deity during a single pilgrimage journey. The more common practice, however, is to import Hindu rituals into Catholic shrines and direct them to a Catholic saint whose personality and power are often modeled after familiar Hindu tutelary deities. Consequently, the recipients of Catholic vows form a curious mixture of Catholic saints and Hindu deities creating an ecumenical pantheon and resulting in a sort of meta-communion of deities.

Conversely, many Hindu pilgrims go on pilgrimage to such popular Catholic shrines to perform *nerccai* rituals to Catholic saints. According to one estimate, about 35 percent of Velankanni pilgrims are non-Catholic. During my fieldwork at Oriyur I met several Hindu families who had come to offer *nerccai* sacrifices to Britto, many of whom regard this European Catholic saint as their *kula teiyvam*. This is also true, as we just noted, of St. Anthony's shrine at Uvari, where Hindus constitute a sizeable segment of all devotees. This number grows still higher during the annual festival in February. In other remote Catholic centers in Tamil Nadu like St. Anthony's shrine at Manganur, near Tiruchirapalli, Hindu devotees outnumber Catholics. Moreover, when they are at a Catholic shrine, Hindus behave and act like Catholics taking part in Catholic rituals. For example, in all the three shrines discussed in this essay, Hindu pilgrims take part in the chariot (*ter*) procession when the statues of the patron saints are drawn through village streets. Many Hindus perceive in these Catholic saints familiar Hindu sacred figures and hence invest in them the powers and attributes they traditionally associate with Hindu deities. This perspective accounts, in part, for the relative ease and comfort with which Hindu devotees recite the Rosary, attend Mass, and receive communion and cross religious and ritual boundaries. Although Corinne Dempsey (2001) speaks of several instances where through sibling stories Keralite Christians and Hindus effect a sort of communion of disparate deities, I did not encounter such stories or strategies in Tamil Nadu.

Thus the Catholic *nerccai* system and practice serve as an important intersection for the dialogue not only of rituals and devotees but of sites and deities as well. This multilayered dialogue does not absolve or remove religious differences. Nor does it erase the boundaries between deities and shrines. Rather, the differences and boundaries are acknowledged as real but temporarily suspended, violated, and transcended. Such violations of normative boundaries, however temporary, are a source of anxiety for the church hierarchy that tends to view these ritual manifestations as signs of a dysfunctional Catholicism and as a "disease" of popular religiosity. The laity on the other hand frequently complains that their priests do not understand or relate to their religious sensibilities. This perspectival disparity between lay devotees and the church hierarchy reveals their mutual misunderstanding and mutual devaluation of each other's religious perspectives and practices. Indeed, many clergy seek to maintain an intellectual distance between the simple faith of the people and their own mature faith, a phenomenon that Behar discovers also among rural Catholics in Spain (1990: 106). Even within the church hierarchy in Tamil Nadu, there is no one uniform voice but multiple—often competing—voices that adopt divergent approaches to this phenomenon. For example, the perspectives of clergy in daily pastoral interaction with common folk significantly differ from those in theological seminaries and administrative centers who generally have little or no pastoral engagement. The former tend to be more tolerant of lay devotionalism—some might call it dysfunction—than the latter. As I have suggested elsewhere (2002), the pastoral clergy in Tamil Nadu regularly find themselves caught between institutional regulations and directives on the one hand and pastoral exigencies predicated by their flock's own cultural and religious liminality on the other. Consequently, though they disapprove of the religious practices of their flock on theological grounds, pastoral realities compel them to look the other way. The recurring demand for pastoral compromises produces in the pastoral clergy a certain personal and theological liminality. The following incident illustrates this tension. A Catholic bishop in Tamil Nadu issued a decree in his diocese banning all *ter* (chariot) processions at Catholic festivals. A few days later, the same bishop presided over festival celebrations in one of his parishes and reiterated the ban he had issued earlier. As the bishop came out of the church, a group of local parishioners asked him to bless a *ter* kept ready for procession. Despite his condemnatory sermon minutes before, the bishop blessed the *ter*. When a priest sought an explanation for his quick turnaround, the bishop simply replied: "We have no choice but to respect the sentiments of our people" (Raj 2002: 13).

Conclusion

The phenomenon of shared vows, shared space, and shared deities exemplified in vow performances amply demonstrates that the issue of religious identity in south India continues to be problematic. The *nerccai* practices of Tamil Catholics vividly show that the boundaries between Hindus and Catholics, as Vasudha Narayanan has argued in the case of Nagore pilgrims (see chapter 5 in this volume), is, to say the least, quite fuzzy and fluid. While the common heritage and the cultural landscape of the Tamils might contribute to this fluidity and ritual hybridity, there is another compelling factor, namely, the need to obtain solution to human crises or problems that threaten life's balance. Tamil-speaking Hindus and Catholics transcend religious and ritual boundaries especially during crisis moments when the devotee deems cross-religious rituals and pilgrimages as necessary and salutary in the quest for solution to a human or spiritual crisis or problem. A Catholic devotee succinctly captured the essence of this religious pragmatism when he said: "The one who helped our family in a past crisis is our answer to the present problem. It does not matter whether that figure is a Catholic saint or a Hindu deity. The one who delivers is indeed our deity, at least for now!"

Notes

1. For a detailed discussion of the nature and type of *nerccai* rituals, see my Ph.D. dissertation (1994: 115–95).

2. Elsewhere (1994, 2002) I have discussed at length the goat sacrificial rituals performed at the shrine of St. John de Britto.

3. In India, sites and shrines associated with St. Anthony frequently are given this honorific title as a way of enhancing their spiritual repute. It also suggests the localization of the saint. Another popular site competing for this title is the shrine of St. Antony at Puliampatti, near Tirunelveli in Tamil Nadu.

4. A mile north of Uvari is a Hindu village known as "Nadar Uvari" that derives its name from the dominant caste group (Nadars) in the village.

5. Today there is a website that provides basic information about the shrine, its history, miraculous powers, and major festivals. See: http://www.rediff.com/travel/1998/dec/19chris.htm.

6. Whereas church historians trace this shrine to the early nineteenth century, local tradition claims that the shrine is at least four hundred years old. Interview with Marion Thomas at Uvari on June 4, 2000.

7. Devotees recount moving stories and experiences about the saint's extraordinary power to deliver those who take refuge in him. The testimonials of miraculous healing are carefully documented and preserved in the church archives. Church authorities gave me permission to review and copy devotees' testimonials.

8. Curiously, although St. Francis Xavier is revered as a great missionary and a saintly figure who initiated the conversion of Parava Catholics, he does not command the intensity and extent of devotional attention which St. Antony enjoys among the masses.

9. Interview with Rosammal at Oriyur on September 8, 1990.

10. For a detailed discussion of the cattle fertility rite in this shrine, see my article (2002: 4–18).

11. Interview with Marion Thomas at Uvari on June 4, 2000.

12. The number 13 has special religious significance since St. Anthony's feast in the Roman Catholic calendar falls on the 13th of June.

13. Though the vast majority of devotees come from humble economic backgrounds, usually *asanam* meals are quite elaborate. For example, during my field research I met at least two families that had brought 75 kilos of rice and three goats for the *asanam* meal. Devotees pay a nominal fee to rent cooking utensils from the shrine.

14. For an analysis of the social and religious implications of this role reversal ritual, see my article (2004: 33–44).

15. In some versions of this story told by Uvari residents, the man who buried the food was an untouchable (Harijan). I have heard a nearly identical story related at the shrine of St. John de Britto (Raj 1994: 150–51).

16. During my field research at Uvari I met several families who had been at the shrine for more than three months. Many remain in the shrine until they are fully cured.

17. Interview with Subha at Uvari on June 9, 2000. While slaughtering goats or chickens is a common *nerccai* ritual in several Tamil Catholic shrines like Oriyur, it is only at Uvari goats are offered in return for healing from demonic possession.

18. Interview with Arockiadas at Oriyur on January 29, 2003.

References

Bayly, Susan. 1989. *Shrines, Saints and Kings: Muslims and Christians in South Indian Society 1700–1900*. Cambridge: Cambridge University Press.

Behar, Ruth. 1990. "The Struggle for the Church: Popular Anticlericalism and Religiosity in Post-Franco Spain." In *Religious Orthodoxy and Popular Faith in European Society,* ed. Ellen Badone, 76–106. Princeton: Princeton University Press.

Dempsey, Corinne, G. 2001. *Kerala Christian Sainthood: Collisions of Culture and Worldview in South India,* New York: Oxford University Press.

Diehl, Carl, G. 1965. *Church and Shrine: Intermingling Patterns of Cultures in the Life of Some Christian Groups in South India*. Lund: Uppsala.

———. 1956. *Instrument and Purpose: Studies on the Rites and Rituals in South India*. Lund: C.W.K. Gleerup.

Raj, Selva J. 2004. "Dialogue 'On the Ground': The Complicated Identities and the Complex Negotiations of Catholics and Hindus in South India." *Journal of Hindu-Christian Studies* 17: 33–44.

———. 2002. "Transgressing Boundaries, Transcending Turner: The Pilgrimage Tradition at the Shrine of St. John de Britto." *Journal of Ritual Studies* 16, 1: 4–18.

———. 1994. *Interactive Religious Systems in Indian Popular Catholcism: The Case of Tamil and Santal Catholics*. Ph.D. dissertation, University of Chicago.

Sauliere, A. 1947. *Red Sand: A Life of St. John de Britto, S.J., Martyr of the Madura Mission*. Madurai: De Nobili Press.

Uvari website, http://www.rediff.com/travel/1998/dec/19chris.htm.

5

Religious Vows at the Shrine of Shahul Hamid

Vasudha Narayanan

Women carrying flower garlands swarmed around me. Men and women carried little baskets of offerings. Some were putting cash and little silver representations of human organs into a large *hundi,* where one traditionally dropped "offerings." People washed themselves in the tank with holy water or drew water from the sacred well and bathed themselves. Children and toddlers, with their newly shaved heads covered with sandalwood paste, ran through the courtyards; courtyards covered with stones donated by grateful devotees.

It was only the murmuring of the Fatiha by a Muslim trustee as he said intercessory prayers for my welfare and the towering minarets that assured me that the physical and spiritual contexts for these activities was Muslim and not Hindu. "Make a promise," urges the person saying the prayers; "promise the saint that if your wish is fulfilled you will come back and offer him ten times what you are giving now." As I make the down payment, I look around. About half the pilgrims at this shrine seem to be Hindu; the other half Muslim. There seemed to be equal numbers of men and women; however, the trustees and their relatives who offered prayers, recited "mantras," and tied protective amulets around the pilgrims' wrists were all male Muslims.

This is the famous Nagore *dargah,* the final resting place of Shahul Hamid (born c. 1491), more respectfully and commonly known as Nagore Andavar ("the ruler or Lord of Nagore"); Hazrath ("his excellency" or "the honorable one"); Qutb ("pole, axis"), or Nayakar (Tamil: the "leader"), or just affectionately as Meeran (from the Persian *mir* or leader) Sahib. This is my first visit. I felt a sense of deja vu: I had just been to the Catholic Velankanni basilica about twenty kilometers down the road and also by the seashore. This cathedral is devoted to *deva mata* ("the divine mother" or "mother of God," a term referring to the Virgin Mary in south Indian Christianity). Not far off are the equally well-known Hindu temples of Nagapattinam. Tiru Nagai is the traditional name for Nagapattinam and the Vishnu temple there was celebrated by Tirumangai Alvar, a poet-saint of the ninth/tenth century, and the temple to Shiva and Saturn (Sanisvara) at Tirunallaru draws hundreds of thousands of Hindu pilgrims. There had been varying levels of disorganization in these institutions; but a remarkable *structural* similarity in pilgrim ritual activity was readily apparent. This perception has only been reinforced in all my subsequent trips.

The pilgrims come from many parts of India, but the Tamil-speaking people and Tamil customs of veneration are easily discernible. They come to pray, to venerate, to give thanks, to petition, to glorify Nagore Andavar, Shahul Hamid Meeran Sahib, and the supreme being whose grace was manifested through his devotee. Shahul Hamid, whose tomb is in Nagore, is perceived as a saint embedded in the local cultural milieu. However, he is also connected with other Muslim figures in India and with Islamic centers of pilgrimage and saints in the Middle East. While the figure of Shahul Hamid and the town of Nagore are constructed in *ritual* as participating in all these intersecting realms, the *texts* that glorify Nagore seem to emphasize a uniquely Tamil milieu, and the Tamil linguistic and cultural identities are emphasized. Shahul Hamid, therefore, is a saint who is at once relevant to Tamil Muslims and yet connects them through his ancestor Muhiyudin Abd al Qadir al-Jilani (1078–1166) to the ancestral Middle Eastern Islam.

This chapter will unpack the ritual context and performance of some votive exercises in the Nagore Dargah Sharif, in the coastal town of Nagore in the Nagapattinam district of Tamil Nadu state. The material is based primarily on the many visits made to the Nagore *dargah* (literally, "doorway"; refers usually to the burial place of saints) in the last few years, as well as on the wide variety of biographical works on Shahul Hamid and descriptions of Nagore. I will be paying particular attention to the many miracles credited to Shahul Hamid. It is based on these miracles and the conviction of Shahul Hamid's "power" that many vows are undertaken and votive exercises performed. Recollection of the miracle, therefore, is at the heart of such rituals.

I will initially relate the life of Shahul Hamid, then briefly talk about the kinds of votive rites one sees at the *dargah*, the model of a vow, and the words used to talk of these rituals. I will then discuss the *dargah* in the larger south Indian devotional context. In the final section on ritual *kitchidi,* I ask: what kinds of words or metaphors can we use to describe the phenomenon of Hindus and Muslims venerating a Muslim saint in a Muslim *dargah* with the ritual idiom of the Tamil culture?

Literature on Shahul Hamid and Nagore

The local *wali* (very loosely translated as "saint") of Nagore, well-known all over Tamil Nadu, is hailed thus in a modern song:
>You are the lord (*yajamana*)
>who came to protect us
>in the city of Nagore.

Hindus of all castes in Tamil Nadu frequent the *dargah* in Nagore as they do many other Muslim shrines. Tamil-speaking Muslims have celebrated this *pir/ wali* in several *kavya* poems and biographies.[1] The saint is also praised extravagantly in many other Tamil poems. Two works celebrate the life and the afterlife miracles of Shahul Hamid. The most important biography is the *Tirukkarana Puranam* ("The Sacred Purana or Narrative of Divine Miracles," henceforth *TKP*) by Ceyk Aptul Kaatiru Nayinar Leppai Alim, also known as Vidvananda Siromani and as Cekuna Pulavar. Cekuna Pulavar says that he is from Kakirur (said to be derived from the Arabic Kahira or Cairo), better known as Kayalpatnam in Tamil Nadu (*TKP: katavul valtu*, 33). The author says that he composed the *Tirukkarana Puranam* in Hijri 1227 (1812 CE; Wednesday, September 9 according to *TKP katavul valtu*, 38.) The colophon at the end of the book says that it was printed on January 5, 1863. The *TKP* is Cekuna Pulavar's second work; his first major work was one on Muhiyudin Abd al-Qadir (Katiru) al-Jilani (1078–1166) of Baghdad.

The *Nakur Puranam* (*NP*) speaks of the miracles of Shahul Hamid in the *dargah* and in Nagore after his death. This text was written in 1882–83 by Kulam Katiru Navalar (b. 1833) and published in 1893.

While the *TKP* and the *NP* are written in the *kavya* mode and are somewhat difficult to read, the prose biography called *Kanjul Karaamattu* by Sri la Sri Kulam Katiru (Ghulam Khader) Navalar (published 1902) is very popular. There are also several modern Tamil biographies of Shahul Hamid.

The Life of Shahul Hamid

Nagore is the burial place of Shahul Hamid (Tamil: Cakul Amitu Nayakar). Shahul Hamid, was apparently a thirteenth-generation descendant of Muhiyudin Abd al-Qadir (Katiru) al-Jilani, a renowned Sufi saint. According to some accounts, Shahul Hamid was born in 1490 in Manikkapur, in the modern state of Uttar Pradesh; others put the date much later. The *Nakur Puranam* says that he lived for sixty-eight years and says that he died in Hijri 978 (10th day of Jamatul Ahir; corresponding to August 7, Friday, 1579); this puts his date of birth at Hijri 919 or 1513 CE. Since many of those reading the biographies are Hindu devotees of the saint, the texts usually say that Manikkapur is near Ayodhya, a place that most Hindus (and now, all Muslims in India) are familiar with. The name given to him at birth was Sayid Abdul Khader. The books recount many miracles even before he was born. When just a child, Shahul Hamid was visited by the prophet Kiliru (Khazir) and blessed by him. Kiliru spit into Shahul Hamid's mouth, thus transmitting divine grace. Transmission of divine grace through bodily substances, especially saliva, is a common motif in a lot of Tamil Islamic poetry.

The saint is said to have left home when he was eighteen and met his parents only eighteen years later. He went in search of spiritual truth and found a teacher in Sayid Muhammad Kavud (Ghouse) of Gwalior. Shahul Hamid stayed with him for ten years. He is credited with a charismatic personality and with hundreds of miracles; most Tamil biographies are filled with accounts of these miracles. In one biography, he is said to have befriended the Hindu saint Mirabai and saved her from drowning.

Shahul Hamid refused to get married, but is said to have spiritually fathered a son. Apparently when he went to Lahore, he met Hazrat Nuruddin Mupti. Nuruddin sorrowfully told Shahul Hamid that he did not have children. Shahul Hamid asked him to bring his wife and also some betel leaves and nuts. He then chewed on the nuts and asked Nuruddin to give the chewed nuts to his wife. Nuruddin was asked to take his wife home and remain celibate for forty days. Shahul Hamid then told Nuruddin that he will have a son soon and he was to be named Muhammad Yusuf; however, he belonged to Shahul Hamid and would be considered to be *his* son. He also predicted that after Yusuf, Nuruddin would get three more sons and two daughters. Shahul Hamid told Nuruddin that when Yusuf turned seven, he would ask for his father; he was then to be given Shahul Hamid's toothbrush and sent to Mecca. There, he would meet with his "real" father. Through Shahul Hamid's grace, Nuruddin and his wife Juhara Bibi got a son who eventually joined his spiritual father, Shahul Hamid. Although Shahul Hamid is said not to have *biologically* fathered a son, Yusuf is considered to be his child.

In this story of how Shahul Hamid spiritually acquired a son, we see elements of votive exercises in later centuries. A person who dearly desires something makes a supplication to the saint. Shahul Hamid fulfills that promise; in this case he asks for the offering of the son himself. In twentieth-century examples, the devotee will make a promise that if the saint were to fulfill his or her desire she or he will make a certain offering.

After extensive travels all over the Middle East, (among the many places Iraq, Mecca, Rum, and Yemen are named) the islands in the Indian Ocean, and with a vast entourage of disciples, Shahul Hamid is said to have reached south India. It is said he had a vision of al-Jilani in Baghdad. He made a pilgrimage to Tiruchirapalli in south India, and the hagiographies say that he had a mystical conversation with the saint entombed there. In all these stories, as well, we see his connections with the Middle East on the one hand and the local milieu on the other. Finally, he entered the city of Nagore when he was forty-four. Apparently Shahul Hamid cured Achutappa Nayakar, the Hindu ruler of Thanjavur, of his physical affliction. Achutappa Nayakar, it is said, was suffering from various physical problems because of some sorcery. Shahul Hamid is said to have divined the cause, found a pigeon stuck with pins in the palace attic, and as he removed the pins, the king's health improved. In remembrance of this event, pilgrims to the Nagore *dargah* buy and release pigeons within the shrine. The ruler then gratefully donated two hundred acres of land to his entourage. Thus, even in the earliest stories of the hagiography, we see the piety of a Hindu ruler to a Muslim saint and rituals marking the miracle.

Eventually, Shahul Hamid died around 1558 when he was sixty-eight years old. The date of his death is variously given as 1558, 1570, and 1579. After his death, his disciples—who numbered 404 by now—split into four groups and spread in different directions, with the idea of gathering once a year during the anniversary (*kanduri*) celebrations. The first *kanduri* celebrations took place a year after his death. This is celebrated annually from the first day of the waxing moon in the month of Jamatul Ahir and reaches the peak of its celebrations on the tenth day. This day is considered by various sources as both his birth day and/or his death day.

The Nagore *dargah,* as it stands now, is about 194,790 square feet. The minarets around the *dargah* were built by devotees whose wishes were fulfilled by Shahul Hamid even after his physical body left this earth. Pratap Singh (1739–1763), the Hindu Maratha ruler of Thanjavur, built the tallest minaret (*periya manara,* towering about 131 feet) after he was blessed with a son. This was erected about 195 years after Shahul Hamid died. Pratap Singh's son, Tulsi, endowed the income of fifteen villages to this *dargah*.

Shahul Hamid's "son" Yusuf and Bibi had six sons and two daughters. Their descendants are the trustees of the Dargah Sharif today. So popular is Shahul Hamid that "memorial" *dargahs* were built in his honor, in the early nineteenth century, in Penang (Malaysia) and Singapore. In both places the memorials are called "Nagore Dargah." The Singapore *dargah* was built between 1827 and 1830 and it has recently been declared as a national monument. The Nagore shrine in Penang was built on a piece of land (about 1,656 square feet) given by the East India Company to the Tamil Muslims in 1810 and is near the large, well-known, Kapitan Kling mosque.

Other Miracles

In addition to the miracles encountered in the aforementioned stories, most Tamil biographies recount dozens (it may not be an exaggeration to say hundreds) of marvels both during his lifetime and after death. Adam and Eve are

Figure 5.1 Water pond behind Shahul Hamid's tomb; the tallest minaret was built by a Hindu devotee

said to have appeared in front of him and gifted him with a bowl that would feed all those who were hungry. During his lifetime Shahul Hamid is said to have saved ships from sinking. A popular story relates how he saved a Dutch ship from drowning by miraculously floating a mirror in the Bay of Bengal. The glass apparently plugged the leak in the ship.

The pattern of miracles that we see in the traditional biographies generally encompass the following areas: 1) blessing couples to have children, wealth, good harvest, et cetera; 2) curing the sick; 3) saving people from calamities including those that arise from "natural" causes and "evil spirits/magicians." (Since the latter are subsumed under "natural" in the local worldview, I am not referring to such phenomena as supernatural). There are also other miracles to convince the skeptics and unbelievers.

Let us begin with the first significant fulfillment of vows that biographical literature speaks about. Through Shahul Hamid's direct grace, his "spiritual" son Yusuf is born; in this case, Shahul Hamid himself asks for the offering. Yusuf is to be sent to him at a particular age. Achutappa Naiker, the king of Thanjavur, is cured, and he gives land to the saint. In later miracles, Pratap Singh gets the son he wants. In appreciation of the saint's favor and to proclaim their indebtedness to the saint, the devotees make significant offerings in a public way.

Almost all written narratives about Nagore miracles include the benefactions of the Hindu businessmen, Palaniyanti Pillai and Tirumalai Chetti, in addition to the donations of the Thanjavur kings, Pratap Singh and Tulasi. They are not fixed in any particular time period but Tirumalai Chetti is spoken of as being a servant of the Dutch colonial establishment. Apparently Palaniyanti Pillai incurred considerable debt and sought help from Shahul Hamid by meditating outside his shrine for three days. Palaniyanti Pillai was able to overcome his financial obligations. The saint had miraculously helped him repay a debt of 19 lakh rupees (Rs. 190,000) and, as a mark of his gratitude, he built the nineteen gateways of the *dargah*. Through the donations of Tirumalai Chetti, another grateful Hindu devotee, major portions of the *dargah* were built.

Outside the doorway of the *dargah,* we see a curious coconut sprouting what seems to be a horn. There is a votive story told about this coconut. Apparently, during a lean year, the trees in a coconut plantation did not bear fruit. The owner promised that if he got a good crop, he would dedicate one tree to the saint and save all the coconuts from that tree as an offering to the Nagore *dargah*. His wish was fulfilled and the owner kept his side of the bargain. One day, a local chieftain came by and demanded the coconuts from the tree dedicated to the saint. When told that it was meant as an offering for Shahul Hamid, the chieftain asked sarcastically: "Does the coconut from that tree have any special mark? Does it have a special, identifying horn?" When someone in his retinue went near the palm, he discovered that the coconuts in that tree had, in fact, miraculously sprouted a little horn. This story has two miracles: one that favors the owner of the grove after he makes a vow and the other that convinces the disbeliever of the saint's power and that helps the owner keep the terms of his vow. In commemoration of these events we find many pilgrims planting palm trees in the *dargah* as offerings to the saint.

Promises, Promises: Kinds of Vows in the Nagore *Dargah*

Pilgrims come to Nagore from many parts of India, and a few come from Singapore and Malaysia. Some of them come to pray, others to petition for specific desires, and others to fulfill their part of the bargain. In talking to pilgrims, I found that their petitions were similar in many ways to what one may encounter in a Hindu temple and to some extent, a "powerful" church like Velankanni a few kilometers away or the more recent Infant Jesus shrine in Bangalore. High on the list of Hindu and Muslim devotees were the following: admission to colleges, getting jobs, children, good health or cures for illness, and getting cars and fishing trawlers. While many narratives talk about marriage and I heard about such petitions in a secondhand manner, I did not hear directly about people petitioning for marriage.

The petitions and procedure for cures are also different here than in other *dargahs*. Here, unlike some other *dargah*s, (like the one near Madurai), there is no active program of curing with a specific list of activities to procure the healing. Nor are there any direct exorcism rituals to effect the cure, like the kind found in the Madurai *dargah* or the Samayapuram temple.

What do pilgrims promise to do if their wishes are fulfilled? There are many rituals that one may classify:

1. Monetary offerings including giving of cash, specific jewelry, and repairs or additions to the *dargah* complex.

2. Devotional offerings: the devotee promises to come and pray in the *dargah* for six (or X number of) Thursdays. If the devotee is from a faraway place, she or he may simply promise one pilgrimage. Other examples include the lighting of oil lamps (south Indian style) or candles in the chandeliers.

3. Personal "offering": the offering of one's hair; men and children have a ceremonial "tonsure" regularly. The hair is not actually offered to the saint; the word is used locally simply for the shaving of a person's head.

4. "Ecological" offering (I use this term for lack of a better word). When a child is born in a family, the parents plant one or two coconut palms near the *dargah*. To be fair, these offerings were made not out of ecological sensibilities, but out of the belief that coconut palms were equal in some way to human beings. A few south Indian communities, under certain circumstances, consider particular kinds of trees as ritual substitutes for human beings. Thus, to ritually demonstrate the vanquishing of opposing people, men from the Coorgi community chop down banana trees on the way to a wedding. The practice of offering the coconut palm, however, did not seem to be very fashionable today and many of the pilgrims I interviewed were not aware of it.

5. Animal offering. Goats or chickens may be ritually sacrificed in a particular area of the *dargah*.

The Model of the Votive Act

Like many other narratives of miracles and vows, the story of the coconut plantation tells us of a devotee's request, his promise to make a *particular* offering if his wish was fulfilled, the external impediment, and the overcoming of the impediment. Sometimes the impediment is internal, as when devotees "forget" to fulfil the vow; in those cases, the saint gives them a friendly reminder. At the simplest level, therefore, we have the following actions in the ritual of vow-fulfillment: (a) we have a devotee who either with belief or occasionally to "test" the deity, the saint, or the person with "power" prays for the fulfillment of a desire, protection, et cetera, which seems to be hard or impossible to obtain; (b) the deity/saint obliges; (c) the devotee acknowledges the act as direct intervention of the deity; and (d) in thanksgiving, the devotee makes a ritual offering of prayers, money, objects such as flowers, coconuts or clothes, or action such as shaving of one's head to the saint/deity.

One may see further variations in this model. There may be generic or particular vows made as thanksgiving offerings. In the case of Shahul Hamid, one sees examples of many types of vows:

1. *Generic thanksgiving*. The petitioner prays for the fulfillment of a desire. When the wish comes true, the petitioner offers something special to the deity or saint. We see this in the case of Achutappa Naiker, the Thanjavur king. He was afflicted with a disease; Shahul Hamid sees this as a result of sorcery, gets rid of the cause, and cures the king. The king, in gratitude, offers land to the saint. Note that the land was not offered before; the king petitions with faith and then makes an offering.

2. *Specific vow*. The petitioner makes a specific promise: If X happens, I will show my gratitude by doing Y. The owner of the coconut plantation makes a specific promise and is eager to fulfill it. The saint is said to rejoice in this devotional offering and helps the devotee overcome the impediments in his or her path

3. A *down-payment vow*. The petitioner makes a particular offering even before the request is fulfilled and promises more when everything comes to pass. Thus, a person with stomach ailments may go to the *dargah* and offer a small silver facsimile of a generic abdomen or person's torso (resembling the stomach). These silver models are bought outside the *dargah* and placed in the offering box. Sometimes a small monetary offering is made and more sent when one's wish is fulfilled.

In all these cases the nature of the vow resembles a memorandum of understanding or a compact made between two persons. If either defaults, the other can ignore it or get out of the relationship. However, if the wish is fulfilled and the petitioner does not make his or her offering in good faith, she or he may be punished by the deity or saint. We do not find too many cases like this in the life of Shahul Hamid, but one incident illustrates it. This is not a story of a vow, but one of arrogance and grief. It is said that Shahul Hamid wanted his son Yusuf to get married to the daughter of a rich man. The rich man haughtily refused, because he considered Shahul Hamid to be below his social status. The rich man lost his wealth and the daughter died. He then offered a younger daughter to Yusuf.

Figure 5.2 Offering box outside the tomb.

What happens if the devotee's wish is not fulfilled? Not surprisingly, I did not find such people in the *dargah*. I have, however, heard of friends who then move on to another place of worship and shift their patronage to a saint or deity who can help them. This is also true after a wish is fulfilled. Saints are consulted and prayed to for specific projects; you would go to Shahul Hamid for certain things and to Tamim Ansari in the Kovalam dargah for others. People with psychological ailments may go to the *dargah* in Madurai. If things do not come to pass, one may move on to the Velankanni cathedral or one of a dozen temples nearby.

Vocabulary for Divine Power and Actions

When one visits the Nagore shrine today, one is struck by the numbers of Hindus offering worship to the saint. According to Thambi Sahib, the managing trustee of the *dargah*, on any given day about 50 to 75 percent of pilgrims are Hindu and about 60 percent of the premises have been built by Hindus. What are the words that these pilgrims, Hindu and Muslim, use for the vows?

Tamil is the native language of a fair number of Hindus and Muslims in the Nagore area. The words used most often are the Tamil pronunciation of the

Figure 5.3   Hindu women devotees in line inside the *dargah*

Figure 5.4 Muslim women praying at the shrine of Shahul Hamid.

Sanskrit *prarthana* and *vrata*. When pilgrims come to fulfil the vow, they say they come to offer or submit (Tamil: *celutal*) the prayer (*prarthanai*). The word *prarthanai* in this context is more than prayer; it is the promise to do something, fulfill a vow. The Tamil *virutam* (Skt. *vrata*) is used for a wide number of activities, including the fast of *Ramzan*.

Not all *dargahs*, and certainly not all churches, attract hordes of Hindu pilgrims. Hindu devotees go to those sites where the deity or presiding saint is, as one Hindu pilgrim said, *varaprasadi*. Varaprasadi ("favorable to wishes") is a term used for Hindu deities like Meenakshi Amman of Madurai or Venkateswara of Tirupati. Any deity or saint who helps one is called *varaprasadi*.

The other words used regularly in describing the Nagore *dargah* were *shakti*, *karamat*, and *barakat*. Just as the deities in Samayapuram or Mel Maruvatur have power (*shakti*), the saint at Nagore has *shakti*. Karamat comes from *karmah*, the gracious power enjoyed by saints through their intimacy with God; it is this power that enables them to perform miracles. *Karamah* refers to "acts of generosity." According to one devotee of Shahul Hamid in Malaysia, "*karamah* also contains the meaning of 'charisma,' which connotes both divine favour and the power to inspire devotion and enthusiasm" (Yousof 1989: 32). The Tamil version of the word *karamattu* is used regularly in talking of the saint at Nagore. The word *karamat* is used, by extension, in Malaysia and Singapore to refer to the actual shrines of the saints. Gulam-Sarwar Yousof also speaks of the use of the word *shakti* in Malaysian *dargahs*. *Barakat* (from the root *baraka*; literally "to settle" or in a derived way, "the kneeling of a camel," but referring to "grace," "blessing," or "spiritual influence which God sends down" (Glasse 1989: 64) is also used to talk about the marvels that occur here; tea shops and little stalls outside the *dargah* have names like "barakat cafe."

This *shakti* or *karamat* obviously does not just last the physical lifetime of the saint; it continues after death. In fact, the whole *Nakur Puranam* focuses on the miracles that happen after Shahul Hamid's death.

The Shrine in the Larger South Indian Context

Pilgrims criss-cross India to visit temples, shrines, *dargah*s, graves, and other sites of intrinsic power. What does the shrine of Shahul Hamid share with other places of worship in the subcontinent, and how does it differ from Hindu places of worship?

The vows practiced in the shrine of Shahul Hamid are strikingly similar to those done in many south Indian Hindu temples. In this respect, the ritual idiom is south Indian, rather than derived from the Middle East. An example is tonsure: Muslims and Hindus come here to shave the head of the child for a first tonsure. While this is also a Muslim custom, most of the participants in the ritual do not know of the Islamic precedent and speak of it as a family custom. During my visit I observed one man speak of it as a Tamil custom. Hindus and Muslims also buy metal or silver plated facsimiles of different body parts, houses, sailboats, motorcycles et cetera and offer them to the saint, just as they would to the deity in a Hindu temple. Images of the body parts are offered when one requests a cure in that part of the body; similarly, when the real ones are prayed for, tiny models or etchings of houses and motorcycles are offered. When the cure is effected, or when one obtains what one wants, a return pilgrimage is made and another facsimile is offered in thanksgiving. While animals are not regularly offered in the brahmanical Hindu temples—a few like Samayapuram offer them at certain ritual times—they are more common here and in many other *dargahs*.

Men and women make offerings and perform vows just as they would in any Hindu temple. Only men are allowed into the inner shrine of Shahul Hamid and one must pass seven doorways to get there. It is difficult to get a clear idea of the caste of Hindu pilgrims. In conversations with pilgrims and trustees, I understood that while people of all castes visited the shrine, there were not too many brahmins.

In Nagore, the ritual prayers are offered by one of Shahul Hamid's descendants (there are dozens of them in the place) and only they have the hereditary right to do so. I was reminded of some Shaivite temples like Vaitheesvaran Koil

Figure 5.5 Women and men worship together at the *dargah*

Figure 5.6 Descendants of Shahul Hamid say prayers for Hindu devotees

and the Murugan temple of Tiruchendur in south India, where priests attach themselves to visiting pilgrims and then offer prayers on their behalf. Such a pattern is not generally seen in many temples in south India, though they are common in Puri, Orissa, and other places in northern India. In Nagore, while men and women congregate together for the whole week, during midday prayers on Friday, there is segregation between Muslim men and women. Hindus do not generally attend this prayer ritual.

But perhaps what is so striking is that this is an actual grave and is referred to as *samadhi* by pilgrims. Devotees do go to Hindu *samadhis* and pray—the *samadhi* of the Madhva saint Raghavendra swami at Mantralayam is a case in point—but one can easily forget that this is a grave, which from a Hindu perspective is polluting. The actual rituals are more like those done to a Hindu deity; during the *kanturi* celebrations in the month of Jamatul akir, the flags are raised, sandalwood paste is brought in ritual containers and used to anoint the tomb in actions similar to those that may take place in a Hindu temple.

The *dargah*, therefore, becomes a negotiated space for Hindus, Muslims, men, and women to come together and worship a common source of power, a power that is called *barakat, karamat,* or *shakti* by the followers. This power bypasses brahmanical notions of purity and pollution and makes the individual be part of a community of believers, part of Shahul Hamid's spiritual family.

Ritual *Kitchidi* or Stew:
Syncretism, Bricolage, and Other Categories

What kinds of words or metaphors can we use to describe the phenomenon of Hindus and Muslims venerating a Muslim saint in a Muslim *dargah* with the ritual idiom of the Tamil culture? Hindus and Muslims in the subcontinent come together in many forums including literary scholarship, rituals, healing, and music. One does not see reified boundaries in all contexts; what constitutes the identity of "Hindu" or "Muslim" is fluid in *some* spaces and times. There has certainly been a history of acrimonious relationship for several centuries connected with acts of temple destruction. Strong boundary markers are seen—and taken for granted—in certain ritual contexts such as arranging marriages and till the mid-twentieth century in inter-dining both between members of different religious traditions and members of different castes within Hinduism. Clear lines between the Hindus and Muslims are now discernible in response to political pressures from within India and as a reaction to acts of violence. While there was a reciprocally creative relationship at many times and in many places, political and economic considerations have now made some communalist elements highlight the antagonistic and suspicious attitudes that have also been part of Hindu-Muslim relations. It is important to note that shared ritual spaces such as the Nagore *dargah* have existed in the subcontinent along with the military conquests.

The boundaries between Tamil-speaking Muslims and Hindus seem fluid in some areas and the common heritage of the language seems to transcend certain differences. The fluidity of this enterprise has to be emphasized; we are not dealing with a fixed or determinate sense of "mixing" of categories from two distinct, bimorphic cultures. Stewart and Shaw's description of the move from "melting-pot" to "multiculturalism" in the United States (a move that is not irreversible) seems to be applicable to the Indian milieu and "syntheses, adaptations, assemblages, incorporations or appropriations are negotiated and sometimes denied and disassembled" (Stewart and Shaw 1994: 6).

By stating that the boundaries are permeable and that the grey areas are noticeable, I am not alleging that there are no boundaries. It is quite clear that Hindu communities and castes know who they are and how different they are from the Muslims; the Hindu castes are quite clear about whom they marry, with whom they eat and with whom they worship in a temple. But these Hindu castes also adopt other rules, other customs, or export their own customs into the worship of powerful beings such as the Muslim saints and some manifestations of the Virgin Mary as in the Velankanni basilica. The terms that one may use to describe these shared, negotiated spaces can be disputed. The term "syncretism" has been problematized in the last few years and if one has to use the term at all, it has to be with caution. Barbara Metcalfe understands the concept of syncretism to be based on the fixed categories of "Hindu" and "Muslim." She adds:

> It encourages what one might call the "vertical fallacy," that it is possible to make lists, even contrasting lists, of what is "Hindu" in one column and "Muslim" in another. It also tends to call "Hindu" or "Muslim" elements in the culture that may be neither or both. (Metcalfe 1995: 959)

Syncretism emerges when "bits of both in some sense mix." What Metcalfe calls "syncretism" is called "bricolage" by some anthropologists; Stewart and Shaw, in their efforts to rehabilitate the word "syncretism," offer many related words. They quote Werbner, who argued that *"the term 'syncretism' should be limited to the domain of religious or ritual phenomena where elements of two different historical 'traditions' interact or combine"* (Stewart and Shaw 1994: 10 emphasis added.) This would distinguish syncretism from "bricolage, the formation of new cultural forms from bits and pieces of cultural practice of diverse origins" (Stewart and Shaw 1994: 10). Like Metcalfe, Stewart and Shaw say that religions cannot be fixed; they go further and say that syncretism itself cannot be essentialized. They initially trace the history of the word "syncretism" from the time that Plutarch used it in an idiosyncratic sense to the positive tones given by Erasmus. Later in the sixteenth and seventeenth centuries the word had negative connotations when George Calixtus argued for the reconciliation of the various Protestant denominations. Opponents of the movement saw these efforts as a jumbled and confusing mixture of religions (Stewart and Shaw 1994: 3-6). In the nineteenth century, the term "syncretism" is again used in a pejorative sense by scholars of comparative religion; the word is used in their examinations of the religion of Rome and Greece. The term is used to indicate disorder and confusion; it is also used to denote an imperialistic strategy by which all "the varieties of mankind would be called in and restamped at the Caesarian Mint" (Stewart and Shaw 1994: 4).

One may also add that "syncretism" is sometimes used in a derogatory fashion, to distinguish what scholars believe to be "hybrid"—and thus "lesser"—religions from what is "pure" and "authentic." It is because of the negative use of the term "syncretism" that scholars of religion shy away from it now. Anthropologists such as Charles Stewart and Rosalind Shaw are rehabilitating the word now, but Tony Stewart and Carl Ernst urge caution in their analysis of the term (Stewart and Ernst 2003).

What then can we call the phenomena in the intersecting realms of Hindu and Muslim experiences in south India? Obviously it would not be sensible to argue that there are no boundaries between the Muslims and Hindus. There are strong boundaries within and between Hindu communities and castes, and all of them do distinguish themselves from the Muslims. As we noted earlier, they all know with whom they eat, marry or live. What I am arguing for is a shaded area of "fuzzy" boundaries that is fairly large and permeable. If syncretism calls for harsh, discernible boundaries, with specific elements from both sides combining to form a third entity, the shared experience is evidently not that. What we find instead are common, intersecting areas of shared experience drawn from the matrix of language, myth, and ritual. One may argue based on these areas that colonial constructions of the labels "Hindu" and "Muslim" as discrete entities are problematic; softer, permeable membranes with bilateral osmosis have to be imagined. Michael Meister argues for the use of the "osmosis" metaphor in his analysis of the styles of eleventh-century architecture in Rajasthan (Meister 1984). This metaphor still uses the concept of boundaries, but at least makes them permeable and open to influences.

Until one can come up with a commonly acceptable term without the baggage that syncretism carries, it is tempting to consider using a variety of words commonly seen in social anthropology to describe the shared areas of culture between Hindu castes and Muslims in South Asia. Since there are diverse experiences, it would make sense to use different terms to describe them. If bricolage means the creation of a new culture with bits and pieces of others, one may point to the experience of the Meherats and the Maule-e-Salaam Garasiyas of Gujarat, who have elements from both religions in their lifestyles. The term "inculturation" can be used with qualifications (and with acknowledgment of limitations) in describing the lifestyle of the Muslims in Tamil Nadu, the modes of worship in *dargahs,* their intense scholarship of the Tamil Ramayana and incorporation of literary tropes from this epic in the *Cira Puranam,* the Tamil epic that describes the life of the prophet Muhammad. J. B. P. More argues that while the Muslims believe in the Five Pillars of Islam among other observances, and share most of the beliefs held by other Muslims in many parts of the world, they adopt local Tamilian practices for the celebration of weddings and other rituals. Stewart and Shaw describe inculturation thus:

> In Catholic theologians' notions of inculturation . . . the Word of God, the message of the Gospel, is knowledge of a transcendental, timeless and transcultural Truth that is not tied to a particular human language or cultural form, but adaptable into local idioms and symbolic repertoires. Indeed the Church now contends that communities will apprehend the Christian message better if they do so in their own terms. (Stewart and Shaw 1994: 11)

One of the problems with this notion, of course, is that Western notions of distinction between culture and religion may not always translate into other geographic regions. Moreover, in the phenomena we are considering, inculturation may be a misleading term at least in one way. Although it is not explicitly stated, inculturation may refer to a conscious adoption of local forms and styles of worship. In the case of the Tamil Muslims, there is no conscious adoption of something local; the Tamil literature and culture is perceived as their birthright and their inheritance. Inculturation also refers to the Muslim side of the phenomena in the worship at *dargahs;* it does not cover the Tamil Hindu's participation in such rituals.

One may also consider using the word "variation" (or "variant") for some aspects of the shared culture in south India, but even if it can be used, this will again be applicable only for the Islamic side of the picture. This term has been used by anthropologists who studied indigenous churches in Africa. Peel (and in another study, Kiernan) have criticized the use of the word "syncretist" in earlier studies on African churches that practice faith healing. Rather than being a Yoruba or a Zulu practice, they argue that the use of faith healing in these churches have roots in Western Christianity; Kiernan "affirms (like Peel) that Zulu Zionism is not syncretic but a thoroughly Christian variant" (Stewart and Shaw 1994: 11). The term "variant" can be used if a "native" of a religion shares a common ritual or concept that is or has been prevalent in another culture. Tamil Muslims who visit the *dargah* at Nagore frequently take their children there to have their heads shaven. This custom is common enough among Hindus in South Asia; a pilgrimage to a sacred site is undertaken when a child is three months or older and the child's head is shaven. This is a Hindu *samskara* or sacrament; however, it is perceived to be a local Tamil (nonreligious) custom by Tamil Muslims who practice this ritual. While they did not show awareness of it, the tonsure of a child's head is, in fact, an Islamic custom. *Aqiqah* refers to the nonobligatory custom of tonsure on the seventh day after the birth of the child. However, the Muslims whom I interviewed in Nagore were not aware of this ritual as an Islamic one; their children whose heads were being shaved were older, and besides, this was just a "family" (and, of course, Tamil) custom. I would argue that for this custom to be properly called an Islamic "variant," at least some of the people in the *dargah* should relate the ritual to the prophet's life or to a textual source.

The term "bricolage," the replacement word for syncretism, can be used only for some restricted phenomena; the terms "inculturation" and "variant" miss the mark in conceptualizing the shared worlds of the Tamil-speaking Hindus and Muslims. One is left with four alternatives; we may go back to the osmosis metaphor of Meister, encourage the rehabilitation of "syncretism," nuance another term like "synergism" (which again presupposes distinct dimorphic entities), or come up with a neologism.

The fuzzy boundaries and overlapping rituals, the shared ritual spaces, are all still evident when we go to the *dargahs* in the late twentieth and early twenty-first centuries. While the *dargahs* are still areas where people of different faiths worship, since the 1990s there has been an extraordinarily heightened consciousness in many parts of south India about religious labeling; identity markers like "Hindu" and "Muslim" are sharply etched in many arenas. Violence between

Figure 5.7 The sacred well inside the *dargah;* the waters of the Zam Zam (the spring in Mecca) are said to flow inside this well. Hindu women bathe here to acquire "merit"

communities is on the rise; bomb blasts like that attributed to terrorists who operated in the name of Islam in February 1996 in Coimbatore, Tamil Nadu rip apart centuries of cordial communal coexistence. While the harmony had continued in south India even throughout the partition of India, we see a slow attrition of rituals that mark that shared culture. The Muslim scholars of the Ramayana may, perhaps, be curiosities of the past. However, the desire for saintly intervention to solve problems and the perceived power of the charisma keep the Hindu devotees coming to the Muslim *dargah,* making and fulfilling vows. In those liminal moments social categories and labeling are suspended and what is foregrounded is the saint's relationship with the devotee and with the larger spiritual community.

Notes

1. The best introduction to Islamic literature in Tamil is the three-volume work of Muhammad Uvais (Uwise), the *Islamiyat tamil ilakkiya varalaru* (Madurai: Kamrajar University, 1990). See especially the second volume on *kavyas.* The work of Uvais and Ajmal Khan as well as the books and articles of M. M. Ismail have informed my research on Tamil Islamic literature.

References

Glasse, Cyril. 1989. *The Concise Encyclopedia of Islam*. San Francisco: Harper and Row.

Meister, Michael. 1994. "The Membrane of Tolerance: Middle and Modern India." In *Art, the Integral Vision,* eds. B. N. Saraswati, S. C. Malik, and Madhu Khanna. 289–98. New Delhi: D. K. Printworld.

Metcalfe, Barbara. 1995. "Presidential Address: Too Little and Too Much." *The Journal of Asian Studies* 34/4 (November): 959.

More, J. B. P. 1991. "The Marakkayar Muslims of Karikal, South India." *Journal of Islamic Studies* 2, 1: 25–44.

Stewart, Tony and Carl Ernst. 2003. "Syncretism." In *South Asian Folklore: An Encyclopedia: Afghanistan, Bangladesh, Nepal, Pakistan, Sri Lanka,* eds. Margaret A. Mills, Peter J. Claus, and Sarah Diamond, 586–88. NY: Routledge.

Stewart, Charles and Rosalind Shaw. 1994. *Syncretism and Anti-syncretism: The Politics of Religious Synthesis*. London: Routledge.

Yousof, Ghulam-Sarwar. 1989. "Lasting Charisma." *Pulau Pinang* 1/2: 31–35.

6

In the Company of *Pirs*: Making Vows, Receiving Favors at Bangladeshi Sufi Shrines

SUFIA UDDIN

In July 2001 Pakistani President Pervez Musharraf visited India for peace talks with his Indian counterpart Prime Minister Atal Bihari Vajpayee. Before the peace talks began, however, Musharraf visited the tomb of the Chisti saint Khwaja Moin uddin Chisti (d. 1236) in Ajmeer, India. In Bangladesh nearly every political campaign commences only after politicians have performed devotional prayers and sought the blessings of saints. This is true for both the Bangladesh National Party (BNP) and the Awami League, whose leaders typically initiate their campaigns at the shrine of Shah Jalal in the northern district of Sylhet, proceeding to the shrine of Bayazid Bistami in Chittagong, and then visiting the shrine of Khan Jahan Ali in Khulna. In spite of revivalist movements that criticize such actions, a large part of religious and cultural life in Bangladesh and elsewhere in South Asia centers around the shrines of Muslim *pirs* or saints.

This chapter examines the nature of *manat* (popular vows) in Bangladesh and its relationship to the shrines (*mazars*) of Muslim saints.[1] The first part introduces three of Bangladesh's most popular saints and their hagiographies, illustrating the connection between the veneration of saints and their perceived power. Next, I examine the notion of power and blessings associated with saints and their shrines, demonstrating how the power of the saint is believed to be transferred to the dedicant via contact with the shrine. Finally, I illustrate how the lack of formal structure associated with vows and visits to shrines is crucial to the continued popularity of these shrines among both Muslims and non-Muslims, marginalized and dominant communities alike, analyzing the wide range of practices and beliefs associated with these shrines.

Mazars, Ziyarat, and Manat

The practice of making vows is not highly formalized. It can, therefore, be an elusive subject of study. There is no universal format or structure that all dedicants subscribe to. Rather, the tradition of making vows is individualized. Vows are, however, always associated with the practice of *ziyarat* or pilgrimage to the shrines of Muslim saints. Shrines are most often referred to as *mazars* and *dargahs*. The Bangladeshi landscape is dotted with shrines of Muslims who are believed to be divinely blessed with the power to help those in need. Three of the most frequently visited shrines in Bangladesh are the shrines of the saints Shah Jalal in the northern district of Sylhet, Bayazid Bistami in Chittagong (also known as Shah Sultan), and Khan Jahan Ali in Khulna. The cult of Muslim saints is a tradition that embraces diversity and has, over the centuries, created and incorporated local nonsectarian traditions. This diversity appeals to a broad scope of Bangladeshi people. Therefore, Muslim and non-Muslim pilgrims alike frequently visit these shrines to seek the intercession of a saint on their behalf, and it is there that they most often perform vows.

Hagiography as Validating Text

Saints' perceived power is based primarily on their hagiographical oral and written texts. For example, Bayazid Bistami's (d. 874) shrine is located on a hilltop in Nasirabad, Chittagong. Upon entering the compound of the shrine there is a pond filled with fish and giant turtles. The giant turtles are said to be *jinn* who, due to their misbehavior, were transformed by Bistami into giant turtles destined to forever occupy this pond.[2] Visitors to the shrine usually feed and pet these turtles before proceeding to Bistami's shrine and the rarity of this species is deemed by the pilgrims to be proof of Bistami's power.[3]

This shrine compound, though dedicated to Bistami, is only one of several tombs in his name. There is also a shrine to Bistami in Zousfana, Morocco; outside Damascus, Syria; and in Bistam, his likely burial place. According to E. Haque, the saint enshrined in Nasirabad is not Bistami but rather the tomb of Shah Sultan Balkhi (Haque 1975: 136). In fact, it is highly doubtful that Bistami ever visited Bengal at all (Schimmel 1975: 51). Nevertheless, Bistami is fondly remembered and his name often invoked.

A second important saint of Bangladesh is Khan Jahan Ali (d. 1459), whose shrine is located in the southwestern village of Bagerhat in the district of Khulna. Khan Jahan Ali was a *zamindar* of the region who turned virgin forests into rice-cultivating lands. He patronized the construction of hundreds of mosques and

Figure 6.1 Women feeding giant turtles at the *mazar* of Bayazid Bistami

tanks in Bara Bazar, north of Jessore and the Bagerhat region, including the sixty-seven-domed mosque, called Saithgumbad Masjid, in Bagerhat. Khan Jahan Ali is believed to have arrived in the Bagerhat region riding on the backs of two crocodiles. These crocodiles became his first disciples whom Khan Jahan Ali loved and adored. Even today it is rumored that crocodiles still live in the lake steps away from Khan Jahan Ali's tomb and they are the descendants of his first disciples.

The third most important saint of Bangladesh is Shah Jalal (d. 1346). The shrine dedicated to Shah Jalal is located in Sylhet, the northeastern district of the country. It is the largest such compound in Bangladesh and is visited by more pilgrims than any other.[4] According to oral and folk hagiographical traditions composed in the mid-nineteenth century, Shah Jalal was an Arab from Yemen. Like many other saints of the Bengal region, Shah Jalal is attributed with conquering the lands and introducing Islam to the people of Sylhet. The earliest accounts of his life dating back to the sixteenth century suggest he was actually from Turkestan (Eaton 1993: 73).

Oral tradition postulates that Shah Jalal entreated his master in Mecca to permit him to embark on the lesser *jihad*.[5] His master consented to his request, dispatching Shah Jalal and 313 disciples east through India to spread Islam. The band eventually settled in Sylhet where they constructed a Sufi hospice and mosque. Once there, Shah Jalal killed the Hindu king Raja Gaur Govind who, according to this legend, had been persecuting the Muslims. Though he never married, Shah Jalal permitted his companions to marry local women and he continued throughout his life to spread Islam and perform miracles (Ahamad 2000: 7–67; Ikram 1957: 66).[6]

For every shrine in Bangladesh there are stories. These hagiographical accounts of the saints affirm the sanctity of the person and so demonstrate how and why the figure deserved to be the recipient of divine blessing or *baraka*. In fact, stories of saints frequently parallel the hagiographical and historical accounts of the Prophet Muhammad's life, validating the saints' Muhammad-like human qualities. For example, a second version of Shah Jalal's arrival to Bengal tells of a conversation between the Prophet Muhammad and Shah Jalal. In a dream, Muhammad instructs Shah Jalal to go to India to save Muslims from persecution. Muhammad's direct communication clearly defines Shah Jalal's mission as a sacred quest. Thus, many of the images in the story mirror Muhammad's life. Just as Muhammad was given a prophetic command by God, so too did Shah Jalal receive his saintly commission from Muhammad. Moreover, Shah Jalal took 313 companions to India just as Muhammad took 313 companions in the victorious Battle of Badr against the Meccans.[7]

All three of these saints are associated with introducing Islam to three major regions of Bangladesh and attributed with playing a pivotal role in converting dense forest into rich cultivated lands. This introduction of Islam, and the general work of the saints, is often equated with "civilization building." In hagiographies even the saints' relationship with the environment was deemed miraculous. This relationship demonstrated the saints' special connection to Bengal's physical and natural environment. More specifically, the saints were endowed with a special power over animals. Bistami (or Shah Sultan) for example, came to Bengal riding a fish, Khan Jahan Ali came to Bengal riding on the backs of two crocodiles, and Shah Jalal was known to tame tigers and protect deer. These myths paradigmatically mark a major economic, social, and cultural transformation of the Bengal landscape. Communities were formed around the construction of mosques and shrines in former forested regions and as time passed the stories surrounding these figures came to include miracles and fantastic abilities that ultimately transformed these ordinary men into saints.[8]

Occasions for Visitations to Shrines

Annually, devotees of particular saints return to the shrines for *mawlids*, or the saint's birth anniversaries, which, ironically, are often celebrated on the anniversary of the saint's death. The largest and most widely celebrated *mawlids* are for the Prophet Muhammad.[9] Hence on the twelfth of the Islamic month of *Rabi al-Awwal* Muslims gather to celebrate Muhammad's birth with panegyrical poems, stories about his mother's pregnancy, his birth, and his life. And as birth anniversaries venerate the role of the Prophet, so too do the *urs* (weddings) celebrate the role of the saint. The employment of the term *urs* confirms the inherent understanding of the death of a divinely blessed person as union with God. Thus, one who is regarded saintly in life is recognized at death as having achieved the ultimate spiritual goal. This divine union propels the saint toward a completely unfettered connection with God.[10] Consequently, devotees of these saints believe these Sufis to be potent sources of blessings and miracles, miracles originally descended from God.[11] To tap into the saint's power and become a recipient or beneficiary of divine blessings, individuals visit the saint's shrine.[12] The transfer of blessings from the saint to the recipient occurs through objects such as a tomb, or through people associated with the saint such as a disciple, a genealogical heir of the saint (*pir*), or a caretaker (*khadim*) of the shrine. Pilgrims visit saints' tombs for numerous reasons such as taking family holidays, seeking solitude or a place to meet friends, or to pay respects to the saint and to participate in *urs* celebrations and make vows.

At the saint's shrine, vows are commonly made requesting God's assistance or the intercession of the saint on their behalf in difficult circumstances. According to more orthodox Islamic doctrine intercession is not necessary. Rather, vows can be made directly with God. In fact, legal scholars such as Ibn Taimiya (d. 1328) believed that the cult of saints and the practice of *ziyarat* (visits to tombs) were idolatrous. More moderate stances on pilgrimage embrace certain aspects of visits to tombs arguing that tomb visitation is acceptable if conducted under certain conditions.[13] For instance, the medieval scholar al-Ghazali (d.1111) not only condoned the practice of tomb visitation, he recommended it. Nevertheless, there were some practices such as rubbing, touching, or kissing graves that he rejected, associating these acts with Christian practices and, therefore, deeming them un-Islamic and impermissible (Taylor 1989: 126). This debate took on renewed vigor in the mid to late nineteenth century, a period of significant religious reform in South Asia, and continued well into the twentieth century. During the nineteenth century there were more than thirty Muslim journals, covering topics of proper religious practice, Islamic history, biographies of famous Muslims, and events affecting Muslims in Bengal specifically and India in general. Even today, despite some tensions and opposition to various practices associated with Sufi saints, shrines continue to be a locus of popular piety and Bangladeshi daily newspapers dedicate regular columns to religious issues including articles on the commands and prohibitions regarding the practice of making vows (Hak 2001: 4).

Activities Surrounding the Cult of Saints or *Pirs*

One of the most important activities at saints' shrines is prayer, which has several forms. The first type is *salah*, or ritual obligatory prayer performed in Arabic five times daily by observant Muslims. The second kind of prayer is *dua*, a petitionary prayer. The third is *munajat*, a devotional prayer, and the last form of prayer is the *dhikr* or remembrance, involving a repetition of Islamic phrases or names of God. These phrases are said either aloud or in silence, individually or in gatherings, and serve as a form of meditation.[14] Finally, many votaries perform silent *dhikr* whenever they visit shrines.[15]

Prayers in any of the forms mentioned above comprise the foundation of visits to tombs for Muslim visitors to shrines. They are usually preceded by the offering of salutations to the Prophet Muhammad and followed by salutations to the *pir*. Blessings to the Prophet Muhammad and the saint are then recited. According to the *adab al-ziyara* (literature on the appropriate behavior for visits to shrines), performance of prayer for the Prophet Muhammad at a gravesite simultaneously benefits the dead (Taylor 1989: 117). In South Asia, visitors to shrines often also complement their prayers with recitations from the Qur'an, most frequently reciting suras from *Ampara*.[16] The most commonly recited sura is *Ya Sin*, for it is considered the heart of the Qur'an. The central points of this sura include prophecy, revelation, and the hereafter.

In addition to prayer and recitation, other popular activities include touching the grating that encloses the tomb, and giving *ataur* (perfume), *gulab jal* (rosewater), money, candles, and incense. Votaries make their vows during the *dua* or after any other prayers are performed. In some shrines votaries tie cloths or strings to a tree or the grating surrounding the tomb to remind the saint of the votary's request. Once the saint has fulfilled the request, the votary returns to remove the cloth or string and fulfill their part of the agreement made with the saint. For those pilgrims who need assistance with these prayers, the shrines provide copies of the Qur'an, sample *dhikrs,* and petitionary prayers with Bengali transliterations.

Not all of these activities enjoy the same level of religious acceptability. The most acceptable are, of course, those validated by the Prophet Muhammad and by verses from the Qur'an. Other more controversial practices developed after Muhammd's death and so have more tenuous connections with the traditions of the Prophet. These include kissing, touching, and rubbing the tomb, performing prostrations before the tomb, and the making of vows. The connection to the actions of the Prophet Muhammad is significant because the legitimacy of Islamic practice is primarily based in the Qur'an and the actions of the Prophet (*Sunna*). Practices falling outside these parameters, or which otherwise have debatable or no basis in the Qur'an, may be regarded by the *ulama* (Muslim scholars) as mere innovations. Yet, these theoretical and legal considerations do not necessarily affect the actual religious practices of individuals. Hence, though many shrines have signboards in Bengali listing in detail the rules of conduct while visiting tombs, these rules often are neither enforced by the caretakers nor acknowledged by the pilgrims. These signboards exist mostly to appease conservatives and Islamist Muslims. Those who participate in *Tabligh Jamaat* and *Jamaat i Islami* oppose many of the practices associated with shrines. The *Jamaat i Islami* is aggressive in their efforts to make Muslims' practice "orthodox." In my interviews with several *khadims*, they expressed concern about my interest in *manat*. Once they learned I was not a journalist planning to write an article for a Bangladeshi newspaper or magazine, they were pleased to talk with me. Many of the shrines' caretakers make every effort to keep a low profile in Bangladesh in fear of Islamist retaliation. Despite their efforts, one will easily find criticisms of *manat* and Sufi practices in Bangladeshi newspapers such as *Inquilab* and *Sangram* whose readership is Islamist oriented. I also met many shrine visitors or saint followers who expressed equal distaste for Islamist intolerance.

Identifying the Votaries and the Nature of Vows

People throughout Bangladesh perform pilgrimages and make vows. Unlike many other parts of the Islamic world where shrines are more often frequented by women pilgrims, in Bangladesh both men and women alike flock in large numbers to the shrines.[17] Yet visitation alone does not necessarily indicate performance of religious acts. Indeed, based on visual observation alone, there is no clear way to know who is and is not making vows because, more often than not, there is little in a pilgrim's outward behavior to suggest whether they are votaries. Nevertheless, discussions with caretakers, holy men associated with shrines, and male and female visitors to shrines suggest that both men and women make vows, though for different reasons. Men's vows are more often associated with business and professional endeavors.[18] Women votaries, on the other hand, commonly seek a saint's assistance with domestic problems, hoping to pacify an angry family member, end a family dispute, heal the sick, ensure the success of a marriage of a son or daughter, or assure the marriage negotiations between two families. An especially common request is the birth of a son.

A more unusual group of votaries are the sex workers from brothel communities whose participation in community worship is nearly impossible. This ostracized group is excluded from *Id, mawlid*, and the Ramadan festivities because of the sin associated with their profession, which in many cases has been forced upon them. Nevertheless, sex workers believe that by making visits to saints' tombs and vows they may be forgiven for their sins. Their vows typically focus on health, the health of their children, avoiding arrest or harassment from police and the wider community.[19] Because they are excluded from community activities and because they struggle with the guilt associated with their work, sex workers mask their identity and, in groups, make pilgrimage to different shrines around the country and even to Ajmeer Sharif in Rajasthan, India. In Bangladesh, women do not typically attend congregational Friday prayers at the mosque. Attending Friday prayers is regarded as a male activity. Thus, not just for sex workers, but women generally, making vows is a means for participating publicly in religious life.

Many votaries believe that gaining spiritual blessings in conjunction with more practical methods is the best way to achieve one's desired gain. For example, if a couple is having difficulty conceiving a child, they might seek medical aid while simultaneously requesting the intercession of a saint. One couple advised me that after a prolonged period of not being able to have a child, they decided to make a pilgrimage to the most important Muslim shrine in South Asia, Ajmeer Sharif. There they paid homage to the saint Khwaja Moin uddin Chisti and made a vow in the hopes of conceiving a child. They then returned to Bangladesh, continued with medical treatment, and later that year conceived their first child.

To others, seeking the aid of a saint may be their last and best hope. At the shrine of Pir Badar in Chittagong district, for example, it is believed that the saint arrived in Chittagong from Panipath floating on a rock. This rock is now kept in a glass case at the shrine and every morning the caretakers of the shrine carefully pour water over it and into containers. This water is believed to have powers to cure nearly any ailment. Thus, pilgrims who visit the shrine leave with a bottle of this "holy" water in exchange for a small donation.

Those involved in a court case experiencing legal problems are likely to visit the shrine of Shah Amanat. According to legend, Shah Amanat was a court clerk for a judge in Chittagong. In a town called Maheshkali, some 170 kilometers away from Chittagong, a man was wrongly accused of a crime and was sentenced to death. He was saved however by Shah Amanat, who had written proof of the man's innocence and miraculously appeared in Maheshkali before the sentence was imposed.

Non-Muslim Votaries of Bangladesh

Many Hindus, Christians, and Buddhists seek the aid of Muslim saints. And, while the majority of visitors to the Muslim shrines are Bengali, there are also Biharis and Adivasis (tribal communities). Among the visitors to the shrines, the identity of the saint as a Muslim has little significance. Indeed, one of the attractions of the shrine and the activities of the shrine to non-Muslims is the lack of formal structure. For instance, one is not required to perform obligatory prayers, a highly ritualized Islamic prayer, at the shrine's mosque. If it were required, all non-Muslim pilgrims would be excluded from the shrine's activities. Rather, non-Muslims are among those who perform *sejda* (a simple prostration with head touching the floor) in front of the tomb, pray, light candles or incense, or give an offering of money or food.[20] From a non-Muslim perspective the saints are viewed as human beings who, because of either their devotion to God or their compassion, have been blessed with the ability to perform miracles and help others.

The Maijbandar *urs* gathering is purported to be the fourth or fifth largest congregation of Muslims in the world. Nevertheless, Hindus play an integral role in the religious ceremony. Approximately five hundred thousand to six hundred thousand people gather for the festivities annually. The Maijbandari *urs* takes place for several days, beginning on the tenth of the Bengali month of *Magh*. The compound consists of thousands of acres of cultivated land, barns, several shrines, the living *pir's darbar* (court), mosque, hostels, kitchens, tea houses, tanks for bathing, and shops to buy shrine-related paraphenalia such as amulets, *ataur* (perfume), incense, and candles. Yet, of the many activities, it is their music that makes the Maijbandaris famous. Indeed, since the 1800s devotees have flocked to Maijbandar to perform devotional music. The instruments used typically include *mandira, dholok,* and harmonium.[21] Interestingly, however, some of the most famous Maijbandari musicians are not Muslims, but Hindus, who sing the praises of the Maijbandari Muslim saints, further reinforcing the view that one need not be a Muslim to enjoy, appreciate, and participate in the Maijbandari celebrations.

Fulfillment of One's Votive Obligation

Once requests are granted by the saint, votaries demonstrate their gratitude in a number of ways. Frequently gifts promised to the saint fall under one of the following categories (strikingly similar to the Five Pillars of Islam): charity, sacrifice, fast, visit to a saint's tomb, pilgrimage to Mecca or prayer. However, it is completely up to the individual votaries to determine the appropriate gesture. Oftentimes, for example, people promise to give animals to the shrine, with poorer pilgrims donating chickens and hens and wealthier pilgrims donating sweets, goats, lambs, calves, and even cows. Those who offer meat or rice as a part of their vow fulfillment pay a small fee to the caretakers to have the food prepared and distributed to the poor. Many of the shrines have outdoor cooking facilities where they can prepare food for hundreds of people. Maijbandar is exceptionally well-equipped, capable of preparing meals for several hundred thousand people for several days. In other cases people donate money for specific projects such as needed renovations or to build a new mosque. Many of the shrines maintain donation boxes for this type of contribution. Other pilgrims simply fast or promise to return to the shrine to perform a prayer.

According to the Hanafi school of law, dominant in South Asia, one may make a vow to God as long as the act promised is similar to the obligatory forms of worship. It should be noted, however, that the Hanafi scholars refer specifically to vows made to God, not saints. Still, it is worthwhile to consider the commentary of legal scholars on the general topic of vows. The Muslim jurist

Figure 6.2 Poor and hungry visitors await a hot meal prepared by *mazar* workers

Ahmad ibn Naqib al-Misri (d.1368), in his manual of Islamic Sacred Law, *Umdat al-Salik*, in part states that "a vow is only valid: (a) if made by a Muslim who is legally responsible; (b) when it concerns some act of worship" (Keller 1999: 368). Sheikh Abd al-Wakil Durubi, who provides commentary on al-Misri's classical manual, suggests that according to the Hanafi school an act of worship refers to "an act that is similar in kind to an *obligatory* form of worship" (Keller 1999: 368). Thus vows to saints appear to be based on the guidelines Hanafi jurists established with regard to vows made to God which include prayer (including recitation), charity, sacrifice, fasting, and pilgrimage.[22] It should also be noted that some votaries make pilgrimage to Mecca to fulfill their vow, whereas others substitute pilgrimage to Mecca with a visit to a saint's shrine.

This element of individuality in the fulfillment of vows is prevalent throughout Bangladesh. A husband and wife I met at the shrine of Shah Jalal perhaps best illustrate individual expression in the fulfillment of vows. When I encountered them, they had just returned to the shrine to fulfill the vow they made prior to the birth of their child when they sought Shah Jalal's assurance for his birth. To fulfill their vow to Shah Jalal they returned with a small goat, and in a symbolic gesture the child held a rope that was tied to the goat. When the child released the rope, the goat was released and the person who caught the goat became its new owner.

The performance of this vow was indeed an unusual method of vow fulfillment and poses significant legal questions for Muslim scholars. An example of a hadith substantiating a Hanafi view, and so providing parameters for the legitimate constitution of a vow, is evidenced in the hadith collection of Bukhari. According to Bukhari, "the Prophet (Allah bless him and give him peace) passed a man standing in the sun without seeking shade, whom he inquired about and was told that it was Abu Isra'il, who had vowed to stand while fasting without sitting, taking shade, or speaking; to which he replied, 'Pass by him and have him sit in the shade and speak, but let him finish fasting'" (Keller 1999: 368). Thus, according to this hadith fasting is a perfectly acceptable manner of vow fulfillment, but standing in the hot sun without speaking does not enhance its merit. Furthermore, it may be regarded as religious innovation, and therefore deemed inappropriate. How an individual chooses to fulfill a vow can vary. Most votaries choose to simply fast, pray, make the *hajj*, visit saints' shrines, give a donation, or sacrifice an animal whose meat will be consumed by the poor. As we shall see in the next section, vow fulfillment that includes return visits to the shrine and donations of food and money contributes to the economic vibrancy of the shrine and the nearby community.

The Economic Vitality of Shrines

Shrines can be centers of economic exchange in Bangladesh. The shrine and its vicinity is a place of exchange mediated through the shrine caretakers and the

Figure 6.3　Husband and wife with son fulfilling a vow at the *mazar* of Shah Jalal

collective belief in the power of the saints. It is here that the votary fulfills vows promising to repay the saint's past assistance. This promised item is then utilized to benefit the poorer members of society, offering both spiritual hope for those in need and the fulfillment of basic needs for the disadvantaged. For example, outside the shrine compounds vendors sell shrine-related paraphernalia, posters in rickshaw-styled art, amulets, *shirni* (a sweet offering to saints), and books about the saints. Inside the shrines, the poor and hungry spend their days waiting to become benefactors of promises made to the saints. It is a veritable locus of vertical and horizontal exchange. If a saint loses popularity, the economic viability of the shrine compound and the vicinity is compromised. Therefore, the caretakers play a vital role in the continuity of shrine activities and in mediating this financial exchange between the shopkeepers, the dedicants, and the poor, collecting monetary donations, sweets and animals, and coordinating the preparation of the meals distributed to the poor. Donations also fund upkeep and renovation of shrines, which in turn assists in attracting more visitors.[23]

The Relation between Sacred Place and the Efficacy of Vows

The first-time experience of making a vow, and the votary's belief that the saint accepted and assisted the votary, has the effect of strengthening the votary's relationship to the saint. The belief in the potency of the saint's power can transform the votary into a follower of the saint. As a devotee the individual may make frequent visits to the saint's tomb to pray for the saint and Prophet Muhammad and, if there is a living holy person associated with the shrine, he or she might choose to become a follower of that holy person as well, participating in activities such as *dhikr* and *majlis*.

Since a popular vow lacks formal structure, there are no guidelines on the necessity of traveling to shrines to make vows. Yet votaries do precisely that. The votary perceives travel to the sanctified site as increasing the possibility of being a recipient of *karamat* (miracle). To understand how miracles relate to sacred sites we need to look only at Mecca, the sacred center and the most potent symbol of sacrality in the Islamic world. For Muslims, the Kaba in Mecca is the house of God built by Ibrahim and his son Isma'il, which was then rededicated to God by Muhammad. It is the direction in which all financially capable Muslims must make their daily *salah* and is the most important pilgrimage site where Muslims must perform the *hajj* at least once in their lifetime.

The multitude of mosques, shrines, Sufi hospices, and religious schools contribute to sacralizing nearly all space in lands distant from Mecca. The shrines and their compounds around the world are extensions of an Islamic notion of sacred place. The Tree of Life symbol commonly employed by Sufis, sometimes depicted with its roots in heaven bearing fruit on the earth, is a useful image for understanding how Muslims may view the extension of sacredness into their physical world (Bennett 1994: 88–114). Like the Tree of Life each of these saints and their shrines are like branches that extend from heaven to earth offering the beneficience of the divine. A visit to the shrine therefore provides the devotee a sense of proximity to God. Moreover, the people associated with the shrines (caretakers and living *pirs*), as well as the activities at the mosques attached to the shrines such as the different types of prayer and Qur'anic recitation, also assist in manifesting this notion of sacredness. Thus, the individual devotee is surrounded by the sacred.

According to folk tradition, some saints came from distant lands to Bengal and performed miracles. Even from a non-Muslim, Bengali perspective, this event bequeaths a sacred quality to the Bengal landscape. Since the sixteenth century, many saints have been associated with local popular deities (Choudhury 1979: 61–69). Some of these figures have been viewed as *pirs* by some and as deities by others as evidenced in literary sources about figures such as Satya pir, also known as Satya-narayan or Pir-narayan (Stewart 1995: 578-97). In addition, the Panch pir (five *pirs*) in Bengal refers to a number of celebrated figures that varies from region to region and religious community to religious community. Thus, while Panch pir has been associated with the Pandavas of the epic Mahabharata, a unique Muslim association includes a quintet popular with boatmen that includes Shah Badar, Shah Sultan, Shah Jalal, Shah Muhsin, and Shaikh Farid (Haq 1987: 231–56).

Conclusion

The performance of vows in Bangladesh enjoys wide appeal precisely because it lacks a formal structure. This lack of formal structure, like elsewhere in the Islamic world where people perform visits to tombs (*ziyarat*), is particularly appealing to Bangladeshi women who customarily do not attend congregational prayers at the mosque. Mosques in Bangladesh generally are not constructed with the separate women's prayer area. Girls often do not receive religious education, especially in poorer families where secular and religious education are viewed as luxuries. As a result, fewer women are able to recite from the Qur'an and so have limited knowledge of obligatory prayers. Therefore, the shrine gives women a public sphere in which they may perform religious acts as a family or in groups of women. And for the more marginalized sex workers who often have little formal knowledge of Islam, or any other religion, the shrine is often their only means of religious expression.

This lack of formal structure makes shrine-related activities accessible to non-Muslims as well. For them there is no obligation to perform Islamic prayers or Qur'anic recitations in order to benefit from the blessings offered by the saints. Thus from a non-Muslim perspective, these saints are associated with local Bengali customs. They are part of the mythological story of Bengal and its traditions. The popular appeal of making vows at shrines among non-Muslims is also attributable to the local and indigenous characteristics of the shrine environment. For example, the Maijbandari *urs* celebration each year takes place in the Bengali month of *Magh*, as opposed to a date based on the Islamic calendar. Furthermore, the Maijbandari *urs* celebration is one of the largest Islamic gatherings in the world that includes the participation of Hindu musicians, a clear indication of their wide popularity in Bangladesh. Many of the activities associated with the Sufi shrines are ritual elements commonly observed in other religious communities of the South Asian subcontinent such as the binding of string to a tree and the presentation of a gift to the saint, particularly incense, candles, and sweets.

The economic exchange at and near shrines is a significant factor in the vitality of these shrines. The caretakers do not exclude people based on their religious identity. All people are welcomed to the shrines to venerate the saints and to petition them for help. All pilgrims are permitted to demonstrate their respect for the saints in their own unique way. This openness encourages more visitors to the shrine, and more visitors translates into greater economic exchange, both at the shrine and in the wider community. Thus, shrines also impact local economies, and to some extent the economic benefit felt by the community of people who visit the shrine may serve to reaffirm belief in the blessings bestowed by the saint on the local community.

Many of the practices of the shrines not only share commonalities with the activities associated with pilgrimage to non-Muslim sacred sites in the subcontinent, but also with visitation to Sufi shrines throughout the Islamic world such as prayer and Qur'anic recitation, *dhikr*, *majlis*, *mawlid*, and *urs* celebrations. I do not intend to argue that the rituals associated with shrines have a universal nature, but rather that some elements are clearly Islamic while others are clearly common cross-cultural practices of the subcontinent. It is not unusual to find Muslims who travel around the world to different shrines to pay their respects and ask favors of saints, an indication of pilgrimage's global Islamic appeal. When visitation to shrines started to gain widespread popularity in the medieval period, legal scholars scrutinized many of the activities and detailed in writing the proper modes of conduct at shrines. The controversy regarding shrines and vows was a reaction to their growing popularity.

One interesting difference between the saints and their shrines in Bangladesh and other parts of the Islamic world where saints' tombs are visited is that there are few female saints in Bangladesh. This phenomenon may be due to the fact that, as early as the sixteenth century, men who were associated with forest clearing and land reclamation were later remembered as saints for their role in transformation of land and impact on culture (Eaton 1993: 207).

The hagiographies affirm an Islamic history of Bengal. In reference to Shah Jalal, later hagiographical texts portray him as an Arab; an Arab ethnic identity lends him more legitimacy and authority. The land of Bengal is also given importance in the legend by way of suggesting its soil is exactly the same as the soil of the Arabian Peninsula, the birthplace of Islam. These elements of hagiography provide Bangladesh a direct connection to the sacred lands of Islam, specifically Mecca and Medina. The story of the Prophet Muhammad giving the charge to Shah Jalal to move to India to defend Muslims there also affirms the notion of a divine decree or religious authority. Like Muhammad at the Battle of Badr, which is arguably Muhammad's most important battle, Shah Jalal was accompanied by 313 companions on his journey to India. Together, these and the stories of hundreds of other saints bring Bengal within an Islamic sacred historical scope for Bengali Muslims.

Yet, Bengali religious history is susceptible to multiple interpretations. Some saints, depending on one's perspective, are remembered in less Islamic terms. This suits those who are less familiar with Islam or who do not consider themselves to be Muslims. Nonetheless, the hagiographical accounts of the saints' lives are vital to the belief in their power, their presence, and place in Bengali culture. These accounts continue to foster a Bengali sacred history and have become the history belonging to all Bangladeshis.

Regardless of whether we look at the performance of popular vows and the ritual of pilgrimage from the perspective of Islamic global practices or Bengali local practices, it is clear that the saints are endowed or blessed with the power to aid those in need without concern for their religious heritage. Indeed, people from all social and economic classes, the educated and illiterate, men and women, and even politicians and sex workers, make vows. It is the elasticity of this custom that allows it to thrive as a popular tradition throughout Bangladeshi society without concern for one's individual religious identity. Thus, Muslim devotees may view it as a Bengali–Islamic tradition that shares characteristics with the global Islamic tradition, but that is also culturally rooted in the Bengal landscape. To those who identify less with Islam and for non-Muslim devotees, it is simply understood as a Bengali tradition.

Notes

1. In Bangladesh and among Bengalis in India vows are commonly referred to as *manat*. Through *manat* a dedicant promises a specific offering to the deity or saint in exchange for the fulfillment of a request. This term is commonly employed by Muslims, Christians, Hindus, Buddhists, and *Adivasis* (tribal communities) in Bangladesh.

2. *Jinn*, according to the Islamic tradition, are one of the creations of God. Where humans are created from clay, *jinn* are invisible spirits who were created from fire.

3. Next to the tank is the mosque and the hostel. To get to Bistami's shrine, the votaries must climb approximately two hundred steps where there are separate places for women and men to offer their prayers. Beyond the shrine is a monument commemorating the meeting place of the twelve *awliya* or saints (plural of *wali*) of Chittagong who are also attributed with spreading Islam in Chittagong and whose identity is unclear.

4. Upon entering the shrine compound there is a large plaza. Straight ahead is the women's section where women may sit, pray, and petition Shah Jalal for his assistance. To the left of the women's section is a staircase that leads to Shah Jalal's tomb where only men are permitted to enter. The compound includes a *khanaqah* (Sufi hospice), mosque for men, a women's section below and to the right of the tomb, a cooking area, an office, a tank with fish that are fed by visitors, a well, and an adjacent graveyard.

5. There are two kinds of *jihad*, the greater and the lesser. The greater *jihad* is the individual spiritual struggle or effort to improve one's faith and worship of God. The lesser *jihad* refers to an armed resistance. In the case of the story of Shah Jalal's *jihad*, it was a matter of protecting Muslims from persecution.

6. Ibn Battuta (d.1377), a great traveler of the fourteenth century, recounts the miracles of Shah Jalal in his travelogue (Husain 1976: 225–42).

7. In a later version of this story, Shah Jalal allegedly told his uncle about a dream he had in which the Prophet Muhammad informed him that Hindus were persecuting Muslims in India. In this dream Muhammad commanded him to engage in the lesser *jihad* by going to India to defend Muslims residing there. Shah Jalal was ready to comply with the Prophet's request but did not know where India was. With a clump of soil in hand, Shah Jalal's uncle commanded Shah Jalal to journey and settle in the first place that had like soil. That place was Sylhet.

8. There are hundreds of other saints in Bangladesh known for fantastic feats, some with more localized followings.

9. For more information on the origins of the *mawlid* celebrations, see *The Encyclopaedia of Islam*, "Mawlid," CD-ROM edition.

10. In Bangladesh saints are generally all male.

11. Sufism is often regarded as the mystical tradition in Islam with numerous orders or *tariqas* around the world. A Sufi understanding of Islam means that the observance of the Five Pillars of Islam is insufficient. To demonstrate their love of Allah and submission to Allah's will, Sufis perform additional practices in the hope that these practices will purify the soul and thus bring them closer to Allah. Yet, this is only a description of Sufis and not their relationship to the wider Muslim community. Sufi teachers, the great masters in particular, affect the world of Muslims outside these orders. Many ordinary Muslims seek their guidance, advice, and assistance in all matters as Sufis are generally respected for their believed proximity to Allah.

12. The *mazar* of a saint is also known as a *dargah* or court. The use of this term may be due to the fact that the saint is still accessible through prayer and meditation at the site where his or her body is laid to rest.

13. For a more detailed discussion of three medieval Muslim scholars' views on the subject, see Taylor (1989: 100–37).

14. *Dhikrs* are usually held on Thursday evenings at *mazars* between '*asr* and *maghrib* prayers.

15. *Dhikr* may be performed on any occasion, in either group or individual settings.

16. *Ampara* is a group of Qur'anic suras that are most commonly recited during *salah*.

17. Fatima Mernissi, a Moroccan sociologist, found that women are more likely than men to visit the shrines of saints (*Marabout*), especially the shrines of the lesser saints. These sanctuaries are a public space dominated by women who seek the aid of saints. These shrines also provide a public space where women may meet and exchange

accounts about personal difficulties, providing each other with potential solutions to problems and emotional support. See Mernissi (1977: 101–12). Also Betteridge's work (1993: 239–47) on shrines in Iran demonstrates that women there are also more likely than men to go on *ziyarat* to the tombs of the Shi'i imams and their families. She explores the reasons for women's *ziyarat*, concluding that *ziyarat* is a central component of women's religious expression regarded by the public as a female activity. As is the case with *ziyarat* in Morocco, women in Shiraz also visit these shrines in order to request the help of saints with individual problems. Here again, it is believed that these saints have been blessed with special powers or have direct access to the divine. Betteridge has also found that some tactics include haranguing of saints. Finally, she argues that men's lack of participation in *ziyarat* is closely associated with the differences between men's and women's ways of religious expression. The formal setting of the mosque is inconvenient for women's participation. In contrast, the shrine's informal atmosphere is more conducive to women's expression of religiosity. See Betteridge (1993: 239–47).

18. There are times when men along with their wives make vows on family related matters such as when they encounter difficulties conceiving a child. University and high school students, too, often turn to the saints during examination periods at the end of the school year.

19. See Save the Children Australia, Services and Solutions International, and Save the Children Sweden, *Childhood in the Red Light Zone: Growing Up in the Daulatdia and Kandapara Brothel Communities of Bangladesh* (Dhaka: Bangladesh, 2001): 29–30 and Sultan Mahmud (Save the Children Australia), personal interview, June 2001.

20. The performance of *sejda* is frowned upon by the most orthodox and even by those who believe in the practice of *ziyarat* and *manat*. Some shrines have signboards that provide the rules for *ziyarat*, which almost always forbids *sejda*. Regardless, visitors to shrines will see *sejda* being performed by both Muslims and non-Muslims alike.

21. The *mandira* are cup-shaped cymbals and the *dholok* is a type of drum.

22. It is important to note that here the Arabic term used for vow is *nadhr* or promise. Legal scholars differ on its legitimacy. Furthermore, the text does not indicate whether or not "promise" means an exchange for divine intervention to benefit the supplicant.

23. For instance in Khulna, the shrine of Zinda Pir, who is said to have risen from his grave, has one *khadim*, few visitors, and no shops located near the shrine. It is not clear, but the shrine may have once been a thriving shrine center.

References

Abedin, Abul Phatah Maolana Jaynul. 1998. *Marahum hajarat pir khanajahan ali*. Khulana: Adam Ali.

Ahamad, Khandakar Reaj Uddin. 2000. *Hajarat shah jalal o hajarat shahparan*. Jindabajar: Oyahab end shans.

Bennett, Clinton. 1994. "Islam." In *Sacred Place,* eds. Jean Holm with John Bowker, 88–114. London: Pinter Publishers.

Betteridge, Anne H. 1993. "Women and Shrines in Shiraz." In *Everyday Life in the Muslim Middle East,* eds. Donna Lee Bowen and Evelyn A. Early, 239–47. Bloomington: Indiana University Press.

Choudhury, Sujit. 1979. "Badsah: A Hindu Godling with a Muslim Background." In *Folkloric Bangladesh,* ed. Mustafa Zaman Abbasi, 61-69. Dhaka: Bangladesh Folklore Parishad.

Eaton, Richard M. 1993. *The Rise of Islam and the Bengal Frontier, 1204-1760.* Berkeley: University of California Press.

Hak, Alimul. 2001. "Manat: jayej ki na-jayej?" *Dainik ittefak* 6 July (5).

Haq, Muhammad Enamul. 1987. "Panch Pir." In *Folklore of Bangladesh,* ed. Shamsuzzaman Khan, 231–56. Dhaka: Bangla Academy.

Haque, Ennamul. 1975. *A History of Sufi-ism in Bengal.* Dacca: Asiatic Society of Bangladesh, 136.

Hoffman, Valerie J. 1995. *Sufism, Mystics, and Saints in Modern Egypt.* Columbia: University of South Carolina Press.

Husain, Mahdi, trans. 1976. *The Rehla of Ibn Battuta (India, Maldive Islands, and Ceylon).* Baroda: Oriental Institute.

Ikram, S. 1957. "An Unnoticed Account of Shaikh Jalal of Sylhet." *Journal of the Asiatic Society of Pakistan* 2: 63–68.

Keller, Nuh Ha Mim, trans. 1999. *Ahmad ibn Naqib al-Misri Reliance of the Traveller: A Classic Manual of Islamic Sacred Law.* Beltsville: Amana Publications.

Levtzion, Nehemia and Gideon Weigert. 1998. "The Muslim Holy Cities as Foci of Islamic Revivalism in the Eighteenth Century." In *Sacred Space: Shrine, City, Land,* eds. Benjamin Z. Kedar and R. J. Zwi Werblowsky, 259–77. New York: New York University Press.

Mernissi, Fatima. 1977. "Women, Saints, and Sanctuaries." *Signs* 3, 1: 101–12.

Qanungo, Suniti Bhushan. 1988. *A History of Chittagong.* Chittagong: Dipankar Qanungo.

Roy, Asim. 1983. *The Islamic Syncretistic Tradition in Bengal.* Dhaka: Academic Publishers.

Schimmel, Annemarie. 1975. *Mystical Dimensions of Islam.* Chapel Hill: University of North Carolina Press.

Stewart, Tony. 1995. "Satya Pir: Muslim Holy Man and Hindu God." In *Religions of India in Practice,* ed. Donald Lopez, 578–97. Princeton: Princeton University Press.

Subhan, John A. 1938. *Sufism Its Saints and Shrines: An Introduction to the Study of Sufism with Special Reference to India.* Lucknow: Lucknow Publishing House.

Taylor, Christopher Schurman. 1989. *The Cult of the Saints in Late Medieval Egypt.* Ph.D. dissertation, Princeton University. Ann Arbor: UMI. 8920361.

Werbner, Pnina and Helene Basu, eds. 1998. *Embodying Charisma: Modernity, Locality and the Performance of Emotion in Sufi Cults.* London: Routledge.

7

Bara: Buddhist Vows at Kataragama

SUNIL GOONASEKERA

A Classification of Buddhist Vows

Are there vows in Buddhism? The answer depends on what is meant by the term "vow." In general, we can say that there are two meanings to the term. On the one hand, a vow is a promise one makes to oneself. On the other, it is a promise made to a supernatural being to propitiate that being for performing a requested favor.

In the Indian religious traditions the former type of vows are known as *vrata*. In Buddhist terminology they are called *sila* in Pali and *sil* in the colloquial Sinhala of Sri Lanka. The *vrata*, *sila,* or *sil* are soteriological and disciplinary. They are behavioral restrictions that a person imposes upon herself in order to stay away from spiritual defilement and to purify herself so that soteriological progress is hastened.

Everyday Buddhist lay practice includes five such promises. These are known as *panchasila* (*pansil* in Sinhala) or the five precepts. On *poya* days,[1] religious virtuosi observe the eight precepts or *astangasilla* (*atasil* in Sinhala). *Atasil* restrict personal and social conduct in three more ways than the everyday five precepts and require temporary abandonment of household activities. The *atasil* holder maintains these vows for the twenty-four hours of *poya* day and then returns to the household by reobserving the five precepts.[2] Occasionally, one comes across individuals who hold *dasasila* (*dasasil* in Sinhala) or ten precepts. These individuals have abandoned all household activities but have not become members of the monastic order, the next step in Sri Lankan Buddhist soteriological progress, where the monks are supposed to hold *kotiyak sanvara sil* or a billion behavioral restraints.[3] My focus here is not these soteriological vows but the latter type introduced above—the vows made to propitiate supernatural beings in return for favors granted by those beings.

In Sri Lanka, vows made to propitiate supernatural beings are known as *bara*.[4] The term *bara* also has a broader application, and means placing an individual under the care of an authority figure. For example, when a parent admits a child to a school she would say, "*lamaya iskoleta bara keruva*" (*lamaya* [child] *iskoleta* [of the school] *bara keruva* [placed under the authority]). When a criminal surrenders himself to the police, he would say "*policiyata bara vuna*" (*policiyata* [to the police] *bara* [surrender] *vuna* [I became]. Thus, the dominant meaning of the concept is surrendering to an authority figure.

In religious contexts, by means of a *bara,* the devotee surrenders herself to a supernatural being and asks for a favor with the promise that she will propitiate the deity in a particular way if the favor is granted. It is thus a contractual agreement that one enters into with a supernatural being. However, unlike in legal contracts, the supernatural's acceptance of the devotee's offer is not a necessary condition for the contract to be effective. The devotee does not have to wait until the supernatural accepts the offer of devotion because it is taken for granted that the supernatural always accepts these offers and will provide the favor if possible. In fact, the devotee's devotion hinges on this continuous availability of relief or *pihita*.

The fulfillment of a promise by the devotee is an ethical obligation. If the devotee has a bad record of nonfulfillment of previous promises, the supernatural is displeased by the devotee's unethical conduct. They punish (*danduvamkaranava*) such parties, sometimes very severely and become reluctant to be of help. As the *kapurala* (temple attendant) of the Kataragama *devalaya* in Kirinda, near Kataragama, emphatically stated, "there is no escape from this responsibility." The well-known statement, that the culprit can run but cannot hide, applies here to the letter. The devotee also knows of her previous breaches for she remembers her failure and remembers the punishment (*danduvama*) that was meted out by the supernatural. But, there is always hope. The supernatural does not reject her and the *pihita* or help requested will never be denied. However, the supernatural only accepts the new offer conditionally, requiring that special rituals be performed in atonement of previous breaches, in addition to the fulfillment of the promise that she now makes. The dependability of the supernatural, realized through the continual availability of his help, thus constitutes the foundation of devotion.

The fulfillment of a *bara* is called the *bara oppukaranava*. Here, *oppu* means "proof" and *karanava* means "doing." *Oppukaranava* means offering the proof, or proving. The term *oppu* also has wider contexts of application. In law, *oppuva* refers to a deed that is the proof of ownership of land or any other item of movable property that has a long life such as an automobile. In science, *oppukaranava* means proving the truth-value of a proposition. In the context of a *bara* it means the fulfillment of the promise that is the proof of the devotee's devotion for the deity.

Sri Lankan Buddhists make vows to two kinds of supernatural beings—gods (*devivaru*) and planets (*grahayo*). Making a vow to a god is called *deviyanta barayak venava* or surrendering to the benevolence of a god. The gods most frequently invoked are, in order of significance, Kanda Kumara, also known as Kataragama Deviyo, Vishnu, Dedimunda Devata Bandara, Suniyam, and Pattini. The social significance of gods changes with time. For example, the god Natha, who is highly venerated because he is identified as the Maitri Bodhisattva, the next Buddha, is socially relatively insignificant in terms of *bara* because he is

Figure 7.1   Kanda Kumara

believed to be distant and uninvolved in mundane affairs due to his impending Buddhahood. Thus, there is no point in making a *bara* with him.[5] Vishnu is also getting closer to his Buddhahood and is distancing himself from the affairs of humans. Still, Vishnu is useful, and is in command of many gods and can be invoked through *bara* for ethically positive purposes.

Kanda Kumara has been an important god from about the fifth century CE, and by the eighteenth century, he was one of the guardian deities of the nation. Nevertheless, as Gombrich and Obeyesekere show,[6] Kanda Kumara declined in significance during the early decades of the nineteenth century because of the fall of the Kandyan kingdom. But, from the late nineteenth century and since the 1930s, particularly among the Buddhists, Kanda Kumara has been regaining popularity. Currently he is propitiated wherever Buddhists live, especially by the urban middle-class milieu. However, identifying the importance of a god with a particular class is risky because, as far as Kanda Kumara is concerned, individuals from the entire Sri Lankan Buddhist social spectrum, including Buddhist monks, propitiate him.

The up-and-coming deities within the institution of *bara* include Alutnuwara Deviyo or Dedimunda Devata Bandara and Suniyam. These gods are not as significant as Kataragama Deviyo, but are more frequently invoked than Vishnu. Goddess Pattini is significant in a limited range of contexts such as pestilence, epidemics, fertility, and the like. Nevertheless, she is not nearly as significant as Kanda Kumara.[7] Because of this overarching importance of Kanda Kumara and because the *baras* to Kanda Kumara involve virtually every conceivable variety of this phenomenon, my focus here is on vows made with Kanda Kumara, the Prince on the Hill. I will return to deal with him after I discuss the other group of Sri Lankan (and South Asian) supernatural beings with whom the Buddhists deal through vows or *bara*, namely, the planets.

The planets (*grahayo*) have a strong say in the life cycle of an individual. When the planets are in bad combinations with other planets or are in unfriendly or enemy (*saturu*) constellations (*rashi*), houses (*bhava*), or asterisms (*naksastra*), they become malevolent and cause harm. Most of these planetary positions are temporary since the planets are constantly on the move in the geocentric cosmology of South Asian astrology. However, some positions are long lasting. Moreover, depending on a person's time of birth, each planet gets a specific period (*dasa*) in his life span during which that planet has a controlling influence. The periods of certain planets such as Saturn and nonplanetary supernaturals such as *Rahu* and *Ketu* are believed to be utterly inauspicious, full of misery and failure. When an individual suffers from the malefic influences of one or more planets, she or her family members, under the advice of an astrologer, make *baras* to the relevant planets. Once the misfortune passes, the relieved believer performs on her promise.

In the Sri Lankan Buddhist cosmology, the planets are either identified with or placed under the control of the major gods. *Kuja* (Mars) is identified with Kanda Kumara, *Senasura* or *Sani* (Saturn) and *Budha* (Mercury) are brought under Vishnu and so on.[8] Thus, a devotee's deal with the controlling god can be used to coax the planets to behave themselves. As a devotee explained, when a request for favor is made, the invoked god takes the case before the assembly of gods (*deva sabhava*) where the planets also sit, but as a minor league of supernaturals. There, the god, pretty much like a plaintiff's attorney, presents his devotee's plight and moves the king of gods to grant him permission to compel the planet to cease its malevolent influence on the devotee. Such permission is automatically granted and the devotee finds relief. In fulfillment of the promise, the devotee performs the appropriate rituals addressing both the god and the planet.

Kataragama

There is greater seriousness in the *baras* made to gods because gods are, in the supernatural hierarchy, above the planets. As stated above, of the *baras* made to gods, the majority is made to Kanda Kumara, and these *baras* represent the phenomenon of *baras* in general because of their numerousness and inclusiveness.

Kanda Kumara is also known as Murugan, Skanda, and Kataragama Deviyo (the god of Kataragama) because Sri Lankan Buddhists and Hindus everywhere believe that Kanda Kumara or Murugan lives in Kataragama, located about two hundred miles southeast of Colombo, the capital city of Sri Lanka.[9] This region is now a nature reserve. Until the 1930s, there were only cart roads and footpaths to link Kataragama with the nearest major town, Tissamaharama. Thus, before the 1930s, a pilgrimage to Kataragama was an arduous task that only a strongly devout person would undertake. Indeed, according to the Sri Lankan Buddhist saying, *denagena giyot kataragama, nodena giyot ataramaga* (if you know where you are going you may arrive in Kataragama, but if you do not know you will most likely be lost on the way). Numerous footpaths and cart roads crisscrossed the jungle infested with bears, leopards, wild buffaloes, elephants, cobras, vipers, and mosquitoes. Water was scarce. A human voice could not be heard for miles. The belief was that the pilgrim must prepare his last will before setting forth to Kataragama, the village in the desert. Unless thoroughly motivated, no one dared to take the risks. Many who took those risks perished. British colonial administrative reports are replete with accounts of the hazards of the journey and people's suffering on the way. Toward the end of the nineteenth century, with the influx of south Indian laborers imported by the British to work on the coffee plantations, the numbers that took the risks increased, leading to epidemics of cholera. The colonial administrators, in an attempt to curb the spread of the epidemic, restricted the number of pilgrims during the festive season that fell between July and August. As the fears of the epidemic waned, the restrictions were removed.

Since the introduction of motor buses, pilgrimages to Kataragama became less arduous. As traffic increased, the government constructed a paved road between Kataragama and Tissamaharama. That opened the floodgates. Today, people of Buddhist, Hindu, Muslim, and Christian faiths flock to Kataragama not only during the festive season, but throughout the year.

Buddhist Vows in Kataragama

The *baras* are made when distressing contexts arise. Elaborate rituals are not necessary. The devotee can mentally commit herself to a *bara* when she feels that only the supernaturals can help her. She focuses on her problem, concentrates on the god or gods who she thinks would be of help, and makes the promise that if the deity helps her then she will offer the god a specific gift.

Thus, the logic of the *bara* is not different from the logic in any other contractual bond. It is based on the "if, then" framework of obligations. The devotee is convinced about the existence of these deities, their connections with humans, the human ability to communicate with them, and the availability of the supernaturals' support. These are axioms from which the logic of the *baras* is derived.

However, many people perform a simple ritual when or after they make *baras*. My grandmother used to make *baras* to Kanda Kumara whenever my siblings or I fell ill. She would take a coin of any value,[10] clean it by rubbing it with a slice of lime, place the coin on a strip of cloth about eight inches long, hold it in her hands as she clasped them in the traditional Buddhist gesture of worship, close her eyes, and silently make the promise. Silently, she would tie the coin on one of the bedposts or on a branch of the lime bush in the garden. A coin tied in this manner is called the *pandura*, a gift offered as a preliminary consideration. Her silence was a sign of her devotion to the god and the solemnity of the occasion. It could also be a sign of secrecy, for, if there is sorcery or witchcraft, the influence of a demon (*yaka*) or the lingering spirit (*atme*) of a dead relative (*preta*), the distress-causing agent might discover the vow and cause temporary relief so that there is nothing for the god to do, rendering the *bara* ineffective. The cunning agent of distress would return once the god dismisses the *bara* and re-inflict torment with even more malevolence. Thus, vows are made in silence.

When we recovered from whatever afflicted us, my grandmother would demand help from all in our joint family to fulfill (*oppukaranna*) the vow. Often her vows were simple. She had promised that she would go to the nearby Buddhist temple (*pansala*), offer the Buddha lamps (*pahan*), incense (*suvanda dum*), flowers (*mal*), fruit juice (*gilanpasa*), betel leaves (*bulath*) to chew after the drink, and a toothpick (*deheti kura*) made out of a whittled twig from a *bombu* bush (*simplocos spicata*) to clean his teeth. We believed, as Buddhists in Sri Lanka still do, that such offerings brought us merit (*pin*).

Figure 7.2   Wrap a coin on a strip of cloth and tie it on a lime bush

My grandmother also promised that after gathering merit she would go to the small shrine room (*devale*) on the temple yard and have an attendant of the *devale* (*kapurala*) chant a prayer (*yatikava*) and transfer merit (*punyanumodana*) to the god. As she left for the temple to fulfill her vow she would untie the *pandura* and carry it with her. At the *devale*, once the *bara* had been fulfilled (*oppukeruwa*), she would drop it into the till in full relinquishment of her obligations.

The making and fulfillment of the *bara*s can be much more elaborate than my grandmother's simple ritual. Some promise to go to Kataragama on a pilgrimage, on the way worshipping the *Tissa Vehera* (the stupa in Tissamaharama) by offering lotus flowers, lamps, and incense, and then offering the same at the *Kiri Vehera* near the Kataragama *mahadevale* (the main shrine of Kanda Kumara). These devotees transfer merit on a grand scale because the worship of these stupas is more meritorious than a simple ritual at a village temple. Having performed this step of the fulfillment ritual (*oppukirima*), the devotee would make a regular *puja* (offering) at the Kataragama *mahadevale*, the great shrine of the god and the focal point of Kataragama. This *puja* consists of a tray containing betel leaves, a coconut, fruits such as bananas and pineapple, a garland, and the cash fee for the *kapurala* who presents the *puja* to the god.

My cousin Berty, then a senior student at the University of Colombo School of Dentistry, was preparing for his final examinations. As with any undergraduate, he was full of anxieties about the forthcoming event. Berty knew he was a good student and would pass the examinations as his grades were good and he was consistently at the top of his class. But he had various fears. He did not want to become ill, meet with an accident, or encounter some such misfortune that would prevent him from taking the examination. One day he appeared at our house in Galle and suggested I accompany him to Kataragama. He said he wanted to make a vow (*barayak venna ona*) so that, with Kanda Kumara's help, he would be able to avoid these adversities. He wanted to make the *bara* in Kataragama so that it would be totally effective and have no room for failure.

I went with him on this pilgrimage. We first stopped in Devundera, where he worshipped Vishnu, then proceeded to Tissamaharama where he made an elaborate offering of flowers, incense, and lamps. Thereafter we went to Kataragama where Berty meticulously observed all the ritual procedures. We bathed in the river, got into freshly laundered white sarongs and shirts and, after smashing coconuts on the granite slab in front of the *mahadevale* to honor Kanda Kumara, went straight to the *Kiri Vehera*. On the way, Berty bought lotus flowers, incense, and oil. At the *Kiri Vehera*, he placed the flowers on one of the granite slabs (remnants of the ancient *mal asane*s or the "altars for the flowers"), lit the incense sticks, and arranged them where many were already burning, then poured the oil into one of the giant brass lamps in the yard of the *Kiri Vehera*. He knelt down facing the stupa and worshipped. Afterward he fell silent for a while, then got up and said we could return to the main ritual arena. In those days there were shops immediately outside the *mahadevale* compound.[11] From one of these shops, Berty had a *puja vattiya* (tray of offerings) custom made with the best ingredients.

We went back to the *mahadevale*. Berty carried the *puja vattiya* on his head, held securely with both hands. He looked very serious. We joined the crowd inside the *mahadevale*. They were all excited. Some devotees cried *"haro hara,"* the traditional incantation, to celebrate the god. Some were in trance states. Our time to hand over the *puja vattiya* to the *kapurala* arrived. Berty gave it to the *kapurala* and we walked to the side. After a while the *kapurala* returned the *puja vattiya* to Berty. The coconut and the money that Berty placed in it were gone. The fruits, which had been cut in half, lay on the betel leaves. We were about to leave the *devale* through the side exit when an elderly *kapurala* standing at the door placed on our foreheads a dot (*pottu*) made of *vibhuti* (holy ash). The rituals were over. We left the *devale* and ate some of the fruit and gave most of it to the poor children who begged for it. I chewed a betel leaf. The future dentist abhorred abusing his dental health and refused to join me and even advised me on my smoking that stains my teeth (all true and very scientific, but . . .). We gave the remaining betel leaves with the *puja* tray to an old woman who pleaded for them. Berty made his *bara*.

Figure 7.3 Puja vattiya—a tray of offerings

I do not know what kind of promise Berty made and whether he fulfilled his *bara*. But I know he passed the examination with flying colors and practiced dentistry in Colombo until he left Sri Lanka for Great Britain. I have no doubt that he fulfilled (*oppukeruva*) his vow just as elaborately as he made it. Perhaps, based on the positive results he obtained from this vow, he made more vows later.

This manner of making and fulfilling vows is quite common, and this is how the vast majority of Sri Lankan Buddhist devotees of Kanda Kumara make and fulfill their vows. Some make very specific promises. When people, especially children, become ill, they or their parents make a vow called *rupeta rupe bara*. Literally, *rupeta rupe* means image (*rupe*) for image of the child (*rupeta*) or figure for figure of the child. This is to promise that if the god helps the child, a miniature figure that represents the child will be offered. The offered figure signifies the child and the devotee's devotion. This also means that the child will become a devotee for life. Making such *rupes* is a cottage industry and these figures are available in Kataragama shops for a few rupees. They are made of strips of tin, about three inches high, cut to look like a human being.[12] Likewise, when an astrologer finds that an individual is adversely affected by the malefic position of a certain planet in his horoscope, a *praneta prane bara* is prescribed. This means a life (*prane*) will be offered if the god saves the life of the sufferer (*praneta*). The proffered *prane* is usually that of an animal caged or condemned to death and, as the *rupe* does, signifies the life (*prane*) of the individual for whose benefit the *bara* is made. Thus, the promisor releases caged birds or chained animals such as pet monkeys, or buys a cow, a bull, a goat, or chickens from butchers and donates them to a Buddhist temple or a *devale*, where the animal, as the god's property, is left to wander and live free from harm.[13] This was what happened when Dr. Amarasinghe married an Irish-American in the United States. His parents, agitated by their son's marriage to a foreign woman in a foreign land, made a *praneta prave bara* and promised the god that they would offer a young bull if their son returned to Sri Lanka alone and remained on the island for the rest of his life. A young bull was bought from a butcher and released as an advanced fulfillment of the *bara*. However, Dr. Amarasinghe returned only five years later, with his American wife and two daughters. That *bara*, needless to say, failed.

Another frequently made promise is that a *tiraya* (curtain), used to cover and adorn the entrance way to the *devale* and/or the *sanctum sanctorum*, would be offered to the god if the god helps the devotee overcome difficulties and dangers during arduous tasks such as foreign travel, passing of examinations, finding employment, and the like. The *tiraya* should be the same height as the devotee, but usually it is taller since the entrances to the *devale* and to the *sanctum sanctorum* are about seven or eight feet in height. A *tiraya* hung before the *sanctum sanctorum* usually carries a large image of the god painted on it, while those hung at the *devale* entrances are embroidered with sequin decorations and verses in honor of the god.

For success in business activities and for general prosperity, a particularly effective *bara* is to offer a *muruten danaya*. Here, *muruten* means the kitchen and *danaya* refers to an offering. The phrase refers to an offering from the kitchen of the devotee. What is proffered is a *peni batha* (sweet rice) made by boiling rice with milk, mung beans, and *hakuru* (solidified treacle) from coconut or *kitul* [14] palms. For this *bara*, the devotee must also offer the demigod Kadavara his share of *peni batha* since Kadavara is believed to be a demonic form of Shiva, Kanda Kumara's father, and the guardian of treasures. Unless Kadavara is offered his share, the offering is not complete and the devotee has failed to fulfill the vow. Those who wish to obtain favorable results from litigation or examinations proffer gold chains, lamps, and other items to decorate the god's statue or his shrine. As the *kapuralas* stated, there are no strict rules regarding the nature of the proffer. Many devotees combine a number of proffers to obtain the best and fastest results.

A more recent trend for vows to recover from illness and to overcome obstacles is to perform *kavati* dance at Kataragama during the festive season in the *Esala* month that falls between July and August.[15] The Buddhists have borrowed this dance form from the Tamil Murugan cultists of south India and Sri Lanka. A *kavati* is a miniature ritual arch attached to a cylindrical wooden bar. The arch is constructed with aluminum sheets and decorated with peacock feathers and symbolizes the peacock, the vehicle of Kanda Kumara. The devotee places the wooden bar on his shoulders and dances to the rhythms provided by a band of musicians who play popular instrumental music. Usually, either a group of devotees hire a band or a band offers services to individual devotees. When a sufficient number of devotees join, the band moves from *devale* to *devale*, stopping at each for a few minutes to play tunes to which the devotees dance in honor of the deity of the shrine. For fulfilling vows to Kanda Kumara devotees spend considerable amount of time and energy in front of and around the *mahadevale*. The dancing involves erotic movements and is popular among the urban lower-class devotees. Gradually, this dance form has become a standard for many middle-class devotees as well.[16]

A minority of Buddhists take drastic steps to fulfill their vows. These individuals experience trance states. They believe that the trance state, called *arude,* results when the god possesses them by entering their bodies.[17] Mr. Edirisinghe was a pious Buddhist. His religiosity increased as he slowly and painfully realized that one of his sons was a victim of a congenital disease. When he found that no medical treatment could make his son a normal person he sought supernatural help. At the same time, his mother was suffering from cancer in the stomach. Numerous visits to allopathic and ayurvedic practitioners of great repute proved fruitless. On several occasions, the tumor was surgically removed but the cancer showed no signs of remission. The Edirisinghe family made many vows to the planets and the gods while medical treatments were being administered. Exorcisms and removal of the effects of evil magic (*kodivina*) were tried. The doctors decided that old Mrs. Edirisinghe was a terminal case.

Then a friend advised the Edirisinghe family to visit a *devale* in a faraway town where a Buddhist monk cum *kapurala* was famous for his knowledge of *mantras* (verbal incantations that invoke supernatural beings), *gurukam* (magical rituals), and his capacity to approach the gods. He was known to be a specialist in invoking Kanda Kumara. The Edirisinghe family took the advice and went to this authority.

The family made a vow to Kanda Kumara. This was a very serious vow because it was made with the services of a ritual specialist. The monk presented an elaborate petition to the god on behalf of the sick Mrs. Edirisinghe. During the rituals, Mr. Edirisinghe started to shiver and exhibit initial signs of an *arude*. The family was embarrassed and perplexed about Mr. Edirisinghe's *arude* because people of their social standing do not engage in such activities. They believed that *arude* was a lower-class phenomenon that was useful when exhibited by those of lower social status. A person who exhibits *arude* is called *arudakaraya*. The Edirisinghe family did not want their family member to be called an *arudakaraya*.

Nevertheless, Mr. Edirisinghe took the matter seriously and wished to establish his *arude*. He complained that most *arudakarayas* were rogues or had only inferior forms of possession. With his son's and his mother's problems heavily on his shoulders, Mr. Edirisinghe wanted to try the *arude* himself to best help these important people in his life. Mr. Edirisinghe became a vegetarian and consulted many experts. The experts watched his *arude* and opined that the god of Kataragama had blessed Mr. Edirisinghe. His was a Kataragama *arude*. They convinced him to make a *bara*. The promise to Kanda Kumara was that if Mr. Edirisinghe's *arude* were genuine and auspicious, he would perform *ginipa gima* or fire-walking during the following Esala festival in Kataragama.

Mr. Edirisinghe was elated by this tremendous gift from the god. It came from none other than Kanda Kumara himself. He went to Kataragama on an auspicious day. By now Mr. Edirisinghe was well-known among the Sinhala Buddhist *samis* or priests of Kataragama who regarded him as a man from a respectable family. They instructed him to make a vow in the most serious manner.

After bathing in the river, he wore a white sarong and a red shawl. The red shawl indicated his special devotion to the god. The white sarong indicated his purity of the body and the mind. Mr. Edirisinghe, carrying a coconut with him and accompanied by influential *samis*, walked to the *mahadevale* compound. In front of the *mahadevale* there is a granite slab with a steel grill around it. Mr. Edirisinghe stood in front of it. One of the *samis* took the coconut from him, placed a few camphor tablets on it and lit them. Then the *sami* began to recite a long and complex pleading (*yatikava*) interspersed with *mantras* and *slokas* (verses in honor of the god). After this long ritual, he returned the coconut to Mr. Edirisinghe and told him to focus his mind on the *arude*, how it would benefit the world if he was blessed with one, how he would serve the god and the world by means of the *arude*, and that he would perform fire-walking to express his gratitude and devotion (*bhaktiya*) if the god granted (*varam*) him the *arude*. The camphor pills were still burning on the coconut. Mr. Edirisinghe closed his eyes and began to tremble and breathe heavily. The *sami*s roared "*haro hara*." Then, suddenly, Mr. Edirisinghe lifted the coconut over his head with both hands and in one dashing motion smashed the coconut on the rock. Mr. Edirisinghe made his *bara*.

Throughout the following year he practiced strict vegetarianism, hardly attended a funeral to avoid ritual pollution, practiced meditation, and daily chanted the Buddhist sutras. He tried his *arude* on auspicious (*kemmura*) days under the instructions of veteran *sami*s. The *sami*s continually noted steady progress and encouraged him to visit powerful *devales* in various places to experience the god's grace. However, Mr. Edirisinghe's family was unimpressed by all these activities and were quite embarrassed by his decision to use his *arude* to deliver relief to others who needed Kanda Kumara's help. They pressured him to restrict his *arude* to the family circle, opposed any exposure of it to the public and, in turn, offered to attend Mr. Edirisinghe's shrine on auspicious days and receive the god's blessings through him. This compromise worked fine for Mr. Edirisinghe and he began to face life with new confidence.

Mr. Edirisinghe prepared for the fire-walking in the three months before the festive season. He had become a celibate when he made his vow and continued the celibacy during these three months. Daily he recited the *tun suttare* (the three basic *sutras: mangala, ratana,* and *karaniyametta* chanted by pious Buddhists) and practiced *maitri bhavana* (meditation on compassion). Thus prepared, he went to Kataragama to fulfill his vow. Mr. Edirisinghe stayed in Kataragama during the entire festive season and visited the *mahadevale* during all the *pujas*. He socialized with the *sami*s who were, by then, his good friends, and made friends with others. The penultimate day of the festive season was his special day. He had obtained permission to perform fire-walking from the *basnayaka nilame*, the chief official caretaker of the Kataragama sacred establishment. By early afternoon he had to join a special *kavati* dancing meant for the hundreds of fire-walkers. This was known as the *gini kavati* (fire *kavati*).[18] Practically all the dancers appeared to be in trance states, dancing in abandon with sweat pouring from their bodies and evaporating in the hot sun. Once the *gini kavati* was over, Edirisinghe and the other aspiring and veteran fire-walkers relaxed and discussed what they felt during the ritual.

By midnight, in front of the *mahadevale*, a huge wood pyre was created. The fire-walkers themselves carried the firewood and the *sami*s set fire to it with

Figure 7.4 Making a vow elaborately by holding a coconut

Figure 7.5 Smashing a coconut on the rock inside the metal

burning camphor tablets. Soon the pyre became a column of fire. Its heat was so intense, the surrounding steel fence that the fire brigade erected to prevent injury to the onlookers became twisted with its joints dislocated. By four in the morning, the pyre was a mass of embers. This was smoothed to a neat walkway of fire about a foot thick, five feet wide, and twenty-five feet long.

The fire-walkers, led by the chief fire-walker, had all gone to the river, bathed, and were lined up in wet clothes outside the premises of the *mahadevale*. The fire-walkers, Mr. Edirisinghe among them, were in trance states making outcries of *haro hara*, the traditional salutation for Kanda Kumara. At the auspicious moment, a *sami* performed *puja*s before this pyre and blessed the chief fire-walker.[19] The chief fire-walker walked on the path of fire and entered the *mahadevale*. He was followed by the other fire-walkers, including Mr. Edirisinghe. Mr. Edirisinghe thus fulfilled (*oppukeruva*) his *bara* and proved to himself and to others that the Kanda Kumara's blessings were in fact with him.

Theodicy and the Baras at Kataragama

The above cases of my grandmother, Berty, Dr. Amarasinghe, and Mr. Edirisinghe illustrate four modal ways of making *baras* at Kataragama. They also illustrate that devotees make *baras* for numerous purposes. What makes Buddhist vows at Kataragama special is the difference between Kanda Kumara and other gods of the Sri Lankan Buddhist pantheon. Buddhists make *baras* with many gods. Which god or goddess is invoked depends on the purpose. Some gods, like Kanda Kumara, are multipurpose and do not expect the devotee to be ethical in his social conduct. Others, like Natha, Vishnu, Pattini, and Saman demand that their devotees be completely ethical and would not entertain requests for favors for unethical purposes such as those that violate the five precepts. From them, one can ask only for protection from various malevolent powers. But Kanda Kumara has two sides. On the one hand, he is believed to be a bodhisattva. On the other hand, he must wait a long time to realize his Buddhahood and is more closely involved with mundane human affairs. Other gods punish wrongdoers but only mildly, whereas Kanda Kumara's wrath is terrible and devastating. Other gods consider their devotees' ethical conduct as a mark of their devotion. Kanda Kumara's only requirement is unfailing devotion. Irrespective of the ethical background of the devotee, Kanda Kumara responds to the requests. Other gods are loved. Kanda Kumara is loved and feared.

Kanda Kumara's Buddhist devotees include Buddhist monks, politicians, students, litigants, and even criminals. Both the plaintiff and the defendant of the same case could make *baras* to Kanda Kumara to obtain positive results from the pending litigation. In politics, all the candidates to a given parliamentary seat could make *baras* hoping to win. How do the devotees reconcile the contradictions involved? How can a bodhisattva be indifferent to the ethical aspects of a *bara*? How can the god support both opponents? How do the devotees resolve problems of meaning arising from such combinations of mutually exclusive premises?

Kanda Kumara is seen as an imperfect god and is therefore inferior to the likes of Natha and Vishnu. The ethical neutrality of the god is a product of his imperfect nature. Higher gods are always ethical and wrongdoers cannot hope to receive relief from them for they are reluctant to exonerate the culprits. Kanda Kumara's ethical indifference is further evidenced by his relationship with Valli, a concubine, a negative characteristic. He is also known for his valor and militarism, a deviation from the bodhisattva norms of compassion and peace that Natha and Buddhist Vishnu represent.

According to Buddhist beliefs, Natha will be the next Buddha Maitri, followed by Vishnu. Kanda Kumara's Buddhahood is projected into the distant future in cosmic time because of his imperfections. This is how the aporias of theodicy are resolved in the Kanda Kumara cult. It also implies that eventually, as Kanda Kumara comes closer to his Buddhahood, he too will become like Natha and Vishnu and the theodicy will resolve itself. When this occurs, Kanda Kumara will be of less use to unethical devotees because his ethical neutrality will also end. But, for now, the imperfect god expects only raw devotion from the devotees.[20]

Nevertheless, how do the devotees conceive of his ability to help, say, both the plaintiff and the defendant of the same litigation or the mutually opposing candidates for the same parliamentary seat? The concept that resolves this conflict is equity. Kanda Kumara lets both parties to the conflict win in the larger cosmic processes by helping them both in different ways. One wins and the other loses, but the "loser" actually gains in some other way. For example, two candidates to a parliamentary seat make vows with Kanda Kumara. One wins and the other loses. But the loser escapes from an assassination attempt. The loser emphasizes this other gain to sustain his devotion and attributes his loss to the inexorable laws of karma that the god cannot alter. That takes us to the domains in which the Buddhist vows in Kataragama operate.

Domains

Are the *baras* contracts? They are because they are promises to do something if there is quid pro quo. But, as stated earlier, they are different from legal contracts because they are not made with a human being belonging to a social legal domain. Rather, *baras* are give-and-take exchanges with a supernatural being within the supernatural domain. They are also different from legal contracts because the god need not accept the devotee's offer to create the relationship. However, this relationship may be seen as semicontractual because the god is believed to accepts all offers at all times, as long as the one who offers is devoted to him. Further, there is also a meeting of minds, an important feature of a valid contract, because the god always agrees with the devotee's side of the deal. The consideration for acceptance of the offer is devotion. In that sense, the *baras* belong to the domain of supernatural law.

In the social domain, contracts are often flouted through overreaching, deceit, negligence, or any number of other means. Unless the aggrieved party takes legal action to recover his losses, the breaching party escapes the legal repercussions and only suffers loss of the good will of the aggrieved party and of those who know about his failure to perform his promise. By contrast, in the *bara*s, the devotee who flouts the contract may run but he cannot hide from the god's inexorable wrath. That is a difference between breaking a promise in the social domain versus breaking a promise in the supernatural domain.

Can the *baras* in Kataragama be considered as magic? Because they operate under quid pro quo contractual logic, the *baras* are not purely magical lines of action. Magic does not involve a promise to another person or a supernatural being in exchange for the desired result. As Frazer conceptualized long ago, magic involves the "like produces like," a "if this, then that" logic. In this conceptualization, the distinguishing feature of magic is its independence of another person. One proficient in magic merely manipulates the cosmic mechanisms using established formulae in order to obtain a specific result. In the magical domain, man deals directly with the cosmos. Thus, magic is not contractual although it is rational action because it is goal-oriented and logical within the worldview of the practitioner. Buddhists in Sri Lanka *do* practice magic. But for magic, special procedures distinct from the *baras* are followed in order to establish the proper parameters for "if this, then that" operations.

Thus, *baras* are neither magic nor contractual obligations though they contain aspects of both. *Baras* are not magic because they involve another party whose favorable disposition is essential for the *bara* to be effective. Unless Kanda Kumara decides that the devotee's offer is acceptable because of his devotion to him, the *baras* are made in vain. Further, even if the devotee is acceptably devoted to Kanda Kumara, if the devotee's karma overwhelms Kanda Kumara's abilities, there is nothing the god can do, and the *bara* fails. However, there is a magical element in the *bara* in that they attempt to transcend the empirical limitations of the everyday world and coax the everyday world to deliver the desired results provided the devotee's karma permits. Frazer's notions of sympathetic and homeopathic magic apply here. The *rupeta rupe* and *praneta prane baras* involve the "like-produces-like logic" of homeopathic magic. However, the *rupeta rupe* and *praneta prane baras* do not allow the distinction between homeopathic and sympathetic magic because they contain elements of both. In any case, this magical effect is controlled by the god. That gives the *baras* an intermediate position between the domains of magic and contract. The god accepts the devotee's offer for the consideration of the devotee's devotion and magically delivers the desired results.

What happens when *baras* fail, as in the case of Dr. Amarasinghe? Empirical common sense suggests that the failure should discredit the institution as a falsehood. In day-to-day life, most people give up what does not work. Nevertheless, people continue to make *baras* in spite of failure.

Baras survive empirical scrutiny because they arise from a worldview that provides acceptable reasons for the failure. The overarching concept of karma steps in to save the *bara* as an enduring institution. In Sri Lankan Buddhist cosmology, gods are not seen as the highest beings. They enjoy very long lives. Their living standards are much higher than that of the humans and they have supernatural powers to know and do things that mere men cannot. Yet they are not perfect. Their knowledge and powers are limited. And above the gods, the Buddhas and the *arahaths* are omniscient and powerful in ways the gods are not. But karma is the most powerful and inexorable phenomenon in the world. The Buddhas, *arahaths,* and the gods all succumb to the unforgiving power of their karma. For people in distress because of their karma, there is nothing anyone can do to bring them relief. If one makes a *bara* to Kanda Kumara or any god in order to find relief from karmic distress, he is bound to fail because the gods are powerless before his bad karma. This is not their fault or a fault of the *bara* but the very nature of reality. The distress arises from the karmic domain and he must face it. But if the distress does not have a karmic origin or arise from the wrath of a greater god, most gods, including Kanda Kumara, can use their influence to remove or alleviate distress. Thus, when a particular *bara* fails, nothing happens to the institution because the failure arises from the cosmic domain of karma. Nor is the position or authority of the gods impacted because it is common knowledge that the gods are powerless before karma.[21]

That was how Dr. Amarasinghe's parents explained the failure of their *bara* with Kanda Kumara. What could the god do when their son's karma was bad? Five years after the *bara,* Dr. Amarasinghe visited his parents. His American wife and two beautiful daughters were with him. They were received very well. Perhaps, his karma was not all that bad!

Notes

1. The *poya* are the sacred days of the lunar calendar. The moon is believed to wax and wane in fifteen curves. The full moon is the most sacred and is called the *pasalosvaka* or the fifteen curves.

2. In Jainism, the prescriptions for laymen are known as *sravaka vratas*. These are more detailed and rigorous than the Buddhist *panchasila*, in keeping with the severe asceticism of Jainism. See Jaini (1979: 157–85) for details.

3. The Jain structural parallel is known as *pratima*. The Jain layman who holds *pratima* is known as a *sramanabhuta*. See Jaini (1999) for details. In the ethnographic reality these terms are obsolete. Nevertheless, most Jains appear to diligently uphold the concepts and the practices.

4. Even the Christians, particularly the Catholics, have adopted this term for vows. Thus, Catholics make *baras* before the Virgin Mary, St. Anthony, or St. Sebastian. Etymologically, the term is related to the Tamil *baram* or *varam*. Both the Sinhala and Tamil terms mean promise to perform a devotional act in order to receive a boon.

5. However, as the *kapurala* (temple attendant) of the Natha *devalaya* in Kandy informed me, in the Kandyan provinces Natha is still important and many Kandyans do make *baras* with him. He is insignificant elsewhere in the island. See Obeyesekere (1978: 377–96) and Gombrich and Obeyesekere (1988: 30–31, 96–132) for detailed discussions of the vicissitudes of the deities plotted against social need and time.

6. See n.3 supra.

7. Obeyesekere (1978) and Gombrich and Obeyesekere (1988).

8. For details of Indian astrology, the frequently used classical treatises are *Brhat Jataka* by Varahamihira and *Hora Sastra* by Parasara. For modern works see Charak (1994), Raman (1982, 1992), and Sharma (1973). Dreyer (1997) is a fine introduction in English. For Sinhala renditions of Indian astrology, see Hettigoda (1980) and Sederaman (1983).

9. Davy (1821), Arunachalam (1924), Pieris (1930), and Wirz (1930) provide early accounts of the cult of Kanda Kumara. Navaratnam (1973) and Rasaiah (1981) outline the theology and ritual activities in Kataragama. Gombrich and Obeyesekere (1988) and Obeyesekere (1978) discuss the vicissitudes of deity cults in time and the social processes that make the Kataragama cult the nation's most important deity cult. Obeyesekere (1978) examines the Sinhala borrowing of the bhakti elements of the Murugan cult. Obeyesekere (1981) discusses the ecstatic religion of and Hindu-Buddhist-Muslim convergence in Kataragama.

10. The coin is the medium of communication between the devotee and the deity. On the other hand, it is a symbolic down payment.

11. Kataragama had been converted into a sacred town in the 1960s, and all the business activities that existed outside the *mahadevale* compound have been shifted to the other side of the river.

12. The nature of the *rupe* depends on the purpose of the vow. For example, for protection of a car, a *rupe* of a car is promised. Here the signification is not that the car would be devoted to the god but its owner would be!

13. An alternative to this is the offering of a coconut sapling (*pol pele*). But the *kapuralas* known to me scornfully spoke of this cheap alternative.

14. *Caryota urens*.

15. Rasaiah (1981).

16. See Obeyesekere (1978, 1981), Rasaiah (1981: 38–45), and Gombrich and Obeyesekere (1988: 191–95) for details.

17. Obeyesekere (1978, 1981) and Gombrich and Obeyesekere (1988) discuss the trance states in detail.

18. This is a recent Buddhist invention. Wirz (1930: 51–52) and Rasaiah (1981: 85–87) who detail the fire-walking ceremony itself do not mention it at all. I have witnessed this ritual in the mid-1960s. The special feature of this ritual is that unlike other *kavati* troupes, this one goes to the *Kiri Vehera* as well.

19. Obeyesekere (1978) and Gombrich and Obeyesekere (1988) say that this ritual has been "Buddhicized."

20. See Obeyesekere (1978) and Gombrich and Obeyesekere (1988: 65–133; 163–201) for a lengthy discussion of Kanda Kumara and his role as a bodhisattva. Recently I interviewed the *mahakapurala* of the Ruhunu Kataragama Mahadevale and found that this *kapurala* and some devotees are revising the bodhisattva model for Kanda Kumara. The new theory arises from an interpretation of the Buddha's visits to Sri Lanka. Apparently, at that time the king Mahasena reigned in Kataragama. The Buddha visited him and delivered a sermon. Upon hearing it, the king achieved the first stage of preparedness for achieving *nibbana*. This stage is called *sovan* (Pali: *sothapanna*: stepping into the path). The king died and was reborn as six infant gods on six lotuses in the lake Saravana in the Himalayas. Later he became one god with six heads and twelve arms known as Kandasami or Skanda Kumara. Now Skanda Kumara retains his *sovan* achievement. As such he cannot be a bodhisattva. In any event, my friends in Kataragama seem to be still stuck with the old problem of theodicy. The same argument can still be raised. How can an individual who has achieved this level of perfection be ethically neutral? Certainly, the argument is academic. My friends do not go that far. They are not interested in our hairsplitting. Like Levi Strauss's bricoleurs, they somehow get around the problem at hand and move on to the next topic!

21. The Sri Lankan Buddhist concept of karma is more complex than this. I have restricted my use of the term to the context of vows. The reader is urged to consult Keyes (1983) and Obeyesekere (2002) for detailed treatments of the concept particularly in contexts such as merit-transference and rebirth.

References

Arunachalam, Ponnambalam. 1924. "The Worship of Muruka or Skanda." *Journal of the Royal Asiatic Society, Ceylon Branch* 29:77 reprinted in W. Lionel Fernando, (1985) *Kataragama and Its Festivals (1819–1939)*, 18–30. Colombo: Ananda Press.

Charak, K. S. 1994. *Elements of Vedic Astrology.* New Delhi: Vision Wordtronic.

Davy, John. 1821. *An Account of the Interior of Ceylon and Its Inhabitants with Travels in the Island.* London.

Dreyer, Ronnie Gale. 1997. *Vedic Astrology: A Guide to the Fundamentals of Jyotish.* York Beach: Samuel Weiser.

Fernando, W. Lionel. 1985. *Kataragama and Its Festivals (1819–1939).* Colombo: Ananda Press.

Frazer, James G. 1979. "Sympathetic Magic." In *Reader in Comparative Religion: An Anthropological Approach,* eds. William A. Lessa and Evon Z. Vogt, 337–52. NY: Harper & Row Publishers.

Gombrich, Richard and Gananath Obeyesekere. 1988. *Buddhism Transformed.* Princeton: Princeton University Press.

Hettigoda, Hendrik de Silva. 1980. *Jivitaya ha Grahayo.* Colombo: Hector Hettigoda.

Jaini, Padmanabh S. 1979. *The Jaina Path of Purification.* First Indian Edition. Delhi: Motilal Banarsidas.

Keyes, Charles F. 1983. "Merit-Transference in the Karmic Theory of Popular Buddhism." In Karma: An Anthropological Inquiry, eds. Charles F. Keyes and E. Valentine Daniel, 261–86. Berkeley: University of California Press.

Levi-Strauss, Claude. 1966. *The Savage Mind.* Chicago: University of Chicago Press.

Navaratnam, Ratna. 1973. *Karttikeya, the Divine Child.* Bombay: Bharatiya Vidya Bhavan.

Obeyesekere, Gananath. 2002. *Imagining Karma—Ethical Transformation in Amerindian, Buddhist, and Greek Rebirth.* Berkeley, Los Angeles, and London: University of California Press.

———. 1981. *Medusa's Hair: An Essay on Personal Symbols and Religious Experience.* Chicago: University of Chicago Press.

———. 1978. "The Firewalkers of Kataragama, the Rise of Bhakti Religiosity in Buddhist Sri Lanka" *Journal of Asian Studies* 37, 3: 457–76.

Parasara. 1991. *Hora Sastra.* New Delhi: Ranjan Publications.

Pieris, Paul E. 1950. *Sinhale and the Patriots, 1815–1818.* (1995 edition) New Delhi: Navarang.

Raman, B. V. 1992. *Hindu Predictive Astrology.* New Delhi: UBS Distributors List.

———. 1982. *Planetary Influences on Human Affairs.* Bangalore: IBH Prakashana.

Rasaiah, A. 1981. *Kataragama: Divine Power of Kathirkamam and Methods of Realization.* Colombo: Publisher unspecified.

Sederaman, J. E. 1983. *Grahabala ha Grahayoga Pilibanda Jyotir Vidyatmaka Siddhantha,* ed. Siri Kolamunnage. Colombo: S. Godage and Brothers.

Sharma, Viswanath Deva. 1973. *Astrology and Jyotirvidya: The Fundamental Principles and Systems of Prognosis.* Calcutta: Viswa Jyotirvid Samgha.

Varahamihira. 1985. *Brihat Jataka.* New Delhi: Sagar Publications.

Wirz, Paul. 1930. *Kataragama, The Holiest Place in Ceylon,* tr. D. B. Pralle (1966) Colombo: Lake House.

8

Performing Vows in Diasporic Contexts: Tamil Hindus, Temples, and Goddesses in Germany

MARTIN BAUMANN

Studying Hindu Traditions in the Diaspora

During the recent two decades, the study of Hindu traditions in regions outside the Indian subcontinent has gained academic credibility. The topic of overseas or diasporic Hindu communities has been addressed in a variety of disciplines. Anthropologists, social scientists, and historians of religions have conducted studies on South Asian Hindus in South and East Africa, the Caribbean, North America, Europe, Australia, and Southeast Asia (Rukmani 1999, Vertovec 2000, Baumann 2003). Similarly, research has been done on Western converts to Hinduism, especially on Westerners who have converted to neo-Hindu groups such as Transcendental Meditation, the International Society for Krishna Consciousness (the "Hare Krishnas"), the Osho Movement, and others.

Among the South Asian overseas Hindus, Tamils from south India and Sri Lanka are characterized by a language, unique cultural customs, and specifically Tamil aspects of the Hindu tradition. Valuable studies have been conducted on early Tamil migrants from south India, focusing on indentured workers who settled in South Africa, Mauritius, and Malaysia. Compared with this wealth of research, however, few studies have been carried out on overseas Tamils from Sri Lanka and their endeavors to reconstruct a familiar religious and cultural setting in diasporic contexts. Certainly the fact that these sociocultural activities have come about since the 1980s only appears to be a major reason for the dearth of scholarly studies. Sri Lankan Tamils fled the island in hundreds of thousands due to the escalating ethnic conflict. They took refuge in south India and overseas, particularly in Canada (some three hundred thousand) and various states of Europe (approximately two hundred thousand).

A second reason for this lack of academic attention is the fact that the overseas presence of Tamil people from Sri Lanka is perceived as transitory. It is assumed that most Tamils will remigrate to Sri Lanka as soon as the political conflict has come to an end. However, as Tamil refugee communities in Europe, Canada, and elsewhere now enter their third decade of exile, it becomes increasingly clear that most erstwhile refugees will not return despite the promising peace talks since 2002. Instead, they have opted to stay in their adopted country of residence. The construction of Hindu temples with traditional architecture in these overseas countries can be taken as a clear indication that Sri Lankan Tamils intend to root their specific cultural and religious traditions in these Western countries. My study of Sri Lankan Hindu Tamils and their temples in Germany is thus intended to complement the recent research on Tamil Hinduism in diasporic settings.[1]

Research on Indian and Sri Lankan overseas communities can provide an important analytical perspective on the study of South Asian culture and society as a whole. Steven Vertovec, who studied Indian Hindus in Trinidad, observes: "The phenomenon of Hinduism in diaspora presents students of Indian culture and society with unique, almost laboratory-like situations for analyzing the impact of varying conditions on processes of retention and change" (1989: 174). In other words, the limits of the diaspora's geographic and historical presences enable an analysis of factors that influence continuities and dynamics of a religious tradition. And, it might be added, the constraints of the diasporic situation might bring to the fore patterns and relationships difficult to detect in the tradition's country of origin.

My perspective on sacred promises and Hindu vows is rooted in my concern to investigate a tradition's geographic transplantation and its continuation in a culturally foreign context. The settlement of a religious tradition and its re-creation of norms and values in new sociocultural environments constitute the general frame of this chapter. More specific, the chapter examines vows and the establishment of Hindu temples built by Sri Lankan Tamils in diasporic context. Both the opening of temples and the performance of vows aim to reconstruct a "sense world" (Orsi 1985: 172) as a means of structuring basic points of orientation for the individual and the community. "Sense world" is taken in a double meaning: the conceptual or cognitive semantics of a world left, geographically, several thousand miles away are sought to be reconstructed by the refugee. These semantics apply to issues such as Hindu ideas about the cosmos, the importance of the horoscope, arranged marriages, and ideas of status and social hierarchy. A second meaning of "sense world" is related to the senses as perceived through the body, such as diet and fasts; restrictions for menstruating women; polluting substances to be avoided; the noise, smell, and images in diasporic Hindu temples; and also physically demanding vows and rituals. Tamil Hindus in Germany, who practice austerities, are reinforcing religious values. This occurs daily and during festivals. Despite inevitable changes and compromises, a close reconstruction of the Sri Lankan model is sought by the *bhaktas* (devotees)—both physically and spiritually. The notion of diaspora neatly encompasses the complex of relations and links between the overseas group of people and the country and culture from which this group fled or emigrated.[2]

Initially, I shall provide a descriptive sketch of the process of establishing twenty-five Hindu temples by Tamil refugees in Germany during the 1980s and 1990s. The size and activities of the temples differ considerably, and so do the opportunities to perform public vows, especially severe ascetic practices. Then I will focus on vows performed during festivals at these temples. Selecting from the wide spectrum of vows (*nertti* [Tam.] or *vrata* [Skt.]), I will focus on sacred promises made by men.

New Homes for Hindu Goddesses and Gods in Germany

Presently, Tamil refugees from Sri Lanka constitute the largest group of Hindu people in Germany. The number of Sri Lankan Tamils comes to some 65,000 people. About three-fourths are Hindus, about 20 percent Catholics, and 5 percent Protestants of various denominations. In addition, there are about 42,000 to 45,000 Tamil Hindus, 50,000 Hindus from India and Afghanistan, as well as Western converts in Hindu-related groups living in Germany.

As in other European states, Tamils from Sri Lanka have come to Germany since the late 1970s. Their number rose significantly in the wake of the escalating civil war in Sri Lanka during the mid-1980s. In Germany, the figure peaked in 1997 with 60,330 Sri Lankans counted in the foreigners' statistics, dropping since then by a fourth to 43,600 (late 2002). To these we need to add those Sri Lankans who have received the status of German citizenship, about 20,300 persons up to late 2002 (27.2 percent of the total 63,900 Sri Lankans/ Tamils). In earlier migrations mainly young men came, fleeing both the persecution by the Sri Lankan army and forced recruitment by the Tamil Tigers. Since the late 1980s women and children succeeded in escaping from terror-ridden northern parts of Sri Lanka.

In Germany during the 1980s there were twice as many men as women, both sexes being comparatively young. In recent years, the population became more balanced (in 2002: 55 percent men to 45 percent women). The legal status of Tamils in Germany varies according to their date of entrance: those coming until 1988 had been granted asylum and a right to stay, but those arriving since 1989 were able to acquire a status of toleration only. The status of being tolerated has to be renewed every six months. All in all the legal status of about half of the Tamil population is comparatively safe whereas the status of the other half varies between different levels of allowances to remain.[3]

In line with the German policy of distributing asylum seekers all across the country, the refugees from Sri Lanka were settled in small numbers in several towns and cities. This policy was intended to prevent the formation of ethnic colonies. Clustering of similar national or cultural peoples is believed to hinder integration of sojourners and migrants. Nevertheless, for several reasons such as a less restrictive jurisdiction, the permission to work legally while still being subjected to the asylum proceedings and the fact that relatives lived there already created a numerical concentration of Tamil people in the Ruhr area (situated in the mid-northern part of Germany). In this region a small Tamil infrastructure has evolved with shops, cultural and political societies, and the founding of Hindu temples.

Despite their insecure legal status, Tamils have started to open small places of worship with permanently installed deities since the late 1980s. Both the sharp increase of the number of refugees and the arrival of women and children played a decisive part. In addition, those Tamils, having lived for several years in Germany by then, had acquired financial resources and administrative skills to get a temple functioning. In 1989 only four small temples, situated in basement rooms existed. In 1994 the number had climbed to ten temples. And again, five years later, in 1999, the number of temples had doubled to twenty. Three years later, in mid-2003, there were twenty-five Hindu temples maintained by Sri Lankan Tamils. Fifteen of the temples are situated in the federal state of North Rhine, Westphalia. A clear concentration of eleven temples is observable in the industrial Ruhr valley, with three temples in the city of Hamm.

The size of the temples varies. Some temples are more or less hidden in small cellars. Others are set up on the ground floor of a residential house while a few temples are arranged in spacious halls of converted industrial buildings. Until 2002, no newly built temple existed. However, in July 2002 in Hamm, Westphalia a south Indian styled temple with a huge *gopuram* (entrance tower) and a *vimana* (smaller tower above the main shrine) was inaugurated, attracting significant media attendance and thousands of visitors. It is this temple that is by far the most prominent and prestigious in continental Europe and that attracts the largest numbers of participants and visitors during its annual temple festival.

Performing Vows at Public Processions

Despite the expansion in terms of space and number of temples, with the exception of the Sri Kamakshi temple in Hamm, Westphalia, the places of worship are hardly known and noticed by the public. In general, the temples are not identifiable as specific sacred localities by their outer design or architecture. A move

Tamil Hindu Temples in Germany, December 2002

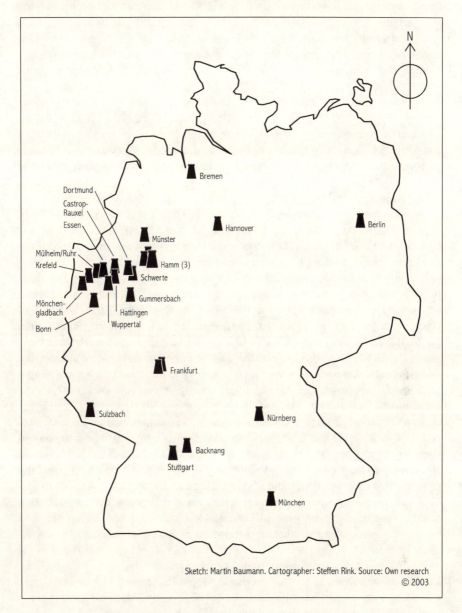

Figure 8.1   Tamil Hindu Temples in Germany, December 2002

into public view and a growing recognition by the neighborhood and local authorities occurred, however, as temples started to carry out processions during their annual temple festivals. At these festivities lasting ten or fourteen days Hindu religiosity and devotional acts became visible and apparent to the wider, non-Tamil population. And it was at the accompanying public processions that women and men undertook to fulfil specific, physically demanding religious vows.

Hindu traditions have a wide spectrum of physical practices associated with a religious vow. The practices can be private or public. A vow, promised to a god or goddess, might be taken to accomplish a wish or a request, to solve a specific problem, or to thank a deity for a given boon. Vows can also be done in advance, that is, before the request is granted. Fulfilling the vow best is done at the deity's main annual festival. In particular this is the case if the vow is public in nature.

Whereas these structures follow established patterns in the South Asian context (Pfaffenberger 1982, Sivathamby 1990, McGilvray 1998), the diasporic context can vary. One main and obvious limitation is that the celebration of the annual temple festival will not necessarily be accompanied by a public procession. The street layout, that is, the specifics of the temple's location, organizational problems, as well as administrative regulations of the town authorities can provide major hindrances. As a consequence of this, most Hindu temples in Germany celebrate their annual temple festival indoors, thus also restricting the possibility to perform vows.

The first public procession, the deity's circumambulation of the temple along the surrounding streets, was carried out at the Sri Kamakshi Ampal temple in Hamm, Westphalia in 1993. Until its legally forced move in 1997 to the outskirts of Hamm (Baumann 2000: 149–55; Luchesi 2003), this temple was set up in a converted laundry in a residential area. Some three hundred participants and visitors attended this first procession. In the following year, the number had risen to several hundred visitors more. Also, for the first time, men rolling clockwise around the temple and men carrying the *kavati* formed a part of the procession. These two demanding bodily practices are specific exercises to fulfill a vow (see figures in this chapter). Likewise, at this procession, women took to their specific forms of vow fulfillment: some carried a heavy clay pot with burning camphor, whereas others prostrated every second step during the procession. In the following years, the number of participants and visitors rose dramatically: In 1996 some four thousand people attended the festival's main day. In 1999 the number came to ten thousand people (the temple is now at its new, more spacious place). The processions in 2002 and 2003 saw some twelve thousand to fourteen thousand Sri Lankan Tamils, coming from all over Germany and from distances as far as Switzerland, France, the Netherlands, Denmark, and Norway.

I address now two public practices of vow fulfilment—that of rolling one's body around the temple and that of carrying the *kavati* (a large, decorated wooden arch). Occasionally the *kavati* carrier is pierced by spears and hooks. Here, the body acts as a domain of expressing devotion as well as authenticating legitimation as the body is subjected to severe pain and exhaustion. The acts are a sacrifice and ritual offering, donated to the deity to whom the vow has been promised. Both kinds of acts can be observed at the annual temple festival of the Sri Kamakshi temple in Hamm, forming spectacular parts of the main procession.

The first time the rolling body circumambulation (Tam. *ankappiratittai*) was performed in Germany was in 1994. It took place at the annual festival of the Sri Kamakshi temple, celebrated for the second time with a public procession. The devotional act at this and the following processions involves lying flat on the street and rolling one's body clockwise along the streets surrounding the temple. The head is always directed towards the temple. The rolling vow fulfillers form a part of the procession. They follow the splendidly decorated procession cart of Sri Kamakshi, the cart itself followed directly by the statue of Candeshvara (carried on a palanquin by four men). The line of rollers is

Figure 8.2 Five men perform the rolling ritual around the Vinayakar temple in Hamm, Germany during the 2005 festival (photo by M. Baumann)

followed by several women kneeling down every few steps and a band of some one hundred girls and women, singing devotional hymns.

Up until 2002, the rolling men had to manage a distance of about 1,000 meters. With the inauguration of the new temple and a change of streets surrounding the building, the distance has grown to an exhausting distance of some 3,500 meters. In contrast to Sri Lanka or south India, in Germany, due to the colder weather even in May, the ground usually is cold and often wet. Also, in the procession the men have to cope with rolling on solid hard tar and numerous small stones pressing into their skin. The shoulders, hips, and knees suffer in particular as these bear the weight while rolling one's body. After a few hundred meters, the exhaustion and pain is literally written in the faces and eyes of the rollers. In a few cases rollers vomit and have severe difficulties continuing. However, encouraging calls of *"arohara"* by the numerous supporters and spectators and the will to fulfill the vow keep the rollers going.

The first time I observed the spectacle of rolling vow fulfillers was in 1996, in Hamm, Westphalia. Some fifteen men rolled in rainy weather, their bodies covered with filth. As I had been introduced to the temple and its priest by a couple of German supporters, I asked them about this strange action. The husband explained to me that the rollers atone for sins done during the last year. And, as he held: "Some of these rascals certainly would deserve a second round to be done." Be that as it may, in the course of asking some rollers myself, I learned more about the reasons and motives to pursue this painful, physically demanding action. And most important, I came across the concept of sacred promises: the rolling is more than just a method to cleanse oneself from wrong deeds. Some indeed roll to purify themselves from immoral action and misconduct done during the past year. "It is like your confession in church," the 22-year-old Jathavan explained to me, comparing Hindu and Catholic methods to wipe out sinful deeds. Some rollers pursued the ordeal to underscore their respect and commitment to the goddess. Another one had taken on the action to thank the goddess for curing a relative, while a third one rolled the distance to beg for the cure of a seriously ill family member. Both rationales are expressed by the rollers, that of fulfilling the given vow to roll around the temple *after* the wish had been granted and that of taking on the demanding action in order to bring a wish to fruition. At times, motives to roll can be very pragmatic and this-worldly: A man had taken on the exercise in order to apply for an official approval to stay in Germany and, as I was told, six months later the permit was granted to him. Finally, I was also told that the demanding action is taken on by the roller himself "because it calms down my mind and mood," as it was explained to me.[4] The more practitioners are asked, the more reasons to roll seem to appear. In general, the motives most often stated have been the expression of thanks and respect to the goddess and the query for the fulfillment of a request or wish.

The second demanding discipline involves the practice of carrying an elaborately decorated wooden arch on one's shoulders, called a *kavati*, during the procession. Some of these *kavati* carriers may additionally have been pierced by a small spear through the cheeks with hooks inserted in one's back. The peacock feathers of the arch point to Murugan and his *vahana* (Skt. vehicle), the peacock. The spear represents the symbol of Murugan, his weapon: the lance (Tam. *vel*). Thus, in general this practice—carrying the *kavati* and being pierced—is performed at Murugan temples and in veneration of Murugan only. In Sri Lanka—in contrast to Tamil Nadu—however, these painful exercises are done at some *amman* or goddess shrines as well (Pfaffenberger 1982: 172–78).

During the procession, the *kavati* carriers walk in front of the festival cart. They are accompanied by a group of drummers and *natasvaram* players. Responding to the demanding rhythm of the music, the men dance in whirling movements, attracting the attention of visitors and cameras. As will be explained in more detail later, carrying a *kavati* and dancing to the sound of the music constitutes a fulfilment of a vow.

The gloriously colorful *kavati* dancers have been a part of the procession at the Kamakshi temple since its inception in 1993. The weight of the arch and the strain of the wheeling dance are physically demanding. However, being

Figure 8.3 *Kavati* dancers fulfilling vows during the Sri Kamakshi Ampal temple festival in Hamm, Germany, 2000 (photo by M. Baumann)

additionally pierced by hooks and a little spear did not occur until six years later in 1999. If the practice of rolling one's body all along the procession's distance aroused the curiosity of most German observers, so even more did the practice of being pierced through the skin.

Let me elaborate the way in which the piercing was done at the Sri Kamakshi temple in Hamm until 2002 (slight changes are noticeable at the new temple in use since July 2002): During the morning *puja* on the festival's main day the young men to be pierced assembled in front of the shrine of Murugan (next to the main shrine of Kamakshi). On silver trays they carried the small spears and hooks. During the *puja* they indicated to Murugan that they would perform the exercise, requesting his grace and support. Following the *puja* the men came together outside the temple in front of the shrine of *Shani* (Saturn). This place for carrying out the piercing had been chosen for simple pragmatic reasons, as other places outside the temple had not been available. In June 2003, at the site of the new temple the piercing was done in a separately set up small tent as limits of space did not enable them to perform the piercing in front of

Figure 8.4 A young man performs the demanding hook swinging vow ritual during the annual festival in 2003 at Sri Kamakshi Ampal temple in Hamm, Germany (photo by M. Baumann)

the shrine of Vairavan (Skt. Bhairava, a forceful manifestation of Shiva). First, the little spear was inserted through the cheeks. A man took the spear and pricked it through the left cheek of the *kavati* carrier. As the needle arrived in the middle of the mouth, a kind of silver tongue (symbolizing a snake, symbol of immortality) that stretches out of the mouth was secured to the spear. Then, the piercer drilled the spear through the right cheek and put an arrowhead, like on the left side, on the spear's end. During this procedure the man was expected to show no signs of pain or emotion. Then the man turned around, sat down, and the fixing of the hooks began. The piercer inserted the hooks in two parallel folds in the back skin running along the shoulder blades. Some seven to twenty little hooks were run through the skin. The number and thickness of the hooks are related to the "problem" for which a solution is sought, as the main temple priest Sri Paskarakurukkal had explained to me in an interview. A reader of the horoscope or a priest might have given advice according to the *kavati* practitioner's horoscope. Once the piercer had set the last hook, small ropes were attached to the hooks. The small ropes were tied into a knot, and a longer, firm rope was attached. Later, during the procession and while dancing, a second man will hold the rope's end, forming a pair of two dancers.

Having gone through this, the pierced man himself started piercing his fellow *kavati* dancers. The whole procedure took about half an hour. It was explained to me that the piercing does not really hurt. "The pricking is like acupuncture," I was told. Be that as it may, relatives and spectators watched with much respect, anxiety, and excitement. Then the men went to the temple's forecourt where the procession was to start. Here they sat, watched by visitors with awe and respect. As the deity (Skt. *utsava murti*) was taken out and fixed on the procession cart, the *kavati* dancers took the decorated arch to the front of the procession. As the musicians started to play their first rhythm, the dancers began their moves and the procession slowly started.[5]

During the 90-minute procession, the *kavati* carriers do not dance all the way. As soon as the drums begin playing, the dancers start to perform. The music's demanding tone and rhythm is intended to invoke the deity into the dancer. Some dancers get possessed or fall into a trance as they dance out of control and seem not to feel the pain of the pulling and dragging hooks in their back. Being possessed or falling into a trance for a short time is interpreted as a sign that Murugan or the goddess has accepted the vow fulfillment and takes pleasure in the sacrifice. At the same time the occurrence of possession or trance states is taken as an indication that the deity does actually reside in the temple and takes care of his or her devotees' mundane problems (Pfaffenberger 1982: 176). In a way, the *kavati* dancers function as a quality mark of a temple—authenticity and authority in the diaspora is reinforced and acted out physically.

As with the vow fulfillers rolling their body around the temple, dancing with the *kavati* is a form of fulfilling a sacred promise. The dancers are expected to have fasted for ten days, taking one meal a day in preparation for the procession. Reasons and motives are more or less similar as explained by the rollers. The devotees perform the demanding activity for Murugan or the goddess in return for a boon either requested or granted. After the procession had ended and the dancers laid aside the *kavati* arch and took off the spears and hooks, I asked several men "Why do you do this?" Perhaps my question was too straightforward or impolite, but several times I did not receive an answer at all. Instead, they only smiled at me. Or they explained in general terms that this exercise is a part of the "Hindu faith." I got the feeling that my inquiry was not a question to be addressed, that for someone who knows the tradition it is self-explanatory.

Conclusion

One of the most interesting facts about the performances of these demanding acts is that they are carried out at all in the diasporic contexts of Germany, Switzerland, and Scandinavia (Baumann, Luchesi, Wilke 2003). Until recently, the Tamil Hindus had very few opportunities to fulfill the specific vows of rolling around a temple or carrying the *kavati*. Other, more pragmatic vows have been performed, such as making generous donations for the opening or enlargement of a temple; or financing an *abhisheka* (bathing or besprinkling ritual in the temple); or bearing the expenses of a festival day or many other possibilities (see Pfaffenberger 1982: 172–78; Collins 1997). Performing the full range of established forms to request a boon, to solve a problem, or to thank for a wish's receipt seems unnecessary to insure the continuation of this transplanted tradition. Rather, a flexible and pragmatic approach enables the Hindu bhaktas (devotees) to cope with their new situation and its restrictions.

In the course of time, as Sri Lankan refugees succeeded in transplanting social, cultural, and religious customs in the new environment, opportunities to choose among vow activities expanded. During recent years the number of rollers and *kavati* dancers' increased and the austerities of the latter intensified. An increasing number of men has chosen to fulfill a vow by performing painful and demanding actions. The statistics of absolute growth are straightforward: During the first processions at the Sri Kamakshi temple only a few men rolled themselves around the temple. In the years 1996 to 1998 some twelve to fifteen men did so; in 1999 there had been eighteen men. At the festivals in 2000 and 2001 we saw some twenty rollers, and in 2002 and 2003 about thirty. In the same way, the number of women who carried a heavy pot of burning camphor increased from an initial few to thirty-four at the 2001 procession. The number of *kavati* dancers rose from ten to twelve (1997 to 1999), up to twenty in 2000, and again rose to about thirty in 2001–2003. In 1999 four dancers got pierced, in the following year ten, in 2001 seventeen, and in 2002 and 2003 there had been twelve to eighteen men pierced with hooks and spears.

It seems plausible to conclude that the increasing number of vow fulfillers points to an intensifying of the practice among the festival participants. This is to jump to conclusions, however. We have to bear in mind that the number of participants at the festivals rose dramatically from some three hundred in 1993, to four thousand in 1996, to some twelve thousand in 2001, up to fifteen thousand to eighteen thousand persons in 2003. Though the statistical number of vow fulfillers did increase, it did not in relational terms. The relation of vow fulfillers to the overall number of participants remained more or less the same.[6] Those other temples in Germany that stage a public procession during the temple festival by no means can compete with the numbers of the Sri Kamakshi temple festival. The Murugan temple founded in 1993 in Gummersbach (mid-Germany) has arranged for a public procession since 1995. In general, some three hundred to five hundred people have taken part at the main festival day. In 2001, ten men carried the *kavati*, seven of them pierced. Two men rolled and a few women carried pots with burning camphor. In Hamm, Westphalia the Sri Sithi Vinayakar Alayam (Ganesha temple) founded in 1989 has sponsored a public circumambulation of the temple since 1996. The number of festival participants has remained steady at about 1,500 to 2,000 people. The number of rollers stayed the same with six to seven men, several firepot carrying women, and two or three prostrating women. There were no *kavati* dancers. Finally, the Sri Muthumariamman temple founded in 1995 in Hannover (northern Germany) had its first public procession in 1996. Participation fluctuates between two hundred to seven hundred visitors. Although it is an *amman* temple, we do not find men rolling the street or others carrying a *kavati*. Vow fulfillers had approached the temple committee to perform the rolling exercise. However, the wish was not approved because the procession takes the route where the public tram passes every 8 to 10 minutes. This would require cancelling the tram two or three times, and the procession would be slowed down considerably. Without rollers the procession is able to pass that part exactly in the interim, causing no cancellation. The committee asked the tram administration to stop the tram but was told that the temple would have to bear the costs of the cancellation.

Obviously, the Kamakshi temple has taken on an exceptional role for and among Sri Lankan Tamils in Germany, and increasingly in Western Europe. The reasons for this success in attracting thousands of people to the main festival and hundreds to calendrical special days and festivities are manifold (Baumann 2000: 147–66; Luchesi 2001, Wilke 2003). One main reason is the fact that the temple, in contrast to all other temples in Germany, is run by the priest himself. The Dravidian priest and former refugee Sri Paskarakurukkal (a German citizen since 2001) is both the main servant of the adorned goddess and the ambitious manager of the temple. Although officially a temple committee exists, it is he, the *kurukkal* (temple priest), who does the organizational work and decides what is to be done. In most other temples a clear division of duties prevails, the priest being responsible for the religious sphere whereas the committee takes care of the management work (Banks 1971: 67; Sivathamby 1990: 162–65). Although at the Sri Kamakshi temple a severe concentration of responsibility and power resides in one person, the temple and priest have gained a positive reputation for punctuality and getting things done. The steady growth of the temple, in terms of size, attendance at the festival, and fame among the Tamil refugees, are interpreted by Hindu bhaktas that the goddess Sri Kamakshi clearly has bestowed her grace on the temple and that her *shakti* (Skt. power) resides in the central *murti* (Skt. deity's statue, Tam. *murtti*). The performance and fulfillment of vows is assumed to be best done at this diasporic shrine.

As Sri Lankan Tamils manage to re-create other customs and known patterns in the new environment, the spectrum of devotional expressions has enlarged. Rather than introducing adapted and new elements to the rituals and exercises, a close resemblance to the Sri Lankan model is sought for (Sivathamby 1990, Veluppillai 1995). Young Tamils who grew up in Germany had not come across such demanding practices. They encountered these disciplines for the first time only at the temples. In this way, the practice of vow fulfillment not only carries an impact for the individual, but also acquires a heightened importance for the tradition as a whole. The practices consolidate the continuation of the transplanted tradition, authenticate young German Sri Lankan Tamils as faithful Hindus, socialize young members into particular aspects of the tradition, and present a model for personal self-sacrifice consonant with South Asian religiosity. Vow fulfillers and their severe bodily acts legitimate the newly ascribed sacredness of diasporic places and reinforce and sustain "sense worlds" both cognitively and somatically.

Notes

1. See the studies by Taylor (1994), McDowell (1996), Jacobsen (1997), Diesel (1998), Steen Preis (1997), Fuglerud (1999), Luchesi (2001), and Baumann, Luchesi, Wilke (2003).

2. For definitional aspects of "diaspora" and "diasporic," I refer to Vertovec (1997), McKeown (1999), and Baumann (2000a, 2003).

3. For details, see Baumann (2000: 96–101) and Baumann, Luchesi, Wilke (2003).

4. This explanation is reminiscent of Anne M. Pearson's book *"Because It Gives Me Peace of Mind"* (1996).

5. At the festival in June 2003, a variation on the normal practice of *kavati* was performed. A young man had a total of eight metal hooks inserted into his back, hips, and legs. Ropes were attached to each hook, and he was hoisted into the air as he hung from the hooks on the rope ends. This extraordinary vow was carried out at the Sri Sivasubramaniar Temple in Adlisweil, Switzerland.

6. The calculation: of some four thousand participants in 1996, fifteen men rolled. This gives us a relational result of 3.7 percent. In 1997–2000 the results for rollers come up to 2 percent, in 2001 to 1.6 percent. For the *kavati* dancers the results are 1 percent for 1997–1999 and some 2 percent in 2000-2003.

References

Banks, Michael. 1971. "Castes in Jaffna." In *Aspects of Caste in South India, Ceylon and North-West Pakistan*, ed. E. R. Leach, 61–77. Cambridge: Cambridge University Press. (originally published 1960).

Baumann, Martin. 2003. *Alte Götter in neuer Heimat: Religionswissenschaftliche Analyse zu Diaspora am Beispiel von Hindus auf Trinidad.* Marburg: Diagonal.

———. 2000a. "Diaspora: Genealogies of Semantics and Transcultural Comparison." *Numen* 47 (3): 313–37.

———. 2000. *Migration, Religion, Integration: Vietnamesische Buddhisten und tamilische Hindus in Deutschland.* Marburg: Diagonal.

Baumann, Martin, Brigitte Luchesi, and Annette Wilke, eds. 2003. *Tempel und Tamilen in zweiter Heimat: Hindus aus Sri Lanka im deutschsprachigen und skandinavischen Raum.* Würzburg: Ergon.

Collins, Elizabeth Fuller. 1997. *Pierced by Murugan's Lance: Ritual, Power, and Moral Redemption among Malaysian Hindus.* DeKalb, IL: Northern Illinois University Press.

Diesel, Alleyn. 1998. "The Empowering Image of the Divine Mother: A South African Hindu Woman Worshipping the Goddess." *Journal of Contemporary Religion* 13 (1): 73–90.

Fuglerud, Oivind. 1999. *Life on the Outside: The Tamil Diaspora and Long-Distance Nationalism.* London: Pluto Press.

Jacobsen, Knut A. 1997. "Hinduismen i diaspora: Religios endring og norsk kontekst." *Kirke og Kultur* (Oslo) 4-5: 441–52.

Luchesi, Brigitte. 2001. "Das hinduistische Tempelfest in Hamm-Uentrup/Westfalen." In *Buddhisten und Hindus im deutschsprachigen Raum,* ed. Manfred Hutter, 61–76. Frankfurt/M: Lang.

Luchesi, Brigitte. 2003. " Hinduistische Sakralarchitektur und Tempelgestaltung in Hamm-Uentrop." In *Tempel und Tamilen in zweiter Heimat: Hindus aus Sri Lanka im deutschsprachigen und skandinavischen Raum,* eds. Martin Baumann, Brigitte Luchesi, Annette Wilke, 223–74. Würzburg: Ergon.

McDowell, Christopher. 1996. *A Tamil Asylum Diaspora: Sri Lankan Migration, Settlement and Politics in Switzerland.* Oxford, Providence, RI: Berghahn Books.

McGilvray, Dennis B. 1998. *Symbolic Heat. Gender, Health and Worship among Tamils of South India and Sri Lanka.* Middletown, NJ: Grantha Corporation.

McKeown, Adam. 1999. "Conceptualizing Chinese Diasporas, 1842 to 1949." *The Journal of Asian Studies* 58 (2): 306–37.

Orsi, Robert. 1985. *The Madonna of 115th Street: Faith and Community in Italian Harlem, 1880-1950.* New Haven: Yale University Press.

Pearson, Anne Mackenzie. 1996. *"Because It Gives Me Peace of Mind": Ritual Fasts in the Religious Lives of Hindu Women.* Albany, NY: State University of New York Press.

Pfaffenberger, Bryan. 1982. *Caste in Tamil Culture: The Religious Foundations of Sudra Domination in Tamil Sri Lanka.* Syracuse, NY: Foreign and Comparative Studies.

Rukmani, T. S., ed. 1999. *Hindu Diaspora: Global Perspectives.* Montreal: Concordia University.

Sivathamby, K. 1990. "Divine Presence and/or Social Prominence: An Inquiry into the Social Role of the Place of Worship in Yalppanam Tamil Society." In *Lanka,* ed. Peter Schalk, 155–75. Uppsala: Universität Uppsala.

Steen Preis, Ann-Belinda. 1997. "Seeking Place: Capsized Identities and Contracted Belonging among Sri Lankan Tamil Refugees." In *Siting Culture. The Shifting Anthropological Object,* eds. Karen Fog Olwig and Kirsten Hastrup 86–100, London, New York: Routledge.

Taylor, Donald. 1994. "The Symbolic Construction of the Sri Lankan Hindu Tamil Community in Britain." Ph.D. dissertation, School of Oriental and African Studies, London, London University.

Veluppillai, A. 1995. "Religious Traditions of the Tamils." *Uppsala Studies in the History of Religions* 2: 11–20.

Vertovec, Steven. 2000. *The Hindu Diaspora: Comparative Patterns.* London, New York: Routledge.

———. 1989. "Hinduism in Diaspora: The Transformation of Tradition in Trinidad." In *Hinduism Reconsidered,* eds. Günther D. Sontheimer and Hermann Kulke, 152–79. New Delhi: Manohar.

———. 1997. "Three Meanings of 'Diaspora', Exemplified among South Asian Religions." *Diaspora* 7 (2): 277–99.

Wilke, Annette. 2003. " 'Traditionenverdichtung' in der Diaspora: Hamm als Bühne der Neuaushandlung von Hindu-Traditionen." In *Tempel und Tamilen in zweiter Heimat: Hindus aus Sri Lanka im deutschsprachigen und skandinavischen Raum,* eds. Martin Baumann, Brigitte Luchesi, Annette Wilke, 125–68.Würzburg: Ergon.

II

Getting What You Need

9

Singing a Vow: Devoting Oneself to Shiva through Song

KAREN PECHILIS

As a category, "vow" has great elasticity: a vow can be long-term or short-term, constitutive or instrumental, ontological or conditional, duty-bound or voluntary, directed toward a specific deity or aimed at transforming one's life path to increase one's spiritual status—or, seemingly, almost any combination thereof.[1] For while these descriptive terms appear to be oppositional, they are not necessarily so. What unites them is that they are facets of an intentional commitment undertaken in an unpredictable world: Vows solicit positive results in an attempt to make life less unpredictable.[2] Like the term, "religion," which may be derived from *religare*, meaning "to tie fast," a vow is bound to human aspirations, and culturally bound theories and practices to achieve them.

Since a vow is generated by humankind, it is this human side of commitment in the face of the unpredictability of life that is an essential feature. As a corollary of this feature, a key classification of vows is whether the vow positions the votary as set apart from the social world or as squarely within the social world. Short-term vows, such as fasting for a day, punctuate everyday life with special, defined periods of spiritual commitment. The context of short-term vows can be either the social world or the spiritual life; in the latter case, it represents an intensification of the spiritual life. There is considerable overlap between, say, wife and nun in terms of the type of short-term vow performed, with fasting and prayer being the most popular. In contrast, the domains of social life and spiritual life are more distinctly represented in long-term vows, since these types of vows, such as becoming an ascetic renouncer (*sannyasin*), or being married in a religious ceremony, define a continuous way of life. In Mary McGee's terminology, they are vows of maintenance, rather than acquisition, for they involve a change in status and maintenance of a certain way of life: *sannyasinhood* is a religious paragon of steadfast set-apartness; while marriage is the householder status, full of auspiciousness as well as worldly concerns and compromise.[3]

Yet even these two seeming extremes in long-term vows are not mutually exclusive. For example, *sannyasins* can be involved in social service, and the *sannyasin* ideal is invoked as a credential for teaching and social work in educational institutions (*matams*) and in the position of the guru.[4] For their part, married householders can become ascetics for a short, defined time period, as Anne Pearson explains in her discussion of women's vows or *vrats*:

> Thus, from its various applications and connotations in earlier literature, as well as quite likely from existing folk rites, the concept of *vrata* was shaped by the Purana and Nibandha writers into the ideal ritual for the householder to express his or her duties, devotion and spiritual aspirations. Within the context of these spiritual aspirations the doctrines, practices and *dharma* ("yogic" values) of the ascetics are "tamed" and harnessed under the control of the this-wordly *dharma* of the householder. (Pearson 1991: 76)

In general, however, each of the two sides of renouncer and householder seeks to encompass and subordinate the other within its worldview: the renouncer seeks to maintain an authoritative religious status with respect to the householder, and the householder seeks to domesticate asceticism.

That one might simultaneously lead a life that is both engaged with the social world *and* spiritually rigorous was the position advanced most prominently by a third perspective, that of bhakti. As a religious path, bhakti brought into dynamic tension the steadfast commitment to the rigorous spiritual life of the *sannyasin* with the very human concerns of the householder. Bhakti sought to encompass these classical paths by understanding their visions of dharma to be related; thus, those on the bhakti path are both set apart from the social world and functional within it. For example, in the Sanskrit *locus classicus* of *bhakti*, the Bhagavad Gita, the theory of *karmayoga* (disciplined action) permits Arjuna to act within the world according to his duty, but to do so under the religious rationale that he is an instrument of Lord Krishna.

Since bhakti understands the two classical categories of *sannyasin* and householder to be simultaneously embodied in each human being—with the commitment to spiritual discipline informing all of one's actions in the world—it is difficult to gloss "bhakti" in English. For example, the common English gloss for *bhakti,* "devotion," is etymologically related to the term "vow," and this gloss does capture the aspect of *bhakti* that one commits oneself to the divine wholeheartedly. Like "vow," bhakti is a term that is used to describe the human response to God and never to characterize God's response to human beings (Carman 1987: 130). However, it is bhakti's nuanced perspective on the human side of religiosity that gets lost in the gloss "devotion," which stresses the commitment while marginalizing the ever-present factor of human concerns. In contrast, bhakti foregrounds the oscillation between commitment to God and human concerns.

Bhakti poetry in the regional languages of India, including Hindi, Tamil, Marathi, and Kannada amplified the Gita's lesson of action in the world by foregrounding the critical dimension inherent in the *sannyasin* position. The regional-language poets highlighted the role of human agency in bhakti by actively encouraging participation (a root meaning of bhakti) in the praise of God through a wide variety of activities, from ritualized practices to everyday acts. Through such commitment, humankind is able to share (another root meaning of bhakti) in the divine essence, which is humankind's true nature. As a theology of embodiment, the path of bhakti is embedded in, yet critical of, the details of human social life (Prentiss 1999).

To illustrate the nature of bhakti as a religious perspective that views the oscillation between commitment and concern as constitutive of a vow, I turn to the Tamil Shiva-bhakti tradition, in which I consider the three celebrated classical poets of the tradition, as well as contemporary performers of their hymns. Both the poets and the contemporary performers devote themselves to Shiva through song, thus undertaking a lifelong vow to remember Shiva first, in and through social life.

The Tamil Shiva-bhakti Poets

In Tamil south Indian tradition, the three classical poets Campantar, Appar, and Cuntarar, whom scholars date to the seventh through ninth centuries, are especially celebrated as the primary proponents of the path of bhakti to Lord Shiva. The three poets share a poetic language that emphasizes praise of Shiva through both pilgrimage and song. Through evidence internal to their compositions, it is possible to suggest that they each traversed the Tamil country, stopping in towns to sing the praises of Lord Shiva in accomplished, metrical Tamil (Prentiss 1999: 47–76).

Within this frame, the poets not only sing of their connection to the Lord; they identify obstacles that they must overcome in realizing that connection. Through their emphasis on human concerns, the poets represent bhakti as an ongoing, lived experience. Indeed, bhakti is often characterized in classical texts as a relationship between friends, lovers, and parent to child. Imagining bhakti through these images captures the oscillation between commitment and concern, for all human relationships have their ups and downs through feelings of connection and estrangement.

In the hymns of the three poets, there is considerable similarity in the way they choose to express their praise of Shiva, including mythologically informed descriptions of his beauty and his actions on behalf of humankind, as well as descriptions of the Tamil towns in which he resides. In contrast, the obstacles are consistently represented as enmeshed with the poets' personal lives, thus contributing to the autobiographical nature of their hymns. Significantly, this critical dimension of the poetry became a locus for tradition to understand and develop biographies of the poets. The conflicts in their lives were a way for Shaiva worshippers both to relate to the poets themselves, and to relate to bhakti as a theology of embodiment.[5]

A common source of conflict represented in the poetry of all three saints is their human weakness in forgetting the Lord; however, Appar is perhaps the most poignant among the three. Appar, whose saint name is Tirunavukkaracar (The king of inspired speech), does not provide many allusions to chronological details of his life; and yet, since he was so frequently disappointed with himself, the internal struggle of a person on the bhakti path is more sharply defined in his poetry than in that of the other poets. He, above others, is an emblem for the human struggle to recognize, and to share in, the divine essence. Some of the poet's disappointment stems from his having been a Jain, which he specifically laments in several of his poems. However, Appar more frequently expresses his frustration with himself in generally applicable human terms, especially his inability to live his life through the experience of God consciousness. A comparison of two of his verses illustrates the oscillation between his criticism of his own failings and his certainty that the Lord will save him.

Appar 6.95.9/7192

I am lacking in family
I am lacking in character
I am lacking in aims;
my faults increase,
and I am lacking in the goodness of beauty.
Inside, I am no good either;
I am not a wise man
I do not join with good people
I am in between being an animal and being human
I am very good at saying hateful things
and I have neither the funds nor the desire to give to those who beg.
Why have I been born? I am impoverished in every way! (trans. Prentiss)

Appar 6.95.2/7185

The severe punishments of Yama will not come to us
the fierce enemy karma will gradually be reduced
we are cured of our distress

we have no afflictions
we are not lowly;
where will the sun arise for us?
The Lord is in my mind
> crowned by the river through His beautiful red matted locks
> dancing with fire
> pleased by bathing with the five substances of the cow
> bearing a red complexion like coral, the hills, the heavens.

(trans. Prentiss)

At first glance, it seems that these two hymns could hardly have been written by the same person: One is helpless in tone, while the other is assured. The first hymn expresses the intensely self-critical mode of bhakti: it links external aspects, such as family identity, physical appearance, and deeds, with the internal state of lacking direction and wisdom. The second hymn describes the solution as living life with the Lord firmly in mind. One acts from a grounding in God-consciousness, and thus one is not "lowly." In this hymn, humankind's tendency toward bad actions, or karma, will "gradually be reduced." As Susan Snow Wadley demonstrates, the neutralizing of karma is a hallmark of *vrats* (Wadley 1983); and this applies to bhakti as well. However, Appar's take on the issue is distinctive: He does not appeal to the bhakti participant's traditional duties or *dharma*, as does the Bhagavad Gita, as a stable, planned path. Nor is the neutralizing of karma a permanent state, as is often the premise of a vow. Instead, Appar represents the oscillation between feeling helpless and feeling assured as itself the dynamic of bhakti.

Contemporary Performers of the Hymns

The performance of the hymns of the three composers, the corpus of which is now known as *Tevaram*, is a living tradition in Tamil India today, primarily in Hindu temple culture. Although Shaiva tradition maintains that the manuscripts of the hymns were lost after the three saints achieved *samadhi*, and then subsequently recovered, organized, and reset to music during the Chola era, the hymns are viewed today as authentically Tamil music.[6] Today, the Tamil hymns have been overshadowed by the popularity and musical sophistication of Carnatic music, which was greatly developed by three musician-saints in the eighteenth and nineteenth centuries. However, though the Tamil hymns are much less complicated musically than Carnatic music, their tunes, known as *pan*, are widely acknowledged to have been a source for the *ragas* of Carnatic music. In addition, the Tamil hymns are in the main comprehensible to Tamil speakers today, whereas many of the Carnatic music pieces are in Telugu or Sanskrit, which are not readily understood by most Tamil speakers. In addition, the *Tevaram* hymns are explicitly identified with bhakti tradition.

Today, adherents of the Tamil Shaiva Siddhanta philosophical school assume responsibility for maintaining and promoting *Tevaram*, in a caretaker role that stems from late medieval times (Prentiss 1996). For example, the group sponsors lectures on and performances of the Tamil bhakti hymns during the yearly music festival in Chennai in December through January (though whether this is envisioned as part of the larger Carnatic music festival or as an alternative to it is an open question); it supports the school of *Tevaram* and Tamil music located at Rajannamalai Hall; and its religious centers (*matams*) in the Chidambaram region both train and employ men to be singers of the hymns in temples, known as *otuvars*. The exclusively male *otuvar* group is, traditionally and in the present day, the authoritative category of singers of *Tevaram*, and they are the ones who can pursue the work professionally as singers in temples, in which context their performance is liturgical.[7] The *otuvars* are not the only contemporary singers of the hymns; there are, for example, groups of women singers of *Tevaram* who perform the hymns publicly at temple festivals and in concert halls. However, the male professional singers do represent the tradition of Tamil Shiva-bhakti at major religious events such as Mahashivaratri, which is the context of the contemporary performances I discuss in this chapter.[8]

Mahashivaratri is the "Great Night of Shiva." "According to classical texts, *Śivarātri* falls on the fourteenth lunar day (*tithi*) of the dark half of the lunar month of January–February or February–March" (Long 1982: 193). The fourteenth *tithi* of the dark half of the lunar month is the last day of the moon's waning cycle, or the new moon, just prior to the commencement of its waxing period, which culminates in the full moon. Thus, there is actually a Shivaratri every lunar month; however, Mahashivaratri (Jan.–Feb. or Feb.–March) is especially important because it is said to be favored by Shiva Himself, because it comes at the end of the lunar calendar, and because of its status as a major *vrat* (vow) in the Hindu calendar.

Through a structuralist analysis, J. Bruce Long understands Mahashivaratri to be a mediation between polarities, including the personality of Shiva and the devotion of humankind. For example, Shiva is both the fearless "night-goer" (*nishacara*) who hangs out with his ghoulish retinue at the cremation ground *and* the benevolent agent of grace who guides humankind to ultimate liberation (*moksha*) (Long 1982: 196–97). As the prime Hindu example of a socially constituted antisocial god, Shiva claims for himself those arenas that humankind avoids, including the cremation ground, midnight, and the darkest night of the month (the fourteenth *tithi*). Furthermore, Mahashivaratri can be viewed as the darkest night of the year, since it falls in the last month of the lunar year: "That night, the night of Shiva is the so-called darkest time of the year in that it comes at the darkest time of the month and at the end of the lunar year. Mythologically speaking, it is the dark night which immediately precedes the dawn of a new day, the death of the old world and the birth of the new" (Long 1982: 209).

Although the time of Mahashivaratri may in social terms appear to be potentially very inauspicious, even dangerous, it is religiously very auspicious, for its liminality captures that of Shiva Himself. As such, Mahashivaratri is a time that demands self-discipline and vigilance on the part of humankind, and, in this state of heightened conscientiousness, it is simultaneously the best time to approach God. Mahashivaratri is widely celebrated; in her book-length study of women and *vrats*, Anne Pearson noted that her subjects participated in the tradition, even when they had dropped their performance of other *vrats* (Pearson 1996: 25, 41–2, 89–90). Classical texts, such as the *Garuda* and *Padma Puranas* and medieval liturgical digests, as well as modern interpretations and local variations, present various authoritative methods for performing the Mahashivaratri *vrat*, but there is a loose consensus that fasting (*upavasa*), worship (*puja*), and the vigil (*jagara*) are constitutive elements (Long 1982: 189–90, 192). These rites are an assertion of the discipline, devotion, and steadfastness of humankind; yet human concern is also very much part of the experience, as J. Bruce Long highlights in his representation of Mahashivaratri as "the Saiva festival of repentance":

> *Śivarātri* commences with a solemn vow to "mend one's ways" and to persevere in the performance of the vow. It concludes with a prayer of repentance, a petition for forgiveness, and a prayer of thanksgiving for the grace to repent which itself is founded upon the love of God which enabled the devotees to repent in the first place. (1982: 212)

The Tamil bhakti hymns are appropriate to Mahashivaratri both for their praise of Shiva and for their joining together of commitment to God and human concern; and they are sung at celebrations of this occasion throughout Tamil Nadu.[9] On March 7, 1997, the night of Mahashivaratri, I attended two performances of *Tevaram* by two distinguished *otuvars*. The evening performance, from 7–9 p.m. at a small temple in Besant Nagar, was by Sami Dandapani, a young yet established performer of the Tamil Shiva-bhakti hymns. An all-night performance was presented by Dharmapuram P. Swaminathan, who is considered to be the seniormost *otuvar* in Chennai today, at a small temple in Mylapore.

During that evening itself, it was quite clear that the two performance styles of the "same" materials diverged quite markedly. Since that time, I have been attempting to articulate those differences and to understand their significance.[10] In the context of thinking about vows, I have come to view the performances as each emphasizing one of the two poles of the oscillation of bhakti. Sami Dandapani's performance was in emulation of the saint-composers: he evoked the dedication of the saints themselves in his passionate solo rendition, in which he imbued the hymns with a profound sense of bhakti. In contrast, Dharmapuram Swaminathan stressed the humanity of the hymns, primarily by contextualizing them in a running discourse of storytelling, especially on the lives of the saints. Each *otuvar*, then, stressed one side of the oscillation, although as I have discussed, the hymns they were singing held the two in dynamic tension. This is not to suggest that the *otuvars* in any sense violated the meanings of the hymns, but instead to suggest that they each privileged a distinctive side of the oscillation as a thesis that guided their interpretive performances of the hymns. Indeed, it enhanced their performances that they each had such a clear focus.

Sami Dandapani

Sami Dandapani is a young man, in his late thirties or early forties, who is known as a traditional performer and interpreter of the *Tevaram* hymns. He is known both in Tamil Nadu and internationally: since 1997 he has traveled on an extensive tour to perform and teach *Tevaram* in prominent Tamil communities abroad, including London, Washington D.C., Toronto, and Durban. I got to know Sami Dandapani when I was researching the current performance and status of *Tevaram* in Chennai in the spring of 1997: as a component of that research, I studied a group of women who sing *Tevaram* in public performances, and Sami Dandapani was the teacher of this group.[11]

Sami Dandapani came to the professional performance of *Tevaram* not through heredity, but through the quality of his singing voice, which is known for its lucidity and poignancy, and he was encouraged to study at the Dharmapuram Atinam, which is a major religious center of the Tamil Shaiva Siddhanta. In 1997, Sami Dandapani lived with his young family on the premises of the Shaiva Siddhanta organization in T. Nagar (Theyagaraya Nagar), and he gave lessons to the Ladies *Tevaram* group in the main hall of the complex. Sami Dandapani told me that the preservation of the traditional style of performing the hymns, including understanding their meaning, is of primary importance to him, and that these concerns inform his methodology of teaching and performance.

On the night of Mahashivaratri, Sami Dandapani performed a selection of *Tevaram* hymns at a small temple in Besant Nagar (the Ratnagireeshwar Temple) in the early evening. He was seated on a raised platform that faced the main shrine, and he was accompanied by a violin player and a drummer. The setting, with the performer facing the deity, evoked the manner in which the saints are said to have performed their hymns, and the violin was suggestive of the *yal*, or ancient stringed instrument, which is believed to have been a traditional accompaniment for the hymns. Sami Dandapani's performance of *Tevaram* verses, in which he selectively repeated words and phrases that he believed were most illustrative of the essence of the hymn, strengthened his association with the saints' bhakti.

For example, Sami Dandapani sang a verse from a hymn on Tiru Valivalam by Campantar, emphasizing through his performance both the name of Shiva and the identification of the singer as the servant to the Lord.[12] My translation of the hymn is as follows:

Tiru Valivalam, Campantar I.50.7 *Pan*: Palantakkarakam

You are my mother; you are my father, Oh Shankara! I am your servant
and my heart desires to love you always;
yet the five senses that dwell within my long-suffering body will
    not allow me to unite with you;
I fear this is *maya* itself—Oh Lord who is Truth at Valivalam!

Sami Dandapani's five-minute rendering of the hymn, translated into English, was the following:

You are my mother; you are my father, Oh Shankara! I am your servant.
[pause, then repeated five times]
Oh Shankara! [repeated twice]
I am your servant [pause]
always loving [repeated three times]
desires
my heart desires [repeated once]
my heart desires to love you always
within my long-suffering body
the five senses that dwell within my long-suffering body will not
    allow me to unite with you
[repeated three times]
I fear this is *maya* itself [repeated once]
I fear this is *maya* itself, Oh Lord who is Truth at Valivalam
[repeated twice]
You are my mother; you are my father, Oh Shankara!
Shankara! [repeated once]
I am your servant

Sami Dandapani framed his performance of this hymn with an emphasis on *atiyen*, "I am [your] servant," by his repetition of the first line of the poem, which concludes with the term, over and above his repetition of other lines, and with his return to this initial line of the poem and its sentiment at the conclusion of his rendition of this hymn. *"Atiyen"* is found throughout the hymns of the three saints, and is understood to be a primary way in which the saints characterized their stance in relation to the Lord. Stressing their dedication to the Lord, the saints viewed themselves as His servants or slaves; their human concerns, expressed in this particular hymn as the distraction of the five senses, are acknowledged within the context of devotion and dedication.

Through his selective repetition of phrases, his rendering of the hymn in the traditional *pan*, and his musical ornamentation of the term *"atiyen,"* Sami Dandapani is a contemporary interpreter of the bhakti hymns. In characterizing the nature of the *otuvars* as interpreters, Indira Peterson contrasts them with virtuoso artists:

> The Tamil Śaiva audience perceives the *ōtuvār* as a medium, in a certain sense, a mediator between the text and itself, rather than as a virtuoso artist. It responds to the performance, rather than to the performer. Listeners more often speak of a "moving rendering" than of "a great singer." In such a view, the *ōtuvār* is seen as a "good" performer when the audience feels that, through creative selection and foregrounding as well as through a "moving" rendering, he has revealed hidden meanings and subtle beauties in the saints' hymns that are by reputation beautiful and rich in devotional themes. (1989: 74–75; cf. 67–75)

Peterson is quite correct to suggest that the ethos of the *otuvars*' performance of the bhakti hymns emphasizes the effective transmission of tradition, in which song and saint are privileged, rather than the contemporary singer. For example, Sami Dandapani is mild-mannered and unassuming in demeanor, and his pedagogy in teaching the hymns to students focuses attention on the hymns' meanings.

On the other hand, considering an *otuvar* such as Sami Dandapani to be a virtuoso, even if it is not in keeping with the ethos of the tradition, does illuminate aspects of his performance. For example, his performance involves natural vocal talent, which is the way many contemporary *otuvars* come to their profession; training over many years in the traditional *pans*; and study to discern the meaning of each hymn, as well as the correct pronunciation of the metered lines. Sami Dandapani's performance captured the persona of the "servant" who is dedicated to the Lord, and the passion and poignancy of that dedication. Emulating the saint, he brought the audience into the emotional experience of bhakti as communion among poet, God, and audience of the hymn, as discussed by Norman Cutler (1987: 19–21). His performance foregrounds the nature of the hymns as "sonic theology" (Beck 1995), and emphasizes the emotional dimension: "While singing one enters into a flow of energy empatterning the mind and nerves with moods of rhythm and sound, as one's feelings are voiced. After one has sung, one's ears ring with silence, the imagination is sensitized, and one is able to listen more intently for the presence of the beloved" (Jackson 1998: 29). This aesthetic-emotional dimension is a hallmark of bhakti, and is often identified as bhakti's distinctive contribution to Hindu worship (Hardy 1983;

Dhavamony 1971). As a virtuoso performance, Sami Dandapani's rendition was a poignant and sincere exploration of the emotional mood of the hymn, especially the affirmation of single-minded dedication to Shiva that is appropriate to the celebration of Mahashivaratri.

Dharmapuram P. Swaminathan

Dharmapuram Swaminathan, who is eighty years old (his devotees held a birthday ceremony for him on June 12, 2003), is considered to be the seniormost *otuvar* and expert of the Tamil Shiva-bhakti hymns in Tamil Nadu; in 1997, he was awarded the prestigious Sangeet Natak Academy award for his lifetime of service to the tradition. I did not have the regular contact with Dharmapuram Swaminathan that I did with Sami Dandapani; however, he did generously grant me a formal interview two months prior to Mahashivaratri.[13]

During the interview, I learned that Dharmapuram Swaminathan is an outspoken preserver of the hymns, and that he uses knowledge of the hymns as a vantage point for critical social commentary. For example, when he discussed his path toward studying *Tevaram*, he described a conflict between film music and classical music that has meaning even today:

> I was born in 1923. In 1935 I came to the *matam* at Dharmapuram. I was a servant and helper to the head of the *matam*. In 1942 there was a Swamikal named Arulnampi Tampiran. He was deeply interested in *Tevaram*. He could sing well. I too could sing well and I would sing film songs. Tampiran told me not to waste my talent on film music and he advised me to sing *Tevaram*. I did not listen to him at that young age, but he went on forcing me and persuading me. On February 2, 1942 I consented to heed his advice. I said I would study *Tevaram*. He was very happy.... There was one Tirunavukkaracu *otuvar* there. He was asked to write the first *Tevaram* and give it to me. I started to study that day. At that time there was a school of *Tevaram* at the Dharmapuram *matam*. It is still there.

Today, he understands the conflict to have been instigated by the secularist Tamil Nadu state government, including such past leaders as Annadurai, E.V. Ramasami Naicker, Karunanidhi and M.G. Ramachandran (M. G. R.), who he says "displaced *Tevaram*" in order to "project propaganda through film music." A particular bone of contention for Swamiji at the time of the interview was the government's failure to replace immediately the second *otuvar* at Mylapore's Kapaleeshvara Temple upon the untimely death of Lalgudi Swaminathan in May of 1996.

According to Swamiji, additional threats to the promotion of the hymns as classical Tamil music include the predominance of Carnatic music and its play on popular media. While he acknowledges the diverse avenues of support that the Shaiva Siddhanta gives to *Tevaram* in the present day, he also leveled a critique at the organization in a comment on the use of the traditional melodies (*pan*) and Carnatic *ragas* in performing *Tevaram*:

> That is how I studied [learning the traditional *paṇs*]. But today there are several new *ragas* used in TV, radio, et cetera There are only around twenty *ragas* used in *Tevaram*. But today several *ragas* are in popular usage. People and musicians listen to these *ragas* and the musician changes the *ragas* in order to gain listeners. I myself do this. If I don't have an audience I cannot earn money. But if staunch supporters of *paṇmurai* and *matam* heads offer to support our pure singing, we will never alter the *paṇmurai* in this way.

Dharmapuram Swaminathan's aim is to popularize the Tamil Shiva-bhakti hymns, which he feels have been eclipsed by these factors. This attempt was immediately apparent when I arrived at the neighborhood Mylapore temple (the Tirumayilai Karaneeccaram Temple) around 10 p.m. Swamiji sat alone on a raised platform in the temple courtyard, surrounded by bhaktas. The program had been advertised, because Swamiji was going to release the first installment of his project to record all of *Tevaram* on audiocassette tapes. The mood was festive, and the night was his as both performer and social commentator.

The traditional *nagaswaram* (a traditional horn) music began, and he sang two hymns on Tillai (Chidambaram), accompanying himself on the harmonium, which lent the performance a festive, almost carnival-like, air.[14] Then he turned abruptly toward the audience, and said: "It seems they are serving only *sambar* rice," a comment that provoked laughter because of its unexpectedness and its critical tone.

He then went into an educational mode, explaining that there are 274 places of pilgrimage celebrated in the hymns of Campantar, Appar, and Cuntarar. He then said that he had asked "a man wearing several *rudraksha* garlands and who appeared to be a bhakta" to name them, and the man could not. Swamiji named the man, who was present and known to be a disciple of his, and the crowd chuckled. Then Swamiji explained that there are two newly discovered places to which the saints pilgrimaged, bringing the total to 276. He held up a book he was releasing that night, explaining that it has hymns on 275 pilgrimage places, and that he himself had written a hymn in honor of all these places. His hymn lists the place names, followed by the phrase, "venerate Shiva!" For example, "*Tirutillai Shivanaip porri!*"

He called a woman to the stage to honor her, which again turned into an opportunity for critical comment on Shaiva devotees: "She was responsible for the publishing of many holy books. It is my opinion that Shaivas do not have the habit of applauding each other. They won't even clap when someone is garlanded! [laughter] They are not in the habit. See the rickshawmen, how they will support each other. But beat me up on the road, even my disciple [the one named previously] will not come!" [laughter].

After garlanding her, he launched into a story about Appar, to set the context for his performance of the next hymn.

> Once Tiruvavukkaracar was staying at Chidambaram, and decided to go to the neighboring town of Tirukkaipparai which was no more than two or three kilometers from Chidambaram. Have you been there? He was going for the Lord's *darshan*. On the way he became aware that he had not been consciously thinking of the Lord for some moments. He became deeply anxious that he should have forgotten the Lord of Tillai even for a moment. He laments that he will not obtain *moksha*. So, within the brief period of walking the three kilometers, he composed the following song: "Would I ever forget the Dancer at Tillai even for a moment of my life?" Imagine, he sang this verse in the time taken to walk three kilometers!

Swamiji started to sing a hymn from Appar (V.2 Koyil), which begins with this verse:

> The one who skinned the crazed elephant
> with a trunk like a palmyra stalk,
> The one who fills the hearts of those who meditate
> in the temple,
> The master of all forms,
> The dancer in the hall—
> If I forget him for a moment as tiny as a grain of millet
> Can I still be saved? (trans. Prentiss)

Swamiji sang the first verse twice, followed by the next two verses. In each case, he sang the verses straight through, repeating only the phrase, *marantu uyvano*, "if I forget, can I be saved?," for emphasis. Then, abruptly, he interrupted his own performance with a question to a member of the audience: "What are you distributing there?" Upon learning that the person was distributing *sambar* rice, Swamiji directed: "Do not give anything now. If you do, they will not listen to the song. As it is they are easily distracted." He then continued singing the rest of the verses of the hymn, again emphasizing *marantu uyvano*.

A major rhetorical theme in this portion of Dharmapuram Swaminathan's all-night performance was the necessity for Shaivas to overcome the human tendency toward forgetfulness, in order to participate actively in the Shiva-bhakti path. This theme informs his criticism of one of his disciples for not knowing the 276 places of pilgrimage in the saints' hymns; his taking to task of the Shaiva community for not supporting each other, in contrast to the rickshawmen; his emphasis on the phrase *marantu uyvano* ("if I forget, can I be saved?") in Appar's hymn; and his scolding of the person distributing food, on the grounds that it would distract the audience from listening to the hymn. Dharmapuram Swaminathan viewed himself as their reminder of the path of Shiva-bhakti.

The major *vrat* of Mahashivaratri is the institutionalized occasion on which Shaiva devotees remember the Lord; many keep all-night vigils. Yet, the *vrat* is also a time to reflect on human concerns, especially human weaknesses that impede progress on the spiritual path; hence, Mahashivaratri is also a time of repentance. The *vrat* provided Swamiji with an audience for his outspoken social criticism; he challenged the bhaktas of Shiva to see themselves in Appar's hymn, for if the saint can forget the Lord even while he is on pilgrimage, how much more so can contemporary humankind forget the Lord on all the other days of the year save Mahashivaratri. His release of resource materials for the study and appreciation of the Tamil Shiva-bhakti hymns and saints provided a way for him to extend his educational message to the bhaktas beyond the Great Night of Shiva, and to others beyond the courtyard of the small Mylapore temple, for Swamiji is insistent that if Tamils are not familiar with the Tamil Shiva-bhakti hymns, they will lose touch with an important part of their heritage.

Bhakti as a Vow

The three classical saints and contemporary performers of their hymns have in common the devotion of themselves to Shiva through song. They are emblematic of Shiva-bhakti as a long-term vow, insofar as their dedication to Shiva is a state of being that informs their life. That their activities take place within the context of social relationships compels an oscillation between the single-mindedness of dedication to the Lord and the negotiable nature of human concerns. That both sides are constitutive of Shiva-bhakti is illustrated by the shared dedication yet distinctive concerns of the Tamil bhakti poets, and by the contrasting contemporary performances of their hymns in a single night of Mahashivaratri. In their performances, Sami Dandapani and Dharmapuram Swaminathan each used the context of a short-term vow, Mahashivaratri, to focus the attention of ordinary people on bhakti as a long-term vow. Sami Dandapani illustrated the bhakti of the classical saints by evoking them in his performance. Dharmapuram Swaminathan's mode was more that of teaching (though he views it as "reminding"): he challenged and chastised his audience into realizing that the bhakti they profess on the Night of Shiva should inform their lives each and every day.

Notes

1. Helpful resources providing general classifications of vows include Elmar Klinger, "Vows and Oaths," and Christian Wedemeyer, "Vows." Full citations are listed in the references for this chapter.

2. In Christianity, a vow is characterized by an oral declaration, often creedal. Thus, Carolyn Walker Bynam distinguishes a medieval women's religious movement from institutional nunneries by noting the absence of vows: "These women [*beguines*] set themselves apart from the world by living austere, poor, chaste lives in which manual labor and charitable service were joined to worship (which was not, however, rigidly prescribed as it was in convents). Initially, at least, their practice contrasted sharply with traditional monasticism, since they took no vows and had no complex organization and rules, no order linking the houses, no hierarchy of officials, no wealthy founders or leaders" (1987: 17). This distinction, while important in Christianity, will not serve as a general classification. A vow is a commitment, which can be expressed in colloquial terms ("I will fast tomorrow"), in creedal terms, or in creative terms (such as the Tamil bhakti poets I discuss later in the essay). Thus it can be argued that the *beguines* did take a long-term vow to live a spiritual life, but that they did not express this commitment in a creedal manner.

3. Vows of maintenance are not limited to long-term ontological vows; as Mary McGee explains, one aspect of short-term *vrats* performed by women is to maintain their auspicious state of being married (1991: 82).

4. See Narayan (1989: 63–81) for interesting comments on the active social service undertaken by *sadhus* and a critique of L. Dumont's separation of the *sannyasin* and the householder along caste lines.

5. Helpful resources in English for the study of the three hymnists' poetry and biographies include I. Peterson (1989: 270–322) and Dehejia (1988: 33–61); see also Prentiss (2001: 11–13).

6. This is the story presented in the *Tirumuraikantapuranam*, probably composed by Umapati Civacaryar. I discuss this text in Prentiss 2001.

7. In contrast to medieval times, from which we have royal inscriptions that suggest that singing the Tamil bhakti hymns was a hereditary occupation, today most of the singers do not come to the profession by inheritance. This is the case with three very well-known singers of *Tevaram* that I have interviewed: the late Lalgudi Swaminathan of the Mylapore Kapaleeshvara Temple, Dharmapuram Swaminathan, and Sami Dandapani; the latter two I profile in this chapter. For further information on the history of singing the hymns in temples, see Prentiss (1999: 89–91, 101-02, 123–25).

8. I performed this research on the contemporary performance of *Tevaram* on the Asian Cultural Council Religion and Art Fellowship in Chennai from December 1996 to May 1997; I am grateful to the ACC for its generous grant for this research.

9. J. Bruce Long's article, "Mahasivaratri," was informed by his research into classical texts as well as fieldwork in Madras in 1968 and 1971; however, since his focus was on discovering a structuralist paradigm, he tended not to include discussion of local variations. Thus, there is nothing in his article about the performance of *Tevaram* during Mahashivaratri.

10. For example, I presented a paper on these two performances, entitled "The Night of Tēvarām," with audiocassette recordings of the performances, at the annual Conference on Religion in South India in Gainsville, Florida in June 1998. Special thanks to ethnomusicologist Zoe Sheridan for her comments on that occasion. I have built upon this paper and the helpful feedback from colleagues at the conference in writing this chapter.

11. Special thanks to Mrs. Champa Kumar for taking a vital and supportive interest in my studies and thus introducing me to Sami Dandapani as well as including me as an observer in the Ladies' *Tevaram* group's practice sessions and performances. Later in 1997, Sami Dandapani moved to London for a long-term stay, where he is currently very successfully teaching and performing the *Tevaram* hymns. A wonderful new scholarly study of a women's devotional singing group is M. Whitney Kelting's recent work (2001).

12. Campantar I.50.7.

13. January 9, 1997. Thanks to one of his disciples, D. Arumugam, and entrepreneur Commander Krishnan for their help in arranging the meeting and accompanying me to Swamiji's home in Kunrattur.

14. He sang Appar IV.81 Koyil and Appar V.1 Koyil.

References

Beck, Guy L. 1995. *Sonic Theology: Hinduism and Sacred Sound.* Delhi: Motilal Banarsidass (1993, University of South Carolina).

Bynam, Carolyn Walker. 1987. *Holy Feast and Holy Fast: The Religious Significance of Food to Medieval Women.* Berkeley: University of California Press.

Carman, John. 1987. "Bhakti." In *The Encyclopedia of Religion,* ed. Mircea Eliade, vol. 2. New York: Macmillan.

Cutler, Norman J. 1987. *Songs of Experience: The Poetics of Tamil Devotion.* Bloomington: Indiana University Press.

Dehejia, Vidya. 1988. *Slaves of the Lord: The Path of the Tamil Saints.* New Delhi: Munshiram Manoharlal Publishers.

Dhavamony, Mariasusai. 1971. *Love of God According to Śaiva Siddhānta: A Study in the Mysticism and Theology of Śaivism.* Oxford: Oxford University Press.

Hardy, Friedhelm Hardy. 1983. *Viraha-Bhakti: The Early History of Krsna Devotion in South India.* Delhi: Oxford University Press.

Jackson, William J. 1998. *Songs of Three Great South Indian Saints.* Delhi: Oxford University Press.

Kelting, Whitney M. 2001. *Singing to the Jinas: Jain Laywomen, Mandal Singing, and the Negotiations of Jain Devotion.* New York: Oxford University Press.

Klinger, Elmar. 1987. "Vows and Oaths." In *The Encyclopedia of Religion,* ed. Mircea Eliade, vol. 15: 301–05. New York: Macmillan Publishing Company.

Long, J. Bruce. 1982. "Mahāśivarātri: The Saiva Festival of Repentance." In *Religious Festivals in South India and Sri Lanka,* eds. Guy R. Welbon and Glenn E. Yocum, 189–217. New Delhi: Manohar.

McGee, Mary. 1991. "Desired Fruits: Motive and Intention in the Votive Rites of Hindu Women." In *Roles and Rituals for Hindu Women,* ed. Julia Leslie, 71–88. Madison, NJ: Fairleigh Dickinson Press.

Narayan, Kiran. 1989. *Storytellers, Saints, and Scoundrels: Fold Narrative in Hindu Religious Teaching.* Philadelphia: University of Pennsylvania Press.

Pearson, Anne Mackenzie. 1996. *"Because It Gives Me Peace of Mind" : Ritual Fasts in the Religious Lives of Hindu Women.* Albany: State University of New York Press.

Peterson, Indira Viswanathan. 1989. *Poems to Śiva: The Hymns of the Tamil Saints.* Princeton: Princeton University Press.

Prentiss, Karen Pechilis. 2001. "On the Making of a Canon: Historicity and Experience in the Tamil Śiva-Bhakti Canon." *International Journal of Hindu Studies* 5, 1: 1–26.

———. 1999. *The Embodiment of Bhakti.* New York: Oxford University Press.

———. 1996. "A Tamil Lineage for Śaiva Siddhānta Philosophy." *History of Religions* 35, 3 (February): 231–57.

Wadley, Susan Snow. 1983. "*Vrats*: Transformers of Destiny." In *Karma: An Anthropological Inquiry,* eds. Charles F. Keyes and E. Valentine Daniel, 147–62. Berkeley: University of California Press.

Wedemeyer, Christian. 1999. "Vows." In *Encyclopedia of Women and World Religion,* ed. Serenity Young, vol. 2, 1016–18. New York: Macmillan Reference U.S.A.

10

Monastic Vows and the Ramananda Sampraday

Ramdas Lamb

India has long been viewed by the West as typifying the "mystic East." Early records of foreign travelers give descriptions of her strange-looking hermits and ascetics, with their matted hair, near-naked bodies, and mysterious practices. More recently, an increasing number of young Westerners and even assorted young urban upper-middle-class Indians have reawakened an outside interest in the lifestyles of Hindu renunciants, collectively referred to herein as "sadhus."[1] From afar, the lives of these ascetics seem intriguing, unique, and liberated. Unencumbered by family, children, job, home, and societal restrictions, or even clothing, they appear to spend their days involved in exotic, often incomprehensible, rituals and other activities. To many, they typify the quintessential free spirit.

However, appearances usually fail to reveal the entire picture and thus are deceptive. In reality, the life of most sadhus is highly structured and disciplined, shaped in large part by self-imposed restrictions, limitations, and various forms of austerity. These, in turn, are initiated and supported by vows and pledges. This is especially true with respect to the Ramananda Sampraday, the largest order of Hindu renunciants today. Thus, the Ramanandi sadhus and the role of vows and associated commitments in their lives are the focus of this chapter.

Monasticism has historically been a predominantly male undertaking, often existing as an antithesis to the material-seeking life in the cultures in which

---

The information provided in this chapter has been gathered by the author over the last three decades, as a Ramanandi sadhu for the first eight years and as a scholar and lay member of the sect since that time.

renunciant traditions have arisen.[2] While most societies have tended to evaluate males in large part by their physical, mental, emotional, and/or material possessions and prowess, monks have typically opted for a different focus, seeking not to possess but to forego, not to obtain but to abstain. Traditionally, males who possess proficiency and prosperity attain power and position. Conversely, those who have little or do little materially are generally regarded as useless, unable, and unworthy. Yet, it is in this latter direction that ascetics and monks have traditionally endeavored to move. For renunciants, it is not one's material accomplishments but one's abstinence that has greater value. Moreover, material rejection and austerity are not only the vehicles but often the goals of the monastic life. As renunciants progress along the path that takes them from possession and sensual pleasure to renunciation and self-control, from material attainment to spiritual prowess, restrictive vows and promises generally become more integral and vital. A common view in Hindu monastic traditions is that a sadhu without renunciation is not a sadhu; a monk who takes no vows is not a monk, because, historically, the renunciant life has been structured by and built around vows of renunciation of and abstinence from the sensuality and materialism of the external world.

At the same time, however, it must be noted that while the process of renunciation followed by most sadhus is in respect to the material realm, it is not a rejection, per se, of accomplishments and attainments. Most sadhus have very specific goals they wish to attain, but these are in the realm of the nonphysical. Hindus traditionally believe that all thoughts, actions, and deeds have karmic results, their fruits, and these are dependent to a large extent upon the intentions of the doer. Actions done with material goals in mind will lead to material results, positive or negative. Even the performance of *sadhana*, or religious practice, done in a selfless manner is believed to generate fruit, although these tend to be nonphysical, in the form of good karma, spiritual virtue, detachment, understanding, or spiritual power. To many ascetics, such results are very real and important attainments in the progression of the ascetic life, for they aid the ascetic in furthering the progress toward his goals, be they wisdom (*gyan*), liberation (*mukti*), or devotion (*bhakti*). The fruit of *sadhana* is believed to be enhanced when religious vows are attached; the more strict the vows and the more severe the practices, the greater the results. Thus, while the life of the sadhu clearly involves a renunciation of involvement with material possessions, for many it also involves an amassing of spiritual fruits and power. It is with this view in mind that many sadhus undertake ascetic practices and vows.

Archaeological evidence from the Indus Valley civilization suggests the early presence of ascetics and ascetic practices. The variety of Sanskrit terms by which these were known suggest a relatively early development and diversification of the concept. Subsequently, various Upanishads emphasize the practice of austerities (*tapas, tapasya*), vows (*vrats*), and restraints (*dama*) as integral to the path of realization; even the gods are believed to undertake these.[3] *Tapas* is not only presented as a requisite for perceiving the Atman, or individual soul, but it is said to facilitate knowing and realizing the Absolute Brahman as well. The religions of Jainism and Buddhism also have their roots in ascetic practices and vows of renunciation, with the founder of each tradition having practiced extreme renunciation as an integral part of his path toward enlightenment. The Hindu Epics and the Puranas are replete with stories of ascetics, yogis, and yoginis taking extreme vows and performing fantastic feats of austerity to obtain worldly and otherworldly goals. Valmiki's Ramayana tells of ascetics committing themselves to intense vows of renunciation and austerities for the purpose of acquiring yogic powers and liberation. The sage Vishwamitra, for example, took vows and endured various forms of *tapasya* for penance, first to gain worldly power and eventually to gain spiritual perfection.[4] The goddess Parvati undertook extreme vows (*ugram suvratam*) and fasted for thousands of years to gain both ascetic power as well as Shiva's favor.[5] Thus, the importance and role of austerities and vows throughout the body of Epic and Puranic literature is immense.

With the rise of the Tantric traditions in both Hinduism and Buddhism during the first millenium, there came a more organized and ritualized rejection of many of the orthodox religious restrictions. However, a rejection of vows and restraints did not occur, per se; instead, they were reformulated and redirected. Moreover, nearly all the ascetic and monastic traditions in Indian history have sought to reconceive and redefine religious and spiritual practice, modifying, and in some cases replacing, one set of doctrines, restrictions, and vows with another. The late medieval Gorakhnath sect, for example, combined elements of the yogic and Tantric traditions in formulating its approach to enlightenment. A major goal of many of the ascetic practices of its practitioners was the attainment of power, for which vows played a pivotal role. Austere vows are said to have granted many of the more famous yogis great powers, both spiritual and profane. As with the prior ascetic groups, the early Ramananda Sampraday drew on this culture and developed its own approach to the practice and role of vows, bringing more of a focus on *bhakti* as integral in both the path and the goal. Therefore, the practices of the present-day order are but the contemporary manifestations of a long literary and pragmatic tradition and evolution of vows and ascetic practices.

History of the Ramananda Sampraday

Most Ramanandis acknowledge Swami Ramananda (circa fourteenth to fifteenth century) to be the founder of their order.[6] However, like with so many celebrated religious figures from India's past, there is little actual evidence about Ramananda, his own religious practices, or the formation and early development of the order that carries his name. There is, however, some evidence to suggest that a collection of ascetics devoted to Ram were present in or around the fifteenth century in north India, and these ascetics may well have been the forerunners or early members of the order.

Tradition has it that Ramananda was initially a renunciant in the lineage of Swami Ramanuja (tenth to eleventh century), but he grew dissatisfied with the order because of its evolving set of doctrines and rules that he came to view as discriminatory and incompatible with his own spiritual path and realizations. Eventually, he left the order and started his own, keeping the Visishtadvaita philosophy of Ramanuja as the basis of much of his theological and philosophical views, while rejecting the caste system and many of its allied narrow social doctrines that the Ramanuja Order had adopted. For Ramananda, the primary emphasis was on the love of God, in the aspect of Ram, which is to be obtained through devotion and renunciation. According to his followers, Ramananda accepted disciples from all castes, creeds, and backgrounds, lecturing to them and writing in the vernacular of the day rather than in Sanskrit. He soon became a popular religious reformer and teacher, and his own ascetic existence attracted to the life of renunciation many Hindus from various castes.

Present-day Ramananda Sampraday

The Ramananda Sampraday currently has the largest number of *virakt*, or renunciant members of any Hindu order, estimated to number nearly one and a half million. Commonly referred to as "Ramanandis," "Vairagis,"[7] or simply "sadhus," its followers come primarily from villages in the northern and western states, especially Uttar Pradesh, Bihar, Madhya Pradesh, Rajasthan, and Gujarat. Since they bring with them elements of their own religious cultures, the corpus of the order's austerities and vow-initiated activities shows not only the influence of previous ascetic movements but also of a variety of regional religious traditions and practices. Adding to those practices the ones that have evolved from within the order, the result is a tradition of vow-taking that, like the broader Hindu world itself, is both unique as well as extremely multivalent.

Contemporary Hindu culture uses an assortment of terms to distinguish various types of vows and promises. Some of the more common words that, in different contexts, can be translated as "vow," "oath," or "promise" are: *bachan* (or *vachan*), *shapath*, and *pratigya* (see the Glossary at the end of this volume). Each of these can be utilized in a variety of contexts. However, because these terms frequently possess a secular connotation, Ramanandis do not find them befitting the ascetic practice of vow-taking. Instead, in addition to their initiatory vows, Ramanandis employ three precise terms that they interpret as integrated but distinct vehicles: these are *vrat, anushthan*, and *sankalp*.[8]

Vrat

The term *vrat* is generally translated as fast, vow, or pledge and typically denotes some form of sensory restriction or regulation. It can refer to limitations on food consumption, speaking, sleeping, sexual relations, clothing, or a variety of other actions or forms of sensory experience. However, a *vrat* can also be a vow to perform a particular practice, such as a ritual for a specific time period. Furthermore, a *vrat* can be of a more traditional nature, such as fasting or keeping silence, or a distinctively and individually formulated endeavor, as will be discussed later in the chapter. Although length of time can vary for all *vrat*s, the term generally refers to vows that are specifically undertaken for a relatively short duration. Finally, the enactment of any type or length of *vrat* is considered a form of *tapasya*.

While all Vairagis perform *vrats* of one sort or another, each is given the freedom and is expected to individualize his vow-taking and associated practices, so that his efforts and undertakings are geared specifically toward his own personality, willpower, and spiritual maturation. While most *vrats* are undertaken for short periods, sadhus may commit to them for more extended periods of time. In such cases, and with respect to certain vows, this period may be for as long as twelve years, the length of time traditionally considered optimal for success in gaining the *siddhi*, or power each *vrat* is believed to produce. Because few Vairagis actually undertake such a lengthy *vrat*, those who commit to vows for an extended period often become identified by and with their undertaking. For example, one who is currently undertaking or has fulfilled a vow to keep silence for a long period, at least several years, might be given the name "Mauni Baba," or "Revered Silent One." If the vow is particularly difficult and is fully completed, then the other monks may, in deference, continue to address a monk with this type of honorific title even after his *vrat* has ended. Thus, there are several well-known sadhus within the order who, although they are no longer in silence, are still refered to as "Mauni Baba."

Anushthan

When a sadhu takes a vow to fulfill a *vrat* or set of *vrats* as part of a larger undertaking, in which the combination of related vows and practices becomes the primary focus of his life during a specific period, then the entire process is known as an *anushthan* ("ritual performance"; "undertaking"). "Spiritual retreat" is probably the closest English phrase to define *anushthan* in the contemporary context, although it does not encompass the breadth of meaning that the term possesses for Ramanandis. Activities designated by *anushthan* are specific intensive disciplines that are usually undertaken for a predetermined period of time. An *anushthan* can last for almost any period, from as few as nine days up to a year or more. Some sadhus will continue practices begun in an *anushthan* for their entire lives. *Anushthans* undertaken for specific periods may involve isolating oneself from other people and devoting all one's energy to the committed practice or set of practices. In some cases, two or more sadhus will engage in an *anushthan* together, with one's primary *sadhana* ("religious effort") consisting of caring for the needs of the other ascetic or ascetics involved. It is felt among Vairagis that a person who serves and cares for one doing an *anushthan* gets half the spiritual merit or power gained by the practice.

During an *anushthan*, a sadhu will likely perform a variety of associated *vrats* and other ritual activities. Typically, newer sadhus will be directed by their primary teachers to undertake certain vows. These initial practices may last for several days up to several weeks and involve such activities as fasting and/or keeping silence, repetition of a specific mantra a certain number of times each day, strict limitations on the amount of sleep or number of meals, and so forth. These early vows serve two primary purposes: to introduce the initiate into the practice of vow-taking, and, more importantly, to serve as a test of his abilities and resolve. If a young renunciant cannot successfully undertake these initial vows, then he is generally not considered to have the qualifications for success as a sadhu, and he may well be encouraged to abandon the lifestyle. However, the new sadhu who succeeds and exhibits the qualities for further success is, as mentioned earlier, then eventually expected to take the initiative in creating and undertaking *anushthans* on his own.

Sankalp

Vairagis underscore the importance of intentionality in the undertaking of any action, especially a religious endeavor, for it is understood that one's objectives and intentions influence not only the success or failure of one's efforts but also the fruit or karma that is accrued as a consequence. Thus, Ramanandis traditionally begin any vow with the taking of a *sankalp* (lit. "definite intention"; "determination"). The mantras used in reciting a *sankalp* typically begin with the propitiation of the deity or form of the divine to whom the efforts are being directed. The sadhu then gives his own name and, in précis, his denominational affiliation and its history, to remind him of the tradition from which he comes and the responsibility he faces in undertaking the vow. Finally, the vows and austerities to be undertaken and the intended goal are specified and verbalized.

Because Ramanandis view *sankalps* as carefully conceived promises and resolve to successfully complete specified actions, *sankalps* are to be taken very seriously and committed to only after deep reflection upon the responsibilities and consequences of the undertaking. Consequently, a vow taken lightly or in haste can not, by definition, be a *sankalp*. Instead, Ramanandis refer to such vows as either a *pratigya* or a *bachan*. While the latter are both types of promises and are thereby considered binding, they are not always enacted with the degree of seriousness and intentionality as a *sankalp*, and so they are not seen to generate the same power and effectiveness in their fulfillment. Additionally, Ramanandis see the making of a *sankalp* as an opportunity to clarify and recall one's resolve and commitment to the ascetic life, framed as it is in vow-taking. Some sadhus will repeat a *sankalp* every morning during their prayer rituals, earmarking the fruits of the day's religious activities. Many see this ritual as a means of keeping their focus and making a daily affirmation to the single-minded attainment of their goal, be it *mukti* or *bhakti*.

Throughout their lives, Vairagis perform multiple *sankalp*-initiated *vrats* and *anushthans*. Even though they may commit to one or more lengthy *anushthan*-like undertakings, as mentioned above, life-long *sankalps* are actually quite rare, since Ramanandis typically avoid binding themselves to many lifetime vows. Because of their open-ended nature, even initiatory vows are not always viewed as demanding, lifelong adherence, at least not in full. The reasoning for the rarity of lifetime vows is two-fold and stems from the seriousness with which *sankalp*-initiated actions are viewed. First and foremost, Vairagis firmly ascribe to the view that all vows are binding contracts that confer on the practitioner power in their fulfillment and negative consequences in their failure. Although the latter can be somewhat mitigated when a *sankalp* is broken because of illness or at the behest of one's guru, there is great care taken to avoid a premature

Figure 10.1 A Ramanandi family, consisting of both Tyagi and Mahatyagi members

ending to any such undertaking. A situation occurred several years ago that illustrates how sadhus may deal with a "broken" *sankalp*. The disciple of a well-respected Mahatyagi teacher became seriously ill after three years of a twelve-year vow. Because of the extreme nature and length of the vow, the teacher made him take a three month hiatus from the commitment in order to regain his physical health, and the other monks in their "family"[9] wholeheartedly agreed it was the best thing to do. Once his health improved, the monk began the *sankalp* again from the beginning, even though his guru had approved the break. When asked his reason for starting anew, the monk noted, "My vow was for twelve years, and I will not personally feel that I completed it unless I do it without a break. What good is the life of a monk if he does not fulfill his vows?"

For this reason, many sadhus do not actually take vows of lifelong celibacy, for example, even though the practice is viewed by most monks, and nearly all householders, as an a priori part of the renunciant life. In this particular case, it is understood that complete control of the sexual urge may take years to accomplish, and, thus, a vow of lifelong celibacy should only be undertaken once an individual has had the training and gained the ability to fulfill it successfully. Otherwise, a sadhu who takes the vow prematurely is setting himself up for failure. At the same time, however, celibacy is considered a prerequisite of any *vrat* or *anushthan*. Finally, since no one knows the future and the goal is freedom, one should not undertake vows that, at some point in one's life and spiritual development, bind one to a commitment that might actually become an obstacle to further spiritual progress.

Vow-taking and the Individual Vairagi

At the time of initiation, all Vairagis take vows of adherence to the ascetic lifestyle, which include restrictions on food and beverage (at minimum, no flesh products, eggs, or alcohol), dress, occupation, association, possessions, habitation, hairstyle, sexual activity, and so forth.[10] These preliminary vows serve as the foundation of the renunciant's life and the basis upon which he organizes and engineers his spiritual path. Some time within a few months to a year after initiation, a sadhu is expected to begin the process of integrating individualized and personalized *vrat*s as a regular part of his daily existence. Such vows are said to symbolize a Vairagi's commitment to the divine, his gradual relinquishing of involvement in, and attachment to, the material world, and his taking charge of his own spiritual progress. These vows also help foster both personal identity formation as well as an affinity to, and an identity within, the broader monastic community.

As mentioned earlier, vows are typically initiated with very specific goals in mind. In this respect, they function as quid pro quo spiritual contracts between the individual renunciant and the divine. On one hand, they may be undertaken as a means of achieving specific worldly objectives, ranging from something as universal as world peace to as specific as helping a follower find a job or overcome an illness. Here, the vowed action or actions are performed primarily for the benefit of another. On the other hand, and perhaps more commonly, vows are used by Vairagis to craft their paths to the realization of the divine, to gain liberation from the cycle of birth and death, or to attain eternal devotion to God. In these cases, the goals are completely personal.

Integral to the daily life of a Vairagi is the performance of any of a variety of *sankalp*-initiated *vrats* and *anushthans*. Ramanandis regularly undertake a diverse range of vows and practices. A sadhu's caste, social, and economic backgrounds, as well as his personality, tendencies, and capabilities all combine to determine the type of vows to which he is drawn. Young ascetics are typically guided by their teachers as to which vows to undertake. It is generally believed, however, that teachers should not force strict disciplines on students but rather suggest and inspire their disciples to place restrictions on themselves. Moreover, any disciplinary practice is considered to be most fruitful when self-imposed. Nevertheless, young sadhus rarely take vows or begin practices without first gaining the approval of their gurus to help assure that the blessings of the latter serve to strengthen both resolve and the likelihood of success. Both for the new sadhu, as well as for the more seasoned renunciant, vows primarily deal with some sort of sensory restriction or discipline, the most common dealing with food, clothing, lodging, and speaking. The inspiration for these vows comes from common practices within one's denomination, as well as from vows completed or being undertaken by one's guru, other members of one's guru family, or other known ascetics.

In addition to the traditional fast days that most Ramanandis observe, for example, Ramnaumi, Navaratri, Tuesdays, et cetera, food restriction vows are generally the *vrats* most frequently undertaken by Vairagis. The specific type of fast often has an individual component. Food-related vows may involve abstinence from all solid foods or from a particular type of food, such as grain products. An even more personalized food *vrat* may consist of a monodiet, or the consumption of only one particular food, such as only fruit, or simply bananas. Food fasts can last for a single day or continue for years. In some cases, sadhus who have initially undertaken monodiets for a specific length of time have subsequently continued them for the remainder of their ascetic lives.

Among the different categories of dietary restriction as recognized by Ramanandis are *anahar*, *phalahar*, *dudhahar*, and *nirahar*. *Anahar* (lit. "grain consumption") diet is essentially the basic Hindu vegetarian diet consisting of grains, beans, nuts, fruits, vegetables, and milk products. Further, a *phalahari* (lit. "fruit eater") abstains from the consumption of all grains and grain products, root vegetables such as carrots and white radish, most legumes, tea, and sea salt. Thus, *phalaharis* limit their diet to fruit, most vegetables, nuts, milk products, and certain kinds of grainlike seeds, such as buckwheat and amaranthus. Most Vairagis will perform *phalahar vrats* on a regular basis, such as on Tuesdays, the full moon, et cetera, while some adopt it as a permanent or semipermanent diet. Sadhus who undertake the diet on a permanent basis are often called "Phalahari Baba." A *dudhahar* diet consists of only dairy products such as milk, yogurt, ghee, butter, buttermilk, and milk sweets. Ramanandis will typically follow this diet for short *anushthan*s only. One following a *nirahar vrat* will consume only water. This latter form of abstinance is a relatively common practice every Tuesday in some families in the order.

Food *vrats* are an important part of the sadhu's life for two principal reasons. First, attachment to taste is regarded as one of the most powerful of the sensual addictions. Therefore, one who learns to control attachment to taste and unnecessary food consumption is believed to have a greater ability to attain *vairagya*, or nonattachment, to other attachments. Additionally, it is believed that those who can control their food intake also have a heightened capacity to control, and eventually transcend, their sexual desires. Thus, fasting and celibacy are directly related.[11] Because learning nonattachment to physical desires is seen as a fundamental aspect of the renunciant life, any practice that helps one develop control of the senses is seen as essential. The second reason that food restriction vows are important concerns matters of purity. For various reasons, even foods acceptable within the typical vegetarian Hindu diet, such as onions, garlic, root vegetables, eggplant, and so forth, are rejected by many Vairagis as being non*sattwic*, or not pure foods. This concept of purity extends to food preparation as well, and it is often given as the primary reason why most Ramanandi sadhus avoid eating in a householder's home or eating food that has been prepared by a householder, irrespective of the latter's caste.[12]

Besides the basic ascetic restrictions on clothing, Ramanandis include a variety of additional clothing limitations in their corpus of vow-defined *tapasya* practices. Such vows are usually undertaken for extended periods of time and may continue for one's lifetime. For most sadhus, initiatory vows proscribe the use of silk and leather (because of the *himsa*, or violence, associated with their production), as well as any type of pants. Some also reject any cloth of artificial fibers, such as nylon. Additionally, those Vairagis known as "Mahatyagis" (see below) traditionally reject the use of cloth altogether. Unlike Shaivite Nagas, however, they are never completely naked. Instead, they wear a genital covering, or *langoti*, fabricated either from the bark of a banana tree or woven from *munja*, a sacred grass. One who wears the latter is called "Munjiya Baba," while a "Loha Langari" rejects even these materials and takes a vow to wear only a steel cup, typically held in place by an iron chain. A "Katiya Baba" takes a vow to wear a wooden *arbandh*, or waist belt, permanently joined together with brass buckles. The wooden belt is purposely large, usually three to four inches thick, and is worn in conjunction with a metal or cloth *langoti*.

Figure 10.2 Munjiya Baba

As with most Ramanandi vows, lodging restrictions are quite varied and have as one of their purposes to distinguish the renunciant's life from that of the householder. Thus, it is common for sadhus to forego sleeping or napping in a householder's dwelling, while some will not even enter such an abode. Others go one step further and refuse to reside in any human-made structure, while still others reject any form of lodging that separates or shields them from the elements of nature, as in the case of Mahatyagis. Because of the tendency to develop an attachment to one's residence, some Vairagis take a vow not to remain in one place for more than three consecutive days. Thus, for example, if they are at a temple or other site where a festival they wish to attend is about to occur three or four days hence, they will leave the place and then return on the day of the event. Such vows also have the added function of limiting a Ramanandi's possessions, since he has to carry with him everything he owns.

A vow of silence, or *maun*, is one of the oldest forms of *tapasya* undertaken by sadhus, and its essential challenge is almost purely psychological. The literal meaning of *maun* is "abstinence from speech," and for short periods of time it is considered an immensely helpful aid to meditation. Depending upon the actual vow, writing and/or chanting may or may not be allowed. Silence is believed to be conducive to developing inner strength and concentration; thus, while the vow deals strictly with the physical act of silence, the objective is to achieve mental silence or stillness of the mind. Since the latter is an extremely difficult aspiration, however, the undertaking can easily fall short and become fraught with negative consequences, such as deep anxiety and frustration, emotional depression, anger, and even physical illness. As a consequence, a practice initiated for attaining peace and happiness can have contrary results. For this reason, many sadhus will practice a *maun vrat* only for short periods of time, typically one to nine days. However, there are ascetics who find this type of *vrat* compatible with their particular personalities, may be drawn deeper into the practice, and end up remaining *maun* for very long periods, some even for the remainder of their lives. In many ways, the practice of *maun* epitomizes the goal of indifference to, or detachment from, the world to which many sadhus aspire. The presence of Mauni Babas, then, has a strong symbolic role in the ascetic community and tradition.

Vows restricting bodily position are some of the most severe, but less frequently practiced, forms of *tapasya* found in the Ramananda Sampraday. These vows require not only a great deal of physical and mental discipline, stamina, and will power, they also demand a willingness to inflict upon one's body great physical discomfort and possibly even permanent disfigurement.[13] Those known as Khardeswari Babas have taken a vow to remain ever-standing. They generally tie a swing or rope from a tree or any sort of structure that can be used to support the upper part of their body when they rest. Problems with blood circulation are inevitable, and in the past many who had undertaken the austerity had to abort it because of acute and dangerous physical complications. Presently, there is but one *khardeshwari* Vairagi, and he has been practicing this austerity for more than fourteen years.[14] A less difficult variant of this practice consists of a vow to not lie down. One who takes this vow is permitted to sit but uses a T-shaped piece of wood or a forked branch to support his upper body when he rests or sleeps.

The practice of *urdhwabahu* (lit. "vertical arm") involves taking a vow to keep one arm permanently elevated above one's head. Indeed, one of the most difficult forms of austerity involving body-position restrictions, it requires substantial will power and commitment to undertake. Circulation problems and the lack of movement in the arm joints lead to stiffening and eventual calcification; thus, any extended performance of *urdhwabahu* inevitably results in the permanent loss of use of the limb.

The purpose of such body-position austerities is clearly to take one beyond attachment to physical comfort. Ascetics who undertake these austerities say that what one loses physically is more than offset by what one gains spiritually. Although they have always been among the less frequently practiced forms of *tapasya,* these vows have nevertheless continued to be options for those who find such austerities useful and compelling. Those who feel the necessity of such extreme practices say that they do so for purification and for freedom from body attachment. As one Mahatyagi sadhu explained,

> Any type of *sadhana* that accomplishes the goal of physical, mental, and spiritual purification is a valid practice. This is so even if the practice results in permanent bodily damage. The body is a vehicle for us to reach liberation. We must drive it hard and not worry about the consequences on the vehicle, for once we succeed, the vehicle can be discarded.

Different Strokes, Different Styles

Danrdiya

The present-day organizational structure of the Ramananda Sampraday encompasses a variety of subgroups, distinguished primarily by the vows they undertake. While all Vairagis adhere to the same foundational vows and restrictions, each subgroup has vows unique to itself. The largest of these groups is that of the Danrdiya, for it is the order in which most Ramanandi ascetics take their primary initiation. However, since "Danrdiya" is an organization term, its members are never referred to as such. Instead, they are most often known by the generic terms "Vairagi" or "Ramanandi." Although they live for the most part in ashrams and temples, they are not bound to these abodes and generally are free to travel as they choose. Their external appearances can vary, but they typically have either long head and facial hair, which is generally groomed, or they have completely shaven heads. Until the 1980s, they nearly always wore white or yellow clothing consisting of a *lungi*, an unsown piece of cotton cloth worn around the waist, and occasionally a shirt as well. During the last two decades, however, many have opted to wear clothing colored in shades of orange and ochre, thereby adopting the colors worn by Shaivite renunciants. Both the *vrats* and the *anushthans* of this suborder tend to include the least physically restrictive vows of the various Ramanandi groups and instead focus upon such actions as eating, speaking, meditation, ritual performance, and prayer practices. Because they tend to have more frequent contact with householders than other Ramanandis, they are most often asked to intercede with the divine for the latter's benefit. Consequently, the *sankalps* of the Danrdiya are more likely to include vows undertaken for the benefit of followers and others than do those of other Ramanandi ascetics.

Tyagis

Those who desire to pursue a more physically austere lifestyle than that of the Danrdiya have the option to take initiation as a Tyagi, literally "renunciant." A Ramanandi may either enter this branch of the order directly at the time of his initiation into the order, or he may take the vows at a later stage in his renunciant life. The name of this initiatory vow is *khak diksha* (lit. "ash initiation") and refers to the daily practice of covering one's body with ashes from the sacred fire that is maintained regularly. Although all Tyagis wear some cloth, it often consists of little more than a *langoti* and possibly a *lungi*, an unsewn piece of cloth wrapped around the lower half of the body. Less tied to temples and ashrams than are Danrdiyas, Tyagis frequently roam the northern and central portions of India. They say of their lifestyle, "*Ramta yogi, bahata pani*." Literally translated as "A wandering yogi is like flowing water," the saying expresses the belief that an ascetic who is not tied to a place has fewer attachments and more freedom, both important to the renunciant life.

Integral to the Tyagi vow is adherence to a set of practices known as *tri tap*, or "three austerities," in which the year is divided into three four-month periods, with a specific daily *tapasya* connected to each period. Basant Panchami, the first day of spring (late January to early February), begins the performance of *dhuni* ("sacred fire") *tap*, an undertaking that consists of sitting in prayer or meditation, surrounded by a set of small fires made of dried cow dung. The number and physical arrangement of these fires is determined by the number of years that the Tyagi has been doing the *tap*. Each day, the practice is to be undertaken for approximately one hour during the hottest time of the afternoon and is preceded by a bath and covering the body with *dhuni* ashes.

Figure 10.3   A young Tyagi, about to begin the practice of *dhuni tap*

Figure 10.4   Several Tyagis performing *dhuni tap;* the various arrangements of dried cow dung piles to be burnt reveals the number of years each has performed the *dhuni tap*

In late May or early June, Tyagis begin the four-month period of *maidan* ("field") *tap*. Performed throughout the monsoon season, the practice involves a restriction against living under any shelter. Some understand this vow to be a prohibition against spending any extended length of time in a shelter, natural or human-created, and thus are not averse to entering a building for a short period or standing under a tree during an intense downpour. Others, however, interpret the vow as prohibiting them from even entering a building or stopping under the shade or protection of a tree.

The four-month period associated with fall and winter is the coldest time of the year and also the time for the performance of *jal* ("water") *tap*. This practice consists of immersing one's body in water up to the waist or even the neck for one hour nightly. The ritual is to be performed between midnight and sunrise and is potentially the most hazardous of the *tri tap*, since the cold temperature can cause hypothermia and loss of muscle control. If this practice is conducted in a body of water with a current, the practitioner can then be easily swept away. Therefore, in some places, Tyagis will extend ropes into the water to help avoid drowning.

Mahatyagis

Sometime during the late nineteenth century, an additional suborder arose from within the Tyagis, whose vows further increase the practitioner's degree of physical renunciation. Known as "Mahatyagis," members of this group take the most physically restrictive vows of any Hindu renunciant order as a whole. In addition to the Tyagi vows described above, Mahatyagis also vow never to cut or comb their hair; thus, they typically have long, matted hair, to which they regularly add ashes from their *dhuni*. In their performance of *tri tap*, they traditionally include the year-round practice of *maidan tap*, rather than the four-month period that Tyagis observe it. Mahatyagis also limit bodily covering to a *langoti* of banana tree bark or munja grass. In addition to the restrictive diet common to all Vairagis, the standard Mahatyagis diet is strict *phalahari*. Some members of the suborder will add further restrictions to this already limited dietary practice, for example, excluding milk products as well.

Like Tyagis, Mahatyagis are typically nomadic and tend to travel in small family groups. Wherever they do decide to stop for any length of time, they erect a *dhuni* around which they eat and sleep. At its high point in the mid-1900s, there were estimated to be more than ten thousand practitioners. However, by the 1970s the number had dwindled to a few thousand. Currently, no more than a few hundred actively maintain all the Mahatyagi vows, and the majority of these have been in the order for at least ten to fifteen years. Presently, most of those who refer to themselves as "Mahatyagi" are elders who have actually retired from adherence to the complete set of austerities. Clearly, very few individuals currently look to this lifestyle today with any eagerness. During the 2001 Kumbha

Figure 10.5 Several of the mahants or heads of the various Ramanandi subgroups joined together in procession to the Ganga during a Kumbha Mela festival in Prayag

Mela, I asked one of the few remaining Mahatyagi teachers who has young initiates why he thinks their numbers have dwindled so drastically and what he thinks of the future of the group and their practices. His answer suggested both resignation and acceptance:

> These days, young people are raised with so much physical comfort that they can hardly bathe in a river, much less practice any austerities. It is no longer the age [*yug*] of renunciation and yoga; it is the age of sensual pleasure. Maybe in the future people will again turn to renunciation, when they realize *atma shanti* (lit., "soul peace") is the fruit of nonattachment, not sensual pleasure.[15]

The Guru

Of all the vows a Ramanandi sadhu may take, arguably the most profound is the vow taken silently, and often secretly, by the guru as he initiates a new disciple. Traditionally, at this time he takes the vow to Lord Ram that he will be responsible for overseeing the spiritual advancement of the disciple to the point of the latter's spiritual realization and subsequent release from the necessity of rebirth, no matter how many lifetimes it may take. Thus, it is a vow that while meant to help secure the disciple's ultimate release, at the same time necessitates subsequent rebirths of the guru, beyond his own karmic needs. In this way, the vow resembles the bodhisattva vow in Mahayana Buddhism, in which the bodhisattva asserts that "I will not take personal enlightenment until all beings are liberated."

The existence of such a vow reveals a variety of beliefs held by Ramanandis. The first is that having a guru is, if not mandatory, highly beneficial in order to traverse the path to enlightenment. The second is that the relationship between guru and disciple is a very strong and long-term commitment for both individuals involved, one that potentially spans many lifetimes. Finally, it suggests that the role of the guru is not limited to the dissemination of teachings, techniques, and practices, but also includes his function as a grantor of blessings and assistance all along the path. Thus, finding a guru in a particular lifetime may actually mean finding one's guru from past lives.

For one who holds the traditional Hindu view that liberation from the cycle of rebirth is the ultimate goal, becoming a guru can be problematic. Holding this view, one of my upa-gurus (teachers from whom one gets teachings, or *siksha*, but not initiation, or *diksha*) once said to me, "I am very hesitant to take on any new disciples. I only want to find those to whom I am already committed. I no longer want to be reborn more lifetimes that I already have to." Because of such a view, some Ramanandi sadhus are hesitant to accept the role of diksha guru for anyone, although they are willing to serve as upa-gurus, since this latter relationship does not have the karmic mandate of the diksha guru. In essence, they do not wish to take on what many ascetics see as the ultimate sacrifice: foregoing one's own enlightenment for the sake of others.

However, there is another view that can be found within the Ram bhakti tradition, both among lay and renunciant adherents, and this has expanded the traditionally held view regarding the ultimate goal of life. This newer view centers on the concept of devotion itself as the goal. For Ramanandis who hold this, liberation is not seen as the ultimate, and thus being reborn for the sake of one's disciples is not viewed as an obstacle. A very popular Tyagi teacher, who has a large number of disciples, quoted a verse from the Ramcharitmanas, the primary scripture in north India today, to explain why he willingly takes on new disciples,

> Wealth, pleasure, religious merit, and liberation, none of these are my aim.
> Birth after birth, all that I want is devotion to the feet of Lord Ram.[16]

Conclusion

People typically define and express their personalities through their beliefs, dress, activities, and pastimes. Ramanandi ascetics define and express themselves, as well as craft their entire existence, by means of ascetic vows and vow-related undertakings. They believe that for any effort to be truly worthwhile, one should first set his or her mind and intention in the proper direction and toward the highest goal. The committed desire for material things can eventually lead to their attainment, while the desire for devotion or liberation, if undertaken with vows and sincere commitment, can eventually lead to these. In other words, because one will ultimately attain whatever one strives for, then striving for less than the ultimate is a waste of valuable time, energy, and effort. Ideally, then, one must direct all one's religious endeavors to the attainment of spiritual fruits that are directly connected with devotion and/or liberation, and these are believed to be best accomplished through vow-inspired and directed practices.

Ascetics have long had important and multivalent roles within Hindu culture. Since ancient times, they have been feared and ridiculed, but also revered and worshipped. They have had reputations as charlatans, fakers, and black magicians, but also as super human, godlike beings. For many Hindus, they are a present-day remnant of and important connection with India's great past, and they often embody the tension between procreation and renunciation. For most villagers, the ascetic is the true guru, a representation of the divine, whose power comes from the vows undertaken and austerities performed. Lay Hindus also take vows, but these generally provide little more than an occasional ritual accent to their lives. In the case of the renunciant, vows are what give life meaning. Ramanandis view vows and fasts, self-imposed restraints, and accompanying aspirations as activities that raise one above mundane life, that are the foundations of religion and spirituality, and that define culture and humanity itself. The importance of vows in the life of the ascetic cannot be overemphasized. To individualize their lives, Vairagis have a vast array of vows from which to choose and can reconstruct and combine them to fit any endeavor they wish to undertake. However, in the end, they believe that what is most important is not necessarily *what* one vows, but *that* one vows, for in vowing life becomes meaningful.

Notes

1. Within the contemporary Hindu ascetic tradition itself, the term "sadhu" used alone tends to denote Vaishnav monks and ascetics, while their counterparts from other denominations are often referred to by names that associate them with their sect affiliation. Thus, Shaivites are typically called "swami," "sannyasi," "naga sannyasi," or "naga sadhu"; Gorakhnath ascetics are known as "Nath yogis" or "Nath sadhus," and so forth. Lay persons, however, will frequently use the term "sadhu" more collectively and generically, as is the case here.

2. Since over 99 percent of Ramanandi ascetics are male, male pronouns are used throughout in reference to them. Although in the past and more commonly in the present,

females have also undertaken the renunciant path in various traditions (especially Buddhist and Catholic), nevertheless, they remain a small percentage of those who have traditionally chosen the lifestyle. The reasons for this are multiple, diverse, and cannot be adequately discussed within the scope and length of the present study.

3. Examples of this can be seen in the *Prasna Upanishad* (I.2, I.10) and the *Taittiriya Upanishad* (IX.1–2).

4. Ramayana (I.51–65).

5. Ramayana (I.35.19–20); *Ramcharitmanas* (I.74–75).

6. There have been several scholarly works that discuss aspects of the Ramananda Sampraday. Peter van der Veer's *Gods on Earth* has some valuable material on the history and development of the order, while William Pinch's *Peasant and Monks in British India* addresses issues surrounding the order and some of the reasons for the lack of much scholarly focus on it. In his *Sadhus of India,* Robert Gross provides more specifics on beliefs and practices within the order.

7. From the Sanskrit *vairagya*, or "nonattachment."

8. In contemporary Hindi, the language used by the vast majority of Ramanandis, the short "a" sound at the end of most words is silent. Thus, the Sanskrit *vrata* becomes *vrat,* and so forth. Transliteration of these terms is consistent with present-day pronunciation.

9. Every Ramanandi sadhu belongs to a particular family, with his own initiation guru as his father figure. Most live and/or travel in family groups, which are generally composed of brother disciples of the guru. If the guru has a large family, he may or may not reside or travel with the particular group. Further, each family tends to emphasize its own corpus of preferred forms of *vrat*, although members can undertake any vows they choose. These are discussed in more detail in the sections on Tyagis and Mahatyagis.

10. While such vows are similar for all Ramanandis, how they are understood and put into practice may vary from region to region or even teacher to teacher.

11. Yogis claim that subtle nerves in the body connect the sex glands and taste buds; therefore, one who can learn to control either of the two can learn better to control the other. Thus, in the yogic system of beliefs and practices, the *chakra*, or energy center, associated with the sex organs is called *swadishtan*, literally, "place of taste."

12. The issue of commensality rules between Vairagis and householders is complex, extremely variable, and is not the focus of this chapter nor can it be adequately covered in the space allotted here.

13. Although also rare in such ascetic groups as the Gorakhnath Sampraday and the Shaivite Nagas, such undertakings are nevertheless a bit more common.

14. There is a well-respected Udasi sadhu who remained standing for twenty-three years, but through a strict regimen of yogic practices, diet, and other exercises, he was able to keep his body joints healthy and in good working condition. He ended the practice in the mid-1990s and currently has four disciples who are performing the practice under his guidance.

15. From an interview with Phalahari Ramcharandas, Kumbha Mela (Prayag, India), 2/2/2001.

16. Ramcharitmanas (2.204).

References

Gross, Robert, L. 1992. *The Sadhus of India*. New Delhi: Rawat Publications.

Pinch, William, R. 1996. *Peasants and Monks in British India*. Berkeley: University of California Press.

van der Veer, Peter. 1988. *Gods on Earth: The Management of Religious Experience and Identity in a North Indian Pilgrimage Centre*. London: Athlone Press.

11

Negotiating Karma, Merit, and Liberation: Vow-taking in the Jain Tradition

M. Whitney Kelting

Lay Jains negotiate the terrain between the path of karma reduction leading to liberation and the acquisition of merit that fosters familial well-being. The nature of Jain vows balances on the fulcrum between vow-taking as a step on the way to karma reduction and ultimately spiritual liberation, and vow-taking as a key element in familial well-being; this can be seen as a negotiation between mendicant liberation ideologies and vow-taking as a part of a valid path of lay religiosity. This discussion will examine a very popular fast, the Ayambil Oli fast, which is widely undertaken for the well-being of the family and the Updhan during which the participants adopt a lifestyle similar to that of the mendicants both to decrease karma and to explicitly indicate their increased involvement in orthodox Jainism.[1] The divide between the goals of liberation and well-being in Jain traditions is challenged in Cort's work (2001); here, the intermingling of these two goals is clearly demonstrated by the crossover in the explanations of why one should undertake these vows and both the stated and apparent results of these vows.

Simply put, vows are an agreement to do or not do something, in the context of a connection (even if one-sided) between a particular individual and

---

This chapter is based in part on research conducted with the generous support of the American Institute of Indian Studies and St. Lawrence University. I want to thank Bill Harman and Selva Raj for including me in this volume and John Cort and Steve Runge for reading this in earlier forms and giving me helpful suggestions.

some being (deity, saint, teacher, relative) who has authority over that individual to approve or disapprove of his or her actions, with the expectation of a particular possible result. For Jains there are a number of acts that fall under the rubric of vow-taking. Jains use many terms to name the phenomenon of vows, most commonly *vrat*—or in Sanskrit and Prakrit, *vrata*—(observance) and *tap* (austerity). Generally *vrata* are vows clearly intended to lead toward liberation and are based in mendicant praxis, and *tap* are complex temporary fasting vows. These vows include the vows taken as a basic statement of Jain identity, the vows undertaken by mendicants, special lay vows taken in parallel with mendicants, lifelong modifications of lay vows, particular vows associated with fasts, and a variety of other austerities. The vows, which are undertaken by mendicants and by lay people in imitation of mendicants, are all understood to be liberation-directed vows—vows with the stated goal of liberation. Jain vows are significant as markers of one's level of dedication to Jain ethics and as an indication of the general support of Jain practice by one's family. It is understood that all Jains will at some time or another participate in vow-taking though for most Jains this means taking short and relatively easy fasting vows. The kinds of vows discussed later in this chapter are understood to mark substantial religious dedication and single out the vow-takers as particularly pious Jains. These vows are also more theologically complex as they work simultaneously to reduce karma and to increase merit.

Jainism in Brief

A quick introduction to Jainism will set my discussion in its context. My research is conducted primarily with Gujarati- and Marwari-speaking Shvetambar Murtipujak Jains in Pune District, Maharashtra. Jains are a minority religious community clustered primarily in western India with a smaller cluster in south India.[2] There are two distinct mendicant lineages (and lay devotees who are associated with them) in Jainism, the Shvetambar (lit., "white clad") identified with southern Rajasthan, Gujarat, and the Bombay area of Maharashtra and the Digambar ("sky-clad"), clustered primarily in Rajasthan, southern Maharashtra and Karnataka. Scholars date the religious movements that are collectively called Jainism from the life of Mahavir, who was teaching in approximately the sixth century BCE. Jains see Mahavir as the most recent of twenty-four enlightened teachers (hereafter, Jinas) who have come to revitalize the Jain faith in this era.[3] Jains describe themselves as a four-fold community of monks, nuns, laymen, and laywomen. The mendicants (monks and nuns) follow a strict regimen of asceticism modeled (more or less) on the accounts of the lives of the Jinas and the instructions for mendicants attributed to Mahavir with the goal of attaining total spiritual release from worldly bonds.

Jain worship includes much that is shared with other South Asian traditions: temple worship, domestic worship and rites, guru veneration, annual and monthly festivals linked to a lunar calendar, pilgrimages, and vow-taking. Jains also share in the pan-Indic concepts of karma and the transmigration of souls, but understand the workings of karma in a unique way. Jain karma is a material substance that binds to the soul when the soul is made sticky with passion or other strong emotions or attachments. This matter prevents the soul from rising to the top of the universe from which it cannot return. Much of the Jain textual tradition is concerned with the workings of karma and the ways to avoid the accrual of karma and to destroy karma that has already bound with one's soul. Contemporary Jains speak of karma in the language of the path of spiritual liberation particularly when explaining the workings of liberation itself. In most discussions with contemporary lay Jains, it was more a question of good karma or merit and bad karma or sin. In the present era of spiritual decline in which Jains believe liberation is not possible, Jains work toward maximizing their merit while decreasing their sin, in hopes of both gaining a good rebirth to enjoy and facilitating the gradual progression of one's soul toward liberation.

The Theologies of Jain Vow-taking

The Jain tradition presents a challenge to the theistic model of vow-taking that most South Asian traditions share. Perhaps the most striking difference between Jainism and the other vow-taking traditions discussed in this volume is the nature of divine beings. Jains worship twenty-four Jinas (lit., "victors") who were perfect humans victorious over their senses and also over the accumulations of karma that bind the soul to rebirth. The Jinas are principally the fully liberated, passionless souls of teachers. Because they are fully liberated souls, there is no possibility for interaction between the Jina and the earth-bound human. Thus the Jina cannot respond to prayers, vows, deals, or threats. Jains must interact with the Jina with the understanding that the Jina is a nontransactional being (Babb 1996). Because Jinas are nontransactional, Jains understand the workings of worship differently; they do not see prayer as a dialogue with Jinas—it is rather directed at the nonresponsive Jinas, and, most obviously different, they do not receive blessings from the Jinas like those so significant to much of Hindu worship.

In fact, the kind of cajoling, praising, and pleading that many of the chapters in this volume speak of are not merely useless, they are in fact sin, for they ask the Jina to diminish the very state of accomplishment that makes the Jina praiseworthy (his state of passionless liberation). This is not to say that Jains do not pray or sing praises to the Jinas (in fact, this is the bulk of the religious practice of most Jains) but rather to note that there is a distinction within the Jain tradition between prayer and praises asking for nothing particular in return, and worldly requests (appropriate for beings other than Jinas) that demand some kind of response. Some of the devotional sentiments found in songs and prayer do present a challenge to nontransactionality, but it is important to note a distinct division in Jainism between the sentiments and wishes expressed in songs (often about the difficulties and frustrations of the demanding lay path) and the intentions and expected results of vows. When we look at the workings of Jain vows, we see no vows taken with the intention of directly affecting a Jina or gaining the Jina's attention. These vows work on the level of karma reduction, the power of *yantras*, and sometimes the grace of unenlightened beings.

While a Jain cannot negotiate with a Jina, there are others with whom it is both acceptable and efficacious to do so. In order to be available for this kind of negotiation the vow receiver must not be a liberated soul such as a Jina, for a liberated soul cannot involve itself in the mundane world. There are three categories of beings who do work in the mundane world: Hindu deities, the magical monks, and the guardian deities. Jains do worship deities who are not specifically Jain (or arguably who are Hindu) but not usually in public Jain events. In many ways these three groups of beings are asked to grant the same kinds of rewards: familial well-being, prosperity, and protection. In their most simple form (in the sense that it produces no theological innovation), Jain vows are efficacious in the worldly realm because one's pious actions are pleasing to fellow Jains (including these various deities) who then reward the vow-taker for her piety.[4]

Regardless of the material benefits one expects to garner from the happiness of the powerful guardian deities, Jains also know that these vows are at the same time working to their benefit on the level of karma. In Jain liberation-directed understandings of the working of karma, the strategy to reach liberation as one's goal—perhaps simplistically put here—is to get rid of all (both good and bad) karma so that the unencumbered soul can rise to the region of liberated souls. Thus, one of the most significant aspects of vow-taking in the Jain context is the construction of asceticism as "not doing" some proscribed act rather than "doing" ascetic acts. The most common acts to "not do" are eating, talking, or moving. Central to many Jain vows taken to decrease karma are fasts, vows of silence for set periods of time, and periods of inactivity or stillness. As opposed to temple worship and many Jain devotional acts that gain a Jain merit (good karma, if you will), the focus of most vows is to "not do" in an effort to stop the influx of karma of any kind. Cort (2002) clearly argues for a strong relationship between asceticism and devotion in the Jain tradition and both of the vows I will discuss later in the piece involve both ascetic and devotional practices. This interlocking pattern is central to the ways that Jains participate in vow-taking.

Liberation-directed Vows

The normative manuals written by monks for lay praxis develop a liberation-directed model for the layman in parallel to the mendicant. They present a structured model of lay development based on a movement through a series of vows or stages of increasing difficulty and withdrawal.[5] The later stages are extensions of the vow-taking culminating in a withdrawal from householder life that can be seen in direct parallel to the ashrama system found in classical Hinduism. The vow to end one's life in fasting meditation is seen as a culmination of this form of Jain praxis. While this model is often presented as the "true path" of lay devotion (Jaini 1979, Williams 1963) and is an important source for understanding some of the contemporary lay vow-taking practices, it cannot be accepted as the sole way that Jains understand vow-taking. Lay vow-taking differs from the mendicant-based model in three important ways: 1) lay Jains rarely formally take even the most basic of the liberation-directed lifelong vows that parallel those of mendicants, 2) when they do take them, lay Jains do not see their acceptance of vows as training for mendicancy as suggested in Jaini (1979), and 3) vow-taking is often a symbol of increased involvement in the Jain community rather than a withdrawal from it.

While lay Jains do accept restrictions that are included in these vows, the way they speak of them is not identical to the model constructed by the mendicants as in the description given above. These restrictions come into Jain lay praxis in less systematic ways. For example, virtually all Jains abstain from eating meat and most from drinking alcohol, but this is usually done as a matter of Jain identity and the adoption of values assumed in the community and not as a formal vow taken in front of a mendicant. Since most vow-takers are women, the effects of a vow can be extended to all areas of the woman's purview; for example, if one member of a family has taken certain formal vows that restrict certain foods, the rest of the family may find that all food in the house is restricted accordingly, so that one meal will suffice for all. This is most common with food restrictions like those against store-bought food or the observation of the ban on greens on certain days of the month where these foods are simply not served at the meals provided. These more pious Jains may take some liberation-directed lifelong vows; more likely, they will participate in temporary vows.

Intention and Karma Reduction

Jains perform a formal statement that binds them to the vow (*pacckkhan*). This is similar to the *sankalp* found in Hindu vow-taking. The oral statement and witnessing of the vow is seen to make the vow efficacious; the omission of this statement makes the vow null and void. These formal statements of intention and their binding nature are key to the effectiveness of the vow in one's striving to decrease karma. All Jain vows must be taken publicly and receiving the vow statement from a senior woman in the family, as most vow-takers do, serves as a way to monitor a person's fasting to make sure he or she is healthy enough to perform the fast, to ensure that there are enough women in the house to perform the household duties, and to check against someone using fasting as a kind of coercion. A Jain vow once taken cannot be broken. If one wishes to undertake a vow to perform a multiple day fast, the vow-taker takes a vow to fast on each day individually. Though a faster may state her intention to her family to do a multiple day fast, the vow formula itself is stated on a day-to-day basis and thus if the vow-taker is too weak to complete the multiple day fast the fast can be broken without breaching a vow.

The Jain tradition also enjoins Jains to perform a ritual confession that works to acknowledge and expiate sins accumulated in a period of time (day, fortnight, year) and therefore reduces karma directly. This confession is part of all lay Jain vow-taking and is a twice-daily practice of all Jain mendicants. Both formal statements of the taking of a vow and the confession are parts of mendicant practice that are enjoined upon pious Jains who wish to reduce their karma and strive toward the goal of spiritual liberation. Lay Jains will perform these two rites at least once a year along with the whole Jain community at the annual festival of Paryusan.

Many popular Jain vows are actually a series of vows taken together in a particular pattern. These vows are usually called *tap,* which means "austerities" but is usually translated in the Jain context as "fasting." *Taps* usually include a complex balance of vows restricting food and vows to perform other ascetic practices such as observing silence or inactivity and certain rituals like meditations, confessions, and other forms of worship particular to the vow being performed. I will now compare the ways that Jains understand the balance of the goals of liberation and well-being in two vow complexes: the Ayambil fasts and the Updhan.

The Ayambil Fasts

Within the Ayambil fast complex, there are three related fasts—a single ayambil fast, the Ayambil Oli, and the Navpad Oli—which differ primarily in terms of the length. Each suggests varying degrees of commitment but all are understood to aim toward the shared goal of familial well-being. An ayambil fast is a one-sitting fast involving the eating of only tasteless foods. The fact of the bad taste, of course, makes the austerity of an ayambil fast substantially greater than a one-sitting fast of regular food. Ayambil fasts are predominantly performed during the twice-annual, nine-day Oli festival, but are also performed on those days where fasting is enjoined upon Jains. Many mendicants take nearly constant

Ayambil vows (Cort 2001), and lay Jains will sometimes take an Ayambil vow in order to ensure that mendicants can come to receive alms at their house (Cort 2001, Kelting 2001, Laidlaw 1995).

The fasts in the ayambil complex are linked to the narrative of Shripal and Maynasundari and to the worship of the *siddhacakra yantra*—a symbolic representation of all those things worthy of worship in the Jain tradition and associated with the powerful Navkar Mantra.[6] This fasting is accompanied by a structured series of additional devotional and ascetic practices including twice-daily confession, extensive temple worship especially focused on the *siddhacakra yantra,* Navkar Mantra recitation, and study of the Shripal and Maynasundari narrative. The participants gather for the better part of the afternoon to eat their single meal, to study the story of Shripal and Maynasundari, and to perform the evening confession as a group. These practices both give women time to spend with other women and provide a break from the heavy demands of housework and cooking. Likewise, women repeatedly spoke of the pleasures of doing communal practices because one has a chance to meet with other women in the congregation. This sociability contrasts with the ascetic nature of these practices and, in this case, the tasteless food.

The study of the story of Shripal and Maynasundari serves to show how vows work on the level of karma while providing a way to understand this fast as one useful for promoting the well-being of one's husband and family. One can compare this with the recitation of fasting narratives that often accompany Hindu women's fasts (McGee 1987, Pearson 1996, Wadley 1975). The story of Shripal and Maynasundari serves as a fasting narrative for the Ayambil Oli fast both by giving instructions for how to perform the fast and its attendant worship and by providing a rationale for performing it. In addition, the narrative illuminates a path for women who wish to glorify the Jain religion. A look at the fasting narrative provides a structure for understanding the vow as performed. Briefly, the story of Shripal and Maynasundari begins with prince Shripal and his mother's exile among a leper colony from whom Shripal contracts leprosy. Meanwhile back in another palace, the princess Maynasundari has reached the age of marriage and the king, her father, asks her to choose a husband. She refuses, saying that choosing her husband would be willed by karma and only her faith in Jainism can provide her a good husband; her father is furious and soon after arranges her marriage (as punishment) to the leper Shripal. After this, people in the kingdom begin to see Jainism as a misguided religion. Greatly concerned, Maynasundari asks the goddess Cakkeshvari for advice on how to prove Jainism's superiority to the kingdom and is told she would meet a mendicant who would show her. Maynasundari then meets the Jain mendicant, Manicandra, who taught her how to worship the *siddhacakra*. She and Shripal perform this worship and he is cured of leprosy and the townspeople are suitably impressed. The story continues with the exploits of Shripal, how his continued worship of the *siddhacakra* brings him great protection and prosperity, and how the couple happily lived as husband and wife in eight more lives before they both achieved liberation.

Because of the fast, the confessions, and the magical *yantra* worship, these vows are understood simultaneously to be efficacious in reducing karmic influx (and destroying existing karma) for the performer and as powerful forces in assisting in the protection of the health of one's family, especially one's husband through a transfer of merit or through magical agency. With this narrative and the worship of the *siddhacakra* at the center of the Ayambil Oli festival, it is no surprise that these fasts are seen as important ways of protecting one's husband and one's marital happiness. Generally, this fast is seen as a married woman's fast. While there are men who performed occasional, single-day ayambil fasts they virtually always do so at the behest of their wives almost as if in imitation of Shripal's performance of *siddhacakra* worship after Maynasundari convinces him. While women are performing the ayambil fast they are hesitant to answer whether their own participation in the fast could be efficacious on the front of familial well-being; instead present participants spoke of the good effect of karma reduction from the fast and its attendant confessions. However, on many other occasions women are quick to say that the ayambil fast is very helpful in promoting the well-being of one's husband and family, usually citing the story of Shripal and Maynasundari as evidence of its effectiveness. The reluctance to attribute particular results to a fast points at the ambivalence Jains show when discussing the results of vow-taking.[7] To directly state that one is performing a vow for a worldly result—even if that result is linked to karma reduction too—seems to indicate what is for Jains a sinful demand for blessings or, more complexly, an uneasy connection to magical *mantra-yantra* worship.

The efficacy of the various Ayambil fasts in worldly matters may arise out of the *siddhacakra* worship as presented in the narrative and out of the other rituals associated with the fast. It is paramount to recall that the *siddhacakra* is the representation of a powerful *mantra* (Dundas 1998) and serves as a Jain *yantra* as well. The *siddhacakra* and the Navkar Mantra, which it represents, are believed to have magical powers, which can be garnered by a Jain through recitation and contact with the *siddhacakra yantra* through worship. The *mantra* is said to be able to protect one from harm, to counteract the negative effects of contact with inauspiciousness, and to stand in for all other ritual utterances. Jains often bless themselves with the bathing water from daily or special worship. Laidlaw found that Jains regularly told him that this water was blessed not by the Jina (who is clearly nontransactional) but by the fact that the water flowed over the *siddhacakra yantra* (Laidlaw 1995). In this way we can see connections between the tantric powers of *mantra* and *yantra,* as they have been expressed in a Jain context, and the worldly efficacy of a Jain fast.

On the other hand, the Ayambil fasts all include the performance of the vow statement and confession—two rites that insure that the fast serves to reduce existing karma. In addition, any reduction in food or in the enjoyment of food is very effective in karma reduction. Thus, the vows to perform the Ayambil fast function on two levels: 1) a magical level where interaction with powerful *mantras* and *yantras* have positive results in the material world, and 2) a karmic level where the decrease in food accompanied by the rites of expiation and confession lead to an overall decrease of karma. When the fasting narrative, the descriptions of the fast by Jains outside the context of the fast itself, and the personal accounts of the fast during and after one's performance are combined, these two ways of benefiting from the ayambil fast were seen to work simultaneously. The workings of merit and karma reduction are more complicated with the Updhan Fast because this vow is definitively liberation-directed in its praxis.

The Updhan Tap

As opposed to fasts undertaken for well-being, the Updhan Fast is rhetorically constructed for goals that fit under the umbrella of the path of liberation. The Updhan Fast is a very complex vow that has recently gained new popularity with lay Jains (Cort 2001).[8] In this vow, the layperson lives like a mendicant for a period of time (often forty-seven days for the first vow, though subsequent Updhan vows are shorter). During this vow the layperson is enjoined to perform the same daily rites (meditation, confession, guru worship, etc.) and general practices (no contact with members of the opposite sex, no nonreligious activities) that mark the mendicant's life, excepting those that arise out of ordination rites and vows (giving blessings and sermons). In addition to the daily rites of mendicants, the Updhan vow-takers observe further restrictions (like the restriction against foods that make sounds), perform additional fasts, and study specific texts, particularly sections of the confession texts.

There is a major four-day program to celebrate the completion of the vow. The most significant moment of the fasters' celebration is when the women are garlanded with the garland of liberation. This blessing signifies a kind of mini-ordination and a person can only wear the garland of liberation one time in her life. This garlanding was followed by relatives of the vow-taker feeding her and giving her presents. After the Updhan is complete, the faster is now permitted to recite certain prayers that form part of the ritual confession that only mendicants and those who have completed an Updhan may recite. After the vow is complete each participant agrees to a number of austerities in order to expiate errors committed during the vow and before taking it. In addition to these austerities, many Updhan participants take lifelong vows at the end of the Updhan; the women I spoke with had all vowed to perform the evening confession daily, to eliminate certain foods (mostly store-bought foods) from their diet, and to fast on the anniversary of their Updhan's completion.

Laidlaw (1995) states that the Updhan is specifically not related to ordination and, in the sense of a permanent vow of renunciation, I agree. That being said, women did speak of this as a cutting of ties to worldly activities and compared it to the ordination of mendicants. Divyaprabhashriji, the nun who guided the women at the 1999–2000 Updhan near Pune, spoke to me explicitly about the connection between the Updhan and ordination explaining that it serves as "practice" for those who might consider ordination. While the idea of the Updhan as practice for ordination was not the way laywomen spoke to me of this Updhan, they did see it as being like a mini-ordination that increased their commitment to liberation-directed praxis while permitting them to remain laywomen. The ability of these women to perform these special prayers serves as a public statement of the woman's religious status. In a sense, those who complete the Updhan serve as surrogate mendicants at events where mendicants are not present. It was clear that as a form of karma reduction the Updhan Fast would unquestionably be effective. To live like a mendicant is to live the life best suited for karma reduction and for orienting oneself toward the goal of liberation. The fasting, meditations, and confessions are key to the overall pattern of mendicant life. The kinds of study and text recitations learned during the Updhan serve to move the vow-takers into a position of greater commitment to Jain praxis and point to them as particularly pious laity.

Laidlaw writes that, for the most part, the Updhan Fast was undertaken by middle-aged or older lay Jains as a rite of passage he likens to "training for retirement" (1995: 174–79). These older Jains have fewer obligations in the home or business. Both Laidlaw (1995) and Cort (2001) observe that this vow is taken primarily by women and give time restraints as a reason why more men cannot perform it. Older women with daughters-in-law available to do the housework might be able both to take the six weeks away from home and to perform the time-consuming daily rituals, which they would be expected to undertake after completing the vow. One young unmarried woman, Dipa, wished to perform this vow before she was married, because she knew that after marriage she would not have the time (at least for a decade or so) to perform complex vows that interfered with her workload in the house. In essence, she participated in the language of retirement here but, perhaps a bit impatiently, wanted the benefits of increased religious involvement now. However, half of the forty-four participants in the Updhan Fast in Pune were unmarried young women and she alone spoke about lack of access to time for religion after marriage, suggesting a new way of seeing the role of the Updhan Fast.

Dipa had reached marriageable age and, as was true for most of the young women who participated with her in the Updhan, nervously awaited her parents' search for a groom. The Updhan Fast gave them all an opportunity to spend time with a group of other unmarried young women faced with the same concerns. Dipa undertook the vow with two very close friends. These young women (and others she met at the Updhan) dominated her social life during and after the Updhan; in a time when her movements were circumscribed by family and religion, her relationships with the other young women who performed the Updhan and her visits with the mendicants following the Updhan were encouraged by her parents. Thus she could have a busy social life without a chaperone from her family. When a Jain completes a fast it is customary to have a celebration during which guests are asked to feed the faster and after which each guest gives the faster some kind of gift commensurate with the perceived difficulty of the fast. Those who completed the Updhan Fast were given substantial gifts of expensive and ornate saris and gold jewelry from family members; the grandest gifts were given to the unmarried women, and I suspect they will contribute substantially to their dowries or at least provide the young women with the tools for dressing to impress potential grooms and their families. In this way an unmarried woman—by completing difficult vows and receiving large gifts—can lessen the financial burden (real or imagined) of her upcoming wedding by "earning" some of her dowry.

This fast accomplishes, in addition to karma reduction, three things simultaneously: 1) the participant demonstrates her religiosity in front a large group of Jain women; 2) the participant and her family demonstrate their overall moral virtue (and the support of that virtue by giving them leave from work); and 3) they display publicly the overall familial prosperity that allows women in a family to perform a public vow that is demonstrated by the grandeur of the fast-breaking celebrations and gifts. In a sense, this is a perfectly respectable way to display a potential bride to a wide community while also proving that she comes from a prosperous, religious, joint-family (all desirable qualities in potential brides).[9] Certainly in this case, the connections made during the Updhan were used by the parents to assist in the marriage arrangements of two of the other young women who performed the vow soon after the vow was completed.

An unmarried young woman undertaking this vow, however, does run the risk of looking too religious for her age to some people. Because I was very close to Dipa, several older women asked me if she was thinking of becoming a nun. When I told her grandmother about these questions, she demanded that her granddaughter be seen in secular contexts, and soon the young woman was being brought along to all weddings and other functions where her presence would be acceptable. Clearly religious virtue must be coupled with a sociability deemed appropriate for a woman's age and status if it is to be helpful in finding a groom. Of the twenty-one unmarried young women who performed the Updhan Fast, there was only one who at the close of the Updhan stated her intention of becoming a nun and one other who chose to become a nun in 2003. The other twenty young women clearly intend to marry and most have by now. While accounts of the Updhan Fast speak of it as an older woman's vow, it seems to have taken on a different character in this performance. The nun Divyaprabhashriji had garnered a substantial following among the young women of Pune District (her other events also featured large groups of unmarried young women) and her charisma must have contributed to the ratio of young women to older women at the Updhan. However, I also think that the roles of public rituals in the presentation of young women as marriageable and the concerns of those young women over their upcoming marriages are central to why these young women signed up for this vow. The tensions over the participation of these young women may well represent a shift in lay understandings of this vow. Linking merit exclusively with lay praxis or worldly concerns while seeing liberation-directed religiosity as the exclusive province of mendicants cannot account for the ways in which the Updhan seems to simultaneously function as a mini-ordination while at the same time demonstrating the marriageability of the young women who undertake the vow.

Conclusion

All of this vow-taking must function on the level of karma (though we see some efficacy stemming from the *mantra-yantra* complex in the Ayambil fasts) because Jains are clear that Jinas—the focus of much devotional activity—are nontransactional and cannot (and will not) interfere for good or ill in the lives of Jain devotees. The results of fasts are the direct results of the actions of lay Jains distinguishing these vows from the theistic understanding of the results of vow-taking usually found in Hindu contexts. Most of the vows—usually complex fasts—taken by Jains are understood to be effective based in the inevitable workings of karma that result from the particulars of the vow. The intended results of the vows included both karma reduction and familial well-being arising out of merit (as a kind of karma). The ayambil fast complex serves to both decrease karma and produce merit, which leads to familial well-being and illuminates the ways in which lay Jains negotiate the narrow terrain between prayerful request and worldly desires. The Updhan clearly decreases karma through fasting, confession, and other practices associated with living as mendicants—the very kind of lives best suited for karma reduction. At the same time, the Updhan provides a religiously sanctioned way to display one's marriageable daughters. Jain vows in practice exhibit complex negotiations between this-worldly and liberation-directed results of vows and between lay and mendicant priorities while underlining the Jain stress on karma as the key force behind the success of one's vows—rather than the grace or deal-making of deities.

Notes

1. The Updhan is a complex vow in which a lay Jain lives like a Jain mendicant for a month and a half.

2. The 1991 census of India gave the total population of Jains in India as 3,352,706 (0.4% of the total population).

3. Jains understand time as a cycle of ascending and descending periods. Each cycle of time has its own set of twenty-four Jinas.

4. In addition to Jain vows, Jains do occasionally take Hindu vows. These vows are usually taken in crisis: for health, children, or special intercession; and not spoken of in public contexts. These vows are understood to be not Jain and incidental enough to remain outside the scope of this chapter. Most significantly, the presence of these Hindu vows and the possibility of taking them may lead to the development of new Jain vows or new ways of understanding the efficacy of existing Jain vows to—in a sense—cover those issues.

5. In the system of vow-taking expounded by Jain mendicants in their texts advising Jain laity, there is a division into three sets: *anuvrata* (derived from the initial vows taken by mendicants, modified for lay life), *gunavrata* (which produce good qualities in the vow-taker), and *dikshavrata* (the adoption of mendicant-like practices).

6. They are represented in nine positions: *arhat, siddha, acharya, upadhyaya, sadhu, darshana, jnan, caritra,* and *tap.* The first five are the five highest beings, the next three are the three jewels of Jainism: right faith (*samyak-darshana*), right knowledge (*samyak-jnana*), and right behavior (*samyak-caritra*); and finally, right austerity (*samyak-tapas*) (Cort 2001: 162). It is, in essence, a representation of the powerful Navkar Mantra.

7. Cort reports that the ayambil fast was believed to be good for creating equanimity of mind and possibly rebirth in a time and place where liberation is possible (Cort 2001). While Laidlaw found that the fast was said to contribute to well-being and health, he also noticed that those performing the fast were hesitant to claim any result beyond the general reduction of karma and some kind of purification of the soul (Laidlaw 1995).

8. The Updhan is first described in the seventh century Mahanishitha Sutra (III.3.15–III.36.1).

9. A joint-family here indicates that the parents, all or most of their sons (along with their wives and children) and any unmarried daughters are a single economic unit usually living in a single dwelling.

References

Babb, Lawrence A. 1996. *Absent Lord: Ascetic and Worldly Values in a Jain Ritual Culture.* Berkeley: University of California Press.

Cort, John E. 2001. *Jains in the World: Religious Values and Ideology in India.* New York: Oxford University Press.

———. 2002. "Singing the Glory of Asceticism: Devotion of Asceticism in Jainism." *Journal of the American Academy of Religion* 70: 719–42.

Dundas, Paul. 1998. "Becoming Gautama." In *Open Boundaries*, ed. John E. Cort, 31–41. Albany: State University of New York Press.

Jaini, Padmanabh S. 1979. *The Jaina Path of Purification.* Berkeley: University of California Press.

Kelting, M. Whitney. 2001. *Singing to the Jinas: Jain Laywomen, Mandal Singing, and the Negotiations of Jain Devotion.* New York: Oxford University Press.

Laidlaw, James. 1995. *Riches and Renunciation: Religion and Economy among the Jains*. Oxford: Oxford University Press.

McGee, Mary. 1987. "Feasting and Fasting: The Vrata Tradition and Its Significance for Hindu Women." Th.D. dissertation, Harvard Univesity.

Pearson, Anne Mackenzie. 1996. *"Because It Gives Me Peace of Mind": Ritual Fasts in the Lives of Hindu Women*. Albany: State University of New York Press.

Reynell, Josephine. 1985. "Honour, Nurture and Festivity: Aspects of Female Religiosity amongst Jain Women in Jaipur." Ph.D. thesis, Cambridge University.

Wadley, Susan S. 1975. *Shakti: Power in the Conceptual Structure of Karimpur Religion*. Chicago: University of Chicago Studies in Anthropology Series.

Williams, R. 1963. *Jaina Yoga*. London: Oxford University Press.

12

Vows in the Sikh Tradition

Louis E. Fenech and Pashaura Singh

Whoever makes truthfulness his vow (bratu nemu) shall not be afflicted with [the pain of] death.

—Gurn Nanak, *Asa ashtapadian* 1:8

Every man ought to be a man of his word: he should not say one thing while practicing another

—*Zafar-Namah* 55

In these two concise statements attributed to the first and tenth Sikh Gurus and penned some two centuries apart is contained the general Sikh attitude with regard to vows and oaths. On the one hand formal religious vows such as those of fasting, celibacy, or any other form of asceticism are not a part of the Sikh religion. To those who know how to properly read the hymns of Guru Nanak, the founder of the Sikh tradition, such an implication is certainly present in the Gurmukhi passage on the left.[1] The Persian couplet, however, shows on the other hand that both oaths and vows of a general sort are understood by Punjabi Sikhs as profoundly binding, their fulfillment a matter of both collective and individual honor and self respect.[2] Indeed, in the Punjabi language one often speaks of "eating" an oath (*sahum khana* or *qasam khana*), making it literally a part of one's own body so that its violation threatens one's individual and collective life.

The first outlook is best observed in statements to this effect which we discover in the sacred Sikh scripture, the Adi Granth. In the majority of

---

Verse 1:8 from *Asa ashtapadian* is found in the Adi Granth (411). The above excerpt from *Zafar-namah* reads, literally, "He should not have one thing in his belly and another in his mouth." This couplet is found in the Dasam Granth (1391). The test of the *Zafar-namah* appears in Gurmukhi script in *Sri Dasam Granth Sahib ji* (1988: 1389–94).

declarations dealing with formal vows the context clearly suggests the specific vows or *vrats* of Hinduism. Such *vrats* would include fasting or any of the unconditioned vows to perform various Hindu religious ceremonies.[3] A hymn representative of the Sikh approach to these is found in Guru Arjan's famous composition, *Sukhmani Sahib*:

> Muttering prayers, meditation, wisdom, and all forms of attentiveness; the six schools of philosophy and sermons on the scriptures; the practice of yoga and righteous conduct; renouncing all and wandering around in the wilderness; the performance of all sorts of works; donations to charities and offerings of jewels to the sacred fire; cutting oneself limb from limb and casting the pieces into the fire as a sacred offering; keeping fasts and making vows of many kinds (*varata nem karai bahu bhati*)—none of these are (*sic*) equal to the contemplation of Ram's blessed Name, O Nanak, even when the Gurmukh recites the Nam just once.[4]

In the pursuit of that knowledge that engenders liberation the Sikh Gurus assign to these *vrats* the same place that is allotted to all external elements of religiosity in their teachings. These outer shows of piety are impediments on the path rather than aids and reliance upon them ensures that one remain fettered to the transmigratory wheel. There are vows, however, which do not discourage one's gradual progress along the spiritual path. Guru Nanak in his own characteristic manner elaborates upon these:

> Those who have truth as their vow of fasting (*vratu*), contentment as their pilgrimage place, spiritual wisdom and meditation as their purifying bath, [those who have] kindness as their deity, and forgiveness as their prayer beads—they are the best people. Those who take the [Sikh] way of living as their loincloth, and intuitive awareness as their purified enclosure, those who mark their foreheads with good deeds, and make the love [of God and others] their food—these people, O Nanak, are very rare indeed.[5]

True piety, in other words, is not to be found in outward shows of religiosity but rather in the inner disciplines of truthfulness, contentment, and love. Only those unpretentious vows that aid in the pursuit of these noble goals may be deemed "true" vows. It is these that, the Sikh Gurus maintain, should be observed.

Notwithstanding the Sikh attitude toward formal religious vows, therefore, we find that there are no derisive statements in the Adi Granth in regard to the general taking of vows and oaths. Indeed, the fulfillment of these it seems is very much enjoined. Such may be inferred, for example, in a hymn by the third

Sikh Master, Guru Amar Das, which immediately follows the hymn above by Guru Nanak in the Adi Granth:

> On the ninth day [of the month] take a vow to speak the truth and so shall you do away with lust, anger, and desire.[6]

It is perhaps from such statements that the attitude demonstrated in the Persian quotation in our opening epigraph derives. According to Sikh tradition, this couplet appears in the scalding admonition to the Mughal emperor Aurangzeb that is found in the *Zafar-namah*, the "Epistle of Victory," a text that, according to Sikh tradition, was prepared by the tenth Sikh Guru, Guru Gobind Singh.

It has long been maintained that during the infamous battle of Anandpur between Mughal and Sikh forces in December 1704 the Muslim emperor had assured Guru Gobind Singh by an oath sworn over the Qur'an that he and his followers would be allowed to safely evacuate the fort of Anandpur to which the emperor's forces along with those of the Hindu hill rajas were laying siege. Neither did Aurangzeb nor the combined forces of the Mughals and Hindu hill chieftains prove true to their word, however, and almost immediately after the fort had been relinquished, the Guru's followers, including his mother and four young children, were quickly followed and dispatched. Managing to flee across the Sirsa River and through the forests of Machhivara, the Guru was told of the emperor's treachery. Rather than fall into a pit of despair at the loss of his family and friends, however, the tenth Guru wrote to the emperor chastising the latter's lack of faith and underscoring the importance of standing true to vows and promises, of honoring pledges and oaths.[7]

Indeed, the entire *Zafar-namah* may be read as advocating such high moral principles. Those who stand by and fulfill these, the Guru declares, even if they have to suffer for such adherence, are the favored of God and shall thus secure divine protection.

> Every person who trusts in both an oath spoken over the Qur'an and upon God as his guide along the path to salvation will be taken along that path by the Lord.
>
> As a result [of such trust] not a single hair on my head was touched, nor was my body molested in any way. For *Khuda*, the destroyer of the unrighteous, pulled me out to safety.[8]

Those who prove deceitful and ignore such vows are men whom the Guru refers to as *paima-shikan*, "oath-breakers," and *iman-fikan* or "those who throw away their faith in God."[9] For the Muslim emperor himself Guru Gobind Singh marshals language of the most unflattering sort implying the depths to which those who break their vows will plummet.

[As a result of your treachery] you are no longer faithful nor do you seek refuge in religion. You have no knowledge of either the Master [of us all] nor of [the Prophet] Muhammad.[10]

A more severe condemnation in the context of the *Zafar-namah* would be difficult to imagine.

Here then we have the context in which our epigraph should be read. Yet despite the fact that vows—although significant from a general point of view—are not a formal part of the Sikh tradition, there are certainly vows that Sikhs are implied to take and observe. These we may extract from both sacred and secular Sikh literature. In the understanding of who is a Sikh, for example, there are certain ethical and ritual observances that are enjoined upon the individual by the Sikh Panth (literally "path" but here understood as community) that he or she accepts. These rites are noted in the Adi Granth and, as well, in the *vars* or odes of its amanuensis, the celebrated Bhai Gurdas Bhalla (d. circa 1637), a relation of Guru Amar Das. These included rising during the last watch of the night (*amrit-vela*) to bathe and recite various compositions of the Sikh Gurus, contemplating the Divine Name (*nam*), visiting the dharamsala for congregational singing (*kirtan*), and charity.[11] Often these early requirements were referred to collectively as *nam dan ishnan*, an easily remembered formula that dates back to the time of Guru Nanak and that finds ample expression in the earliest hagiographies of the Guru.[12]

Details of these nascent Sikh rituals are sketchy at best, but it is safe to assume that certain vows were taken by initiates. The twenty-third *pauri* of Bhai Gurdas's first *var* implies that vows would certainly accompany the footwash ritual (*charan-amrit*) by which disciples were initiated into the early Sikh or Nanak Panth.

> Having a prepared *charan-amrit* [to drink] by washing the Guru's foot in water according to the ritual serve the water to Sikhs.[13]

Implicitly therefore vows abound in Sikhism, especially Khalsa Sikhism, and as one may infer it is to a large extent the taking of such vows and the dedication to their observance and fulfillment that today aids in that all-important quest for a separate Sikh identity. This differentiates Sikhs generally and Khalsa Sikhs in particular from both the Hindu and Muslim cultures of northern India respectively.

Within the Sikh tradition vows tend to be more corporate and not personal (there is an exception to this rule). In a community such as the Sikh Panth, which has been particularly cognizant of its minority status in India since the late nineteenth century, a great deal of effort has been spent in the attempt to distinguish itself from the majority communities of the subcontinent, especially the Hindu community. This in turn has tacitly encouraged a vibrant Sikh religious nationalism.[14] The implicit vows in the Sikh tradition to which we shall become privy therefore function in the way that rituals do cross-culturally in that these, also, are the means by which groups send collective messages to themselves, confirming their social substance and endorsing their world view, delineating their group consciousness. The taking of such vows in other words is what makes one a Khalsa Sikh. This is, it seems, a far cry from the attitude of Guru Nanak in regard to formal vow-taking yet an inevitable step toward greater cohesion and Sikh self-definition.[15]

In the attempt to distinguish Khalsa Sikhs from all others there was and perhaps is nothing in Sikh literature as significant as the Khalsa Code of Conduct, the Rahit. Today the Rahit has been formalized in a document known generally as the *Sikh Rahit Maryada,* a text profoundly influenced by the modern ideas and attitudes of the nineteenth-century Singh Sabha reform movement.[16] In this code the implicit taking of vows is recognized on virtually every page. The opening statement, for example, in its definition of "Sikh" implies that those who consider themselves Sikh will vow to uphold these specifications:

> That woman or man is a Sikh who believes in one Akal Purakh, the ten [Sikh] Gurus (Guru Nanak Dev ji to Guru Gobind Singh Sahib [only]), the [guruship of] the Guru Granth Sahib, the sacred utterings and teachings of the ten Sikh Gurus, and the amrit ceremony [inaugurated] by the tenth Lord. [Those so believing must also] accept no other religion.[17]

We also see the acceptance of vows in particular during both the Anand marriage ceremony (*anand karaj*) and the initiation ritual into Khalsa Sikhism, namely *khande di pahul* or the Ceremony of the Double-edged Sword. Seated in front of five Amritdhari Khalsa Sikhs in full Singh regalia, the Sikhs desirous of initiation are instructed on the principles of Khalsa Sikhism by one of the Cherished Five (*panj piare*):

> The Sikh religion renounces the worship of any created thing and advocates the loving devotion and worship of the one creator. The principal means to achieve the perfection of this devotion is reflection on the sacred utterances of the Gurus contained within Sikh scripture [and putting these tenets into practice by] selflessly serving one's own congregation as well as the entire collective Sikh Panth, cultivating benevolence [for the welfare of all humanity], and living one's life according to the Rahit and other Sikh principles (*rahit-bahit*) after having received the nectar of the double-edged sword.[18]

Immediately after this explanation the initiates are then asked, Do you accept these principles gladly?

It is this last passage that certainly implies that Sikhs vow to observe these principles.

Let us look closely at the actual initiation ceremony. When Sikhs are knighted as Khalsa, they take three specific vows at the time of initiation. Much like an oath-taking ceremony, the initiates repeat the Khalsa vows after the Cherished Five a number of times. The Cherished Five conduct the ceremony with the use of the following five substances: 1) a double-edged sword (*khanda*) symbolizing the divine attributes of justice and grace; 2) a steel bowl (*sarab loh da batta*) symbolizing the unbending nature of character and the courage of conviction; 3) water (*jal*) symbolizing purity; 4) sugar crystals (*patashas*) symbolizing the virtues of sweetness and humility; and 5) five liturgical prayers (*panj banis*) symbolizing the transforming power of the divine Word. Thus the Cherished Five prepare the nectar of immortality (*amrit*) by stirring the water with a double-edged sword and reciting five liturgical prayers from memory while sitting in what Sikhs refer to as the heroic posture (*bir asan*), keeping the right knee on the ground and holding the left knee upright.

When the *amrit* is ready, it is given to the novice who drinks it five times so that his body is purified from the influence of five vices (lust, anger, greed, attachment and pride), and five times it is sprinkled on his eyes to transform his outlook toward life. Finally, it is poured five times on his head to sanctify his hair so that he preserves his natural form and listens to the voice of conscience. Throughout this whole procedure the initiated Sikh formally takes the oath each time by repeating the following vow:

vahiguru ji ka khalsa // vahiguru ji ki fateh

The Khalsa belongs to the Wonderful Lord. Victory belongs to the Wonderful Lord.

In fact this first vow has become one of the standard Khalsa Sikh greetings. In Sikh teachings, the goal of human life is to achieve union with Akal Purakh. The main obstacle to this is self-centerdness, *haumai* (lit., "I-me"), the root cause of one's separation from Akal Purakh and fellow human beings. The Khalsa Sikh greeting constantly reminds one to rise above self-centerdness by performing selfless service (*seva*) to others. Even in their hour of triumph, Khalsa Sikhs must remember Akal Purakh instead of exulting in their own courage and valor.

The second Khalsa Sikh vow relates to the "slogan of victory," *jaikara*. It is an integral part of Sikh liturgy and is shouted at the end of congregational prayer in every Sikh ceremony. It is raised as a spirited war-cry:

jo bole so nihal // sat sri akal

Whosoever utters: "Truth is Immortal," shall be blessed with everlasting happiness.

This is an oath to follow the path of Truth. In answering the fundamental question, How is Truth realized? Guru Nanak proclaimed at the beginning of his famous composition *Japji*: Truth is obtained not by intellectual effort or by cunning, but by personal commitment. To know it we must live in it.[19] He says: "Truth is the highest virtue, but higher still is truthful living."[20] Guru Gobind Singh taught the Khalsa to have a firm belief in the ultimate victory of Truth over falsehood. He declared that no sacrifice is too great for the sake of truth. Not surprisingly, when a spirited *jaikara* is raised after much deliberation on any issue within a Sikh congregation, the decision taken at that time becomes binding on the congregation. Actually the second line of the jaikara (*sat sri akal*) is also a common Sikh greeting.

The third Khalsa vow relates to identity and discipline. According to tradition, Guru Gobind Singh ordered the Sikhs to take on external insignia so that they could be easily recognized in a public setting. As part of the Khalsa discipline, all initiated Sikhs must observe the Rahit (Code of Conduct) as enunciated by Guru Gobind Singh and subsequently elaborated. The most significant part of the Rahit is the enjoinder to wear five items of external identity known from their Punjabi names as the Five Ks. These are unshorn hair (*kes*), a wooden comb (*kangha*), a steel wrist-ring (*kara*), and a pair of short breeches (*kacchahira*). In Sikh self-understanding the Five Ks are understood as outer symbols of the divine Word, implying a direct correlation between *bani* (the divine Word) and *bana* (Khalsa dress). Putting on the Five Ks along with the turban (in the case of male Sikhs) while reciting prayers symbolizes that the Khalsa Sikh is dressed in the word of God.[21] Their minds are thus purified and inspired, and their bodies girded to do battle with daily temptations. They are also prohibited from the "four gross transgressions of the Rahit" (*char kurahits*): cutting the hair, using tobacco, committing adultery, and eating meat that has not come from an animal killed with a single blow (*jhataka*).

Along with these injunctions, we also discover ones that outline the specific discipline enjoined upon a newly initiated Khalsa Sikh. Here men and women are instructed that they shall not worship any but the one Akal Purakh nor think of anyone or thing apart from the ten Gurus and Gurbani as providing that knowledge whereby liberation is secured. They are also instructed on both practices and people to avoid lest they be declared apostates (*patit*) or those deserving of some punitive redress (*tankhahie*).[22] Breaking the four cardinal vows results in one's banishment from the Khalsa Panth. Those who do so intentionally may seek to be readmitted into the Khalsa fold but only after undergoing the ceremony of initiation once again. The breaking of the minor vows of observance, however, results in punitive action.[23] Usually the guilty party undertakes to sweep the floor of the *parikarma*, the circumambulatory walkway around the Golden Temple or to clean the shoes of the many pilgrims who daily visit this historic shrine.

The Khalsa intiation ritual thus involves a series of vows. As may be easily inferred these vows are made to both the divine (that is to Akal Purakh or Vahiguru) as well as to the gathered Sikh community, that is represented by the five initiated Khalsa Sikhs or *panj piare*. The two, the eternal Guru and the Panth (particularly the Khalsa Panth), are in effect quite similar in Sikh theology. According to Sikh tradition, prior to his death in 1708 Guru Gobind Singh invested both the Sikh scripture and the gathered Sikh community with guruship. It is for this reason that the scripture is often referred to by devout Sikhs as the Guru (rather than Adi) Granth Sahib or the Granth in whose pages mystically dwells the presence of God, and that the Sikh community itself is understood as the Guru Panth or the Khalsa Sikh community in its capacity as the Guru. The second part of the Guru Granth/Guru Panth doctrine holds that whenever five Khalsa Sikhs are gathered together the eternal Guru is mystically present. It thus identifies the Sikh community itself with the eternal Guru. This doctrine first appears in an early eighteenth-century Sikh work entitled *Gur-Sobha* (Radiance of the Guru):

> On an earlier occasion the Guru had been approached by his Sikhs and had been asked what form the [eternal] Guru would assume [after he had departed this earthly life]. He had replied that it would be the Khalsa. "The Khalsa is now the focus of all my hopes and desires," he declared, "Upon the Khalsa which I have created 1 shall bestow the succession. The Khalsa is my physical form and I am one with the Khalsa. To all eternity I shall be manifest in the Khalsa. They whose hearts are purged of falsehood will be known as the true Khalsa; and the Khalsa, freed from error and illusion, will be my true Guru."[24]

As noted in the introduction to this book, vows are made in a relationship to a transcendent reality. In the Sikh tradition this is very much underscored as Sikhs vow to observe the standards of the Rahit physically before the repository of divinity, namely the Khalsa Panth. In this way vows and oaths taken by Sikhs are a way of thus identifying with the divine and the traditons of the Panth, setting Sikhs apart from all other communities within the subcontinent.

A Sikh wedding, according to the Anand (bliss) rite, also underscores such identification, taking place in the presence of the first repository of divintiy, the Guru Granth Sahib. The performance of the actual marriage requires the couple to circumambulate the sacred scripture four times in order to take four vows. Before the bridegroom and the bride make each round they listen to a verse of Guru Ram Das's *Suhi Chhant* 2 read by a *granthi* or scriptural reader.[25] They then touch their foreheads to the floor in humility before the scripture and walk around it while the same verse is being sung by both professional *ragis* (hymn singers) and the congregation. During their fourfold movement around the scripture they take the following four vows: 1) to lead an action-oriented life (*pravirati karam*) based upon righteousness and never to shun the obligations of family and society; 2) to maintain a bond of reverence (*niramal bhau*) and dignity between one another; 3) to keep the enthusiasm for life alive in the face of adverse circumstances and to remain removed from worldly attachments (*chau bhaia bairagia*); and 4) to cultivate a balanced approach (*sahaj*) in life, avoiding all extremes. The pattern of circumambulation in the Anand marriage ceremony is in fact the reactualization of the primordial movement of life in which there is no beginning and no end. The continuous remembrance of the four marital vows is meant to ensure that the couple's married life is one filled with happiness and joy.

Apart from vows to observe certain beliefs and disciplines there are as well others that the individual Sikh imposes upon himself or herself to develop their spiritual lives or express some gratitude to the eternal Guru for some special mercy. These latter go by many names but are generally referred to as either *mannat* or *sukh* and are characteristically the prerogative of Sikh women. These vows in the form of *mannat manani* or *sukh sukhani* are taken secretly by Sikh women by offering an Ardas at a particular *gurdwara* to seek a boon.[26] For instance, a woman desirous of the birth of a son would normally go to Baba Buddha's Bir *gurdwara* in Amritsar District and offer her prayer secretly.[27] She will fulfill her vow by visiting the same *gurdwara* with gifts after the birth of the son. Further, Sikh women secretly offer prayers for healing from sickness, the welfare of their husbands and children, and other family-related issues and businesses. They normally vow to arrange the continuous recitation (*akhand path*) of the Guru Granth Sahib at home if their desires for particular boons are fulfilled. These are perhaps those "other Sikh principles" to which the aforementioned portion from the *Sikh Rahit Maryada* may allude. Included in these other principles would also be other vows, ones which today play a significant part in the construction of Sikh personhood. These are indeed amongst the most important and best known ones a Sikh takes on initiation into the Khalsa and are intimately related with the fundamental notions of honor and self-respect that have been a part of Punjabi Sikh society since its foundation in the late fifteenth century. These implied vows and their fulfillment are features of Sikh tradition and culture that are set in the Sikh psyche at a very early age, yet do not seem to receive formal treatment. By way of example let us begin with a passage from a contemporary children's primary school reader dealing with the life and sacrifice of the famous eighteenth-century Sikh martyr, Bhai Taru Singh. Having watched a number of brave Singh warriors rescue a Hindu female from the clutches of a group of rapacious Muslim soldiers, Taru Singh makes a decision that will affect the rest of his life:

> ... as the Singhs began to walk away from there Taru Singh made a request: "Please let me, too, join you [all]."
>
> One Singh spoke, ["Travelling the path of a true Singh] is difficult work. You must be willing to sacrifice your life for the sake of righteousness if need be" [literally, "you must place your head on the palm of your hand"].[28]
>
> "This is no problem," [said Taru Singh], "I will endeavour to do so."
>
> Taru Singh began to prepare himself to forever lead the Singh way of life. "I will become a Singh! I will destroy tyranny. I will protect my sisters [from the clutches of all those deemed unrighteous]."[29]

After a day or two Taru Singh and his childhood companions arrive at the secret camp of the Singhs and ask the *jathedar* (leader) to initiate them into the Khalsa through the Amrit ceremony. The jathedar looks them over and then

> The jathedar of the Singhs said, "Young men, becoming a Singh is very hard. You must place your head on the palm of your hand ... you must walk a path thinner than the edge of sword."[30] All [the boys] then replied "We are ready."[31]

There is of course a great deal that is both implied and explicit within these brief passages. The description of the true Singh, for example, follows clearly from what Taru Singh vows to himself. The ability to sacrifice oneself if need be for a righteous (i.e., Panthic) cause. That such straightforward statements are directed toward Sikh children also prepares them for vows that they will later take if they choose to abide by the precepts of the *Sikh Rahit Maryada*.

The general history of Khalsa Sikhism is populated with narratives of Sikhs holding true to the vows made by our young Taru Singh mentioned earlier. During the early twentieth century, for example, such material became grist for the Singh Sabha's mill. One need only read the novels of Vir Singh or the histories of Gian Singh to be made aware of the importance in upholding such oaths. Even death, it is suggested in the work of Gian Singh, should not keep one from fulfilling a vow made with the eternal Guru as one's witness. In the popular legend of Baba Dip Singh, for example, a Singh warrior reminds Dip Singh of his vow to reach the precincts of Harimandir Sahib (the latter-day

Golden Temple) after this exemplary Jat warrior's head has been severed from his body:

> *Wah*, Singh ji! You said that you would become a martyr only after having reached Amritsar. Have you now pitched up your tent right here?[32]

Hearing these words Dip Singh stood up with a supernatural effort and, retrieving his severed head, continued toward the city. The symbolism in this episode is no doubt purposeful. It is in a sense the desire to fulfill his vow that allows Dip Singh to grasp his head, the center of intellect and cognition. It is the desire to fulfill his vow that literally brings Dip Singh back to life.

Such stories seem to have had quite an effect on the general Sikh populace during the famous Gurdwara Reform Movement of 1920 to 1925. The entire movement aimed to place Sikh shrines and *gurdwaras* into the hands of Khalsa Sikh managers rather than their present non-Sikh *mahant* managers. The problem in such an endeavor, however, was that these *mahants* were the legal owners of the *gurdwaras* who relied on the British to support their claims. The struggle therefore pitted Akali Sikhs against both the *mahants* and the British Indian government. This was a *dharam yudh* or righteous battle, however, which was fought while keeping the best Sikh traditions of sacrifice and martyrdom in mind.

Advocating parallels between the effort to reform the *gurdwaras* and the protracted struggles that dominate the well-known eighteenth-century history of the Sikhs, the leaders and publicists of the movement portrayed this contemporary Sikh exertion in a profound rhetoric of martyrdom in which vows and oaths had figured prominently. This emphasis certainly remains as, according to G. S. Talib, perhaps the most prolific promoter of a Sikh tradition of martyrdom stretching back to Guru Nanak. The *sankalpa*, the vow or firm resolve, in this case the vow to achieve martyrdom is "the spiritual preparatory stage towards martyrdom" (Talib 1976: 181). This is, of course, debatable but it does underscore the importance attached to vows and oaths in the context of martyrdom.

The leaders were well aware of such cultural conventions and ensured that prospective Akali Sikhs would not just vow to take back the *gurdwaras* but would in fact take oaths in front of the Akal Takhat, the Throne of the Immortal One itself. An appeal in the newspaper *Punch* two days after the infamous massacre at Nankana Sahib (February 21, 1921) indicates the significance of such vows and oaths:

> Sikh heroes! If this sacrifice affects your hearts, if those martyred in the name of religion enthuse you [to follow their example] then placing your own life on the palm of your hand in the name of faith

take a resolution, make a promise, that Sri Nankana Sahib will [now remain] in the possession of the [Sikh] Panth, and will certainly continue to do so [forever]. Let no Udasi mahant stay in the service of any place of the Guru unless he surrenders the gurdwara to the Panth.[33]

It is very well-known that many Akali Sikhs whose hearts were indeed affected by the many Sikh sacrifices vowed to suffer privation and even death to ensure that the *gurdwaras* were kept out of the hands of the mahants and their British overlords. These vows were fulfilled in some cases unto the death.[34] Apart from these there are two very famous instances of taking such vows literally that we come across in the Sikh literature of this period. In the first example an Akali received a severe rebuke when he looked behind him during the march to Guru ka Bagh in 1922, thus inadvertently breaking his vow to abstain from turning his back on his objective. The second saw an observer witnessing a *jatha* marching through fields deep with water rather than turning around after having missed the side road to the shrine.[35]

Not all Sikhs of course take such vows literally and indeed like all human beings many Sikhs tend to break vows and go back on oaths. But as in many cultures and religious traditions, there are repercussions for such activity. How seriously Sikhs react to these depend upon the individual and the particular *sangat* with which he or she is associated. But it is safe to say that for public figures who are Sikh such actions as not standing true to vows and oaths can have devastating results, making or breaking political careers. The two best-known careers to have suffered such defeats are those of Master Tara Singh and Sant Fateh Singh in the mid 1960s. Both of these men lost their political clout after prematurely ending their "fasts unto the death," thus in effect breaking their vows to do so.[36] These failures were considerably exacerbated when Jathedar Darshan Singh Pheruman decided to show these now-humiliated politicians and all such irresolute Sikhs how true Sikhs behave. In August 1969 Pheruman went on such a fast to secure for the new city of Chandigarh its legitimate status as the sole capital of the Punjab (rather than the joint capital of the Punjab and Haryana). On October 27, 1969 Pheruman held true to his vow, laying down his life for the ultimate objective of a Sikh homeland.

The last two decades of the twentieth century were marked by the period of Sikh militancy. Sant Jarnail Singh Bhindranwale and his close followers had begun to use the Akal Takhat (Throne of the Immortal, the building directly across from the Golden Temple) as a base of operations and vowed to defend it to the last breath if the Indian state, concerned with the indiscriminate killings in the Punjab attributed to Bhindranwale, tried to assault the Golden Temple complex to flush him out. The Indian army eventually attacked in June of 1984 on the orders of Prime Minister Indira Gandhi, who in late October of that year paid for her decision with her own life. In the light of the impact such a desecration of the Golden Temple by the Indian army had on the Sikh psyche both within India and abroad it is no wonder that Sant Jarnail Singh Bhindranwale achieved worldwide attention when he died along with many others during that fateful event. Since that time Bhindranwale has become an object of respect and adulation within the larger segment of the Sikh Panth (even more so than when he was alive), especially for the fulfillment of his vow, though it should also be noted that many Sikhs despised and feared him for his role in the resurgence of militancy in the Punjab. At times scholars fail to understand the phenomenon of Sikh vows, how they operate in the minds and hearts of people. Bhindranwale had always thought of himself as the one who belonged to the glorious tradition of the aforementioned Baba Dip Singh, who had achieved martyrdom in defending the Darbar Sahib (Golden Temple). Undoubtedly, Sant Jarnail Singh Bhindranwale "has carved for himself a martyr's niche in the Panth's tradition and no amount of academic or journalistic reassessment will dislodge him from that place in the popular affections" (McLeod 1989b: 116).

In conclusion, it may be stated that in spite of the indifferent attitude of Guru Nanak and his early successors toward *vrats* related to vows and other outward rituals, vows and oaths have played a significant role in the evolution of the Sikh Panth. As a normative part of the tradition, Khalsa Sikh vows keep on inspiring the Sikhs to maintain their visible identity. These vows are constant reminders to Khalsa Sikhs that they must act and behave according to the standards expected of them in the Rahit. The four marital vows, moreover, encourage Sikhs to lead successful family lives. It is thus no wonder that the Sikh religion is frequently referred to as the religion of the householder. At the popular level, Sikh women also observe secret vows by performing Ardas at particular gurdwaras to achieve particular boons, and they pay their visits to those places with gifts when their desires have been fulfilled. They may also organize the unbroken reading (*akhand path*) of the Adi Granth at home when the objectives of their prayers have been achieved. Moreover, the history of the Sikh community shows that once a Sikh takes an oath by offering an Ardas, he even lays down his life to demonstrate the steadfastness of his resolve. Anyone who shirks from his resolve after the prayer suffers much humiliation within the Panth. On the whole, vows and oaths have their legitimate place within the Sikh tradition.

Notes

1. As we will later see Guru Nanak often contrasts external rituals and observances (fasting, for example) with inner qualities (mercy and compassion, for example) implying the impotence of the former as these are generally understood. See his *Japji* 28, Adi Granth, (6–7).

2. It is well known that the difference between oaths and vows is a significant one. Oaths are taken before authorities and are thus binding while vows are generally personal

and in many cases private, involving complete dedication and promises of future action. In the Sikh tradition, however, this distinction is not particularly important. As we will see the emphasis in the Sikh tradition is on group vows that ultimately become group oaths. For vows generally see Klinger (1987: 301–5).

3. In the language of the Adi Granth the term *vratu* (also *bratu*) can mean vow or fast depending upon the context. The two understandings are of course intimately related as those Hindus who undertake *vrats* are quite meticulous about observing restrictions on certain types of speech, dress, and especially food. This last type of *vrat* is by far the most common. See Jolly (1922: 656–57).

4. Guru Arjan, *Gauri sukhmani ashtapadi* 3:1, Adi Granth, (265). Other examples of the uselessness of such vows are Guru Arjan, *Asa* 2:2:151 and Guru Nanak, *Parabhati bibhas chapade* 4:4, Adi Granth (408, 1328).

5. Guru Nanak, *Sarang ki var* 21:1, Adi Granth, (1245).

6. Guru Amar Das, *Sarang ki var*, 21:2, Adi Granth, (1245).

7. These traditions are recorded in numerous texts. For an example, see Joginder Singh's translation of Ishar Singh Nara, *Safarnama and Zafarnama* (1985: 93–130). The address to Aurangzeb begins with the thirteenth couplet:

I have no faith in the oath for which you requested the one, almighty God to testify.

Zafar-namah 13, Dasam Granth (1389).

8. *Zafar-namah* 43, 44, Dasam Granth, (1389-90).

9. *Zafar-namah* 20, 45, Dasam Granth, (1389, 1390).

10. *Zafar-namah* 46, Dasam Granth, (1390).

11. One amongst many such hymns is Guru Ram Das, *Gauri ki var* 11:2, Adi Granth, (305–6). A number of the *vars* of Bhai Gurdas also mention these observances, for example, *var* 12:2 and 26:4. These are found in V. Singh (1997: 197, 404–5). (Hereafter BG).

12. Guru Nanak, *Siddh Gosht* 36, Adi Granth, (942):

The one who faces the Guru [recites] the Divine Name, [gives] alms to the needy, [and] bathes [in the presence of the divine thus living a life of] purity.

13. BG (18).

14. For Sikh religious nationalism, see Fenech (2002: 827–70).

15. The evolution of Guru Nanak's ideas in terms of furthering cohesive ideals among members of the Sikh Panth is described in W. H. McLeod's now famous article (1976: 37–58).

16. For a vivid history of the Rahit, see W. H. McLeod (2003). The Singh Sabha project is described in Oberoi (1994).

17. *Sikh Rahit Maryada* (1995: 8).

18. Ibid. (24).

19. Guru Nanak, *Japji* 1, Adi Granth (1).

20. Guru Nanak, *Siri rag ashtapadian* 14, Adi Granth (62).

21. Although the Five Ks are also mandatory for Sikh women initiated into the Khalsa they may choose not to wear a turban.

22. *Sikh Rahit Maryada* (1995: 26). These are the four *kurahits* mentioned previously. There are also seven groups of people that Sikhs should vow to avoid, which include the infamous *panj mel*, "five reprobate groups," such as the followers of the recalcitrant sons of the Gurus and those who commit female infanticide.

23. Although the actual terminology adopted here is not as direct as noted earlier, the spirit of the recommendation certainly indicates the breaking of vows: *jis kise sikh pason rahit di koi bhul ho jave tan. . .* "Any Sikh who has committed any default in the observance of the Rahit shall. . ." *Sikh Rahit Maryada* (28).

24. The translation belongs to W. H. McLeod and appears in his *Who Is a Sikh? The Problem of Sikh Identity* (1989a: 52).

25. Guru Ram Das, *Suhi Chhant* 2, Adi Granth (773–74).

26. The Ardas is the Khalsa Sikh prayer that is offered at the end of all Sikh rituals.

27. According to a strong Sikh tradition, Baba Buddha was a pious Sikh who lived through the guruship of the first five Sikh Gurus. When Mata Ganga, the wife of the fifth Guru, Guru Arjan, repeatedly failed to have a child, she sought out Baba Buddha and requested his blessing in the hope that such blessing would allow her to conceive. The women who visit the shrine of Baba Buddha in Amritsar usually do so to take vows here in order to produce male offspring. They are almost always secretive about such vows although it is commonly well-known that any woman who goes out of her way to visit the *gurdwara* will go with this request in mind.

28. The allusion here is to Guru Nanak's hymn *Slok varan te vadhik* 20, Adi Granth (1412).

29. *Pañjabi Path Mala* 5 (1990: 88).

30. This wording suggests that the statement is probably an allusion to Guru Nanak, *Maru Solhe* 8: 10, Adi Granth (1028).

31. *Pañjabi Path Mala* 5 (1990: 90).

32. Gin Singh (1987: 198). For an analysis of the recurring taunt in Sikh martyrologies, see Fenech (1996: 177–92).

33. Noted in Fenech (2000: chapter 7). Some of the appeals directed toward Sikhs in front of the Akal Takhat during the Gurdwara Reform Movement may be found in Ganda Singh (1965).

34. See Fenech (2000).

35. These two incidents may be found in Sahni (143–44).

36. Both Sant Fateh Singh and Master Tara Singh vowed to fast to death or until Jawaharlal Nehru conceded the Sikh demand for a Punjabi Province purely on a linguistic basis. Sant Fateh Singh began his fast in December 1960, and Master Tara Singh began his in August 1961.

References

Fenech, L. E. 2002. "Contested Nationalisms; Negotiated Terrains: The Way Sikhs Remember Udham Singh 'Shahid' (1899–1941)." *Modern Asian Studies* 36, 4: 827–70.

———. 2000. *Martyrdom in the Sikh Tradition: Playing the "Game of Love."* Delhi: Oxford University Press.

———. 1996. "The Taunt in Popular Sikh Martyrologies." In *The Transmission of Sikh Heritage in the Diaspora*. eds. Pashaura Singh and N. G. Barrier. 177–92. Delhi: Manohar.

Jolly, J. 1922. "Vows (Hindu)." In *The Encyclopedia of Religion and Ethics*. eds. James Hastings et al. 656–57. New York: Charles Scribner's Sons.

Klinger, Elmar. 1987. "Vows and Oaths." In *The Encyclopedia of Religion,* ed. Mircea Eliade. 15: 301–5, New York: Macmillan.

McLeod, W. H. 2003. *Sikhs of the Khalsa*. New Delhi: Oxford University Press.

———. 1989a. *Who Is a Sikh? The Problem of Sikh Identity*. Oxford: Clarendon Press.

———. 1989b. *The Sikhs: History, Religion and Society*. New York: Columbia University Press.

———. 1976. "Cohesive Ideals and Institutions in the History of the Sikh Panth." In *The Evolution of the Sikh Community: Five Essays*, W. H. McLeod 37–58. Oxford: Clarendon Press.

Oberoi, Harjot. 1994. *The Construction of Religious Boundaries: Culture, Identity and Diversity in the Sikh Tradition*. Delhi: Oxford University Press.

Pañjabi Path Mala 5. 1990. Jalandhar: Amrdeep Prakashan.

Sahni, Ruchi Ram. n.d. *The Struggle for Reform in Sikh Shrines.* (Amritsar: n.p.)

Sikh Rahit Maryada. 1995. Amritsar: SGPC.

Singh, Ganda, ed. 1965. *Some Confidential Papers of the Akali Movement*. Amritsar: np.

Singh, Gian. 1987. *Tavarikh Guru Khalsa* II. Patiala: Bhasha Vibhag Punjab.

Singh, Joginder. 1985. Translation of Ishar Singh Nara, *Safarnama and Zafarnama* 93–103. New Delhi: Nara Publications.

Singh, Vir, ed. 1997. *Sri Guru Granth Sahib ja da kunja arthat Varan Bhai Gurdas Satik Bhav Prakashani Tika Samet Mukammal* 197, 404–5. Delhi: Bhai Vir Singh Sahit Sadan.

Sri Dasam Granth Sahib ji. 1988. Amritsar: Bhai Chatar Singh Jivan Singh, 1389–94.

Talib, G. S. 1976. "The Concept and Tradition of Martyrdom in Sikhism." In *Guru Tegh Bahadar: Background and Supreme Sacrifice*, ed. G. S. Talib, 179–200. Patiala: Punjabi University.

III

Getting Nothing At All

13

When Vows Fail to Deliver What They Promise: The Case of Shyamavati

TRACY PINTCHMAN

Although the Hindi term *vrat* (Sakt. *vrata*) is often translated into English as "vow," there is much that is lost in translation. Mary McGee describes *vrats* in their contemporary form as acts of self-discipline "dedicated to a particular deity and having a specified, personal desire or outcome in mind" (1987: 33). As a type of religious observance, *vrats* may involve a variety of activities, including fasting or some form of food abstention, ritual worship (*puja*) of a deity or deities, recitation of narratives associated with the observance, the giving of gifts or offerings (*dan*), and so forth (Pearson 1996: 2–3). Here I shall take the English term "vow" to refer to the type of ritual known in north India as *vrat*, and I will use the Hindi term throughout.

Vrats may be observed primarily as a means of expressing religious piety. Generally, however, they presume some kind of positive response from the particular deity to whom they are directed. Austerities normally associated with *vrats* such as fasting, sleeping on the floor, and so forth, function as signals of one's faith and devotion, and the assumption is that "the deity will reward this faith and service with some kind of boon" (Wadley 1983: 149). Stories and popular beliefs about *vrats* clearly link their performance to good outcomes, and in many contexts *vrats* are thought to bring worldly, as well as spiritual, benefits to the person who undertakes them. While *vrat*-related traditions establish such expectations, however, those expectations may not necessarily be met. In contrast with what *vrats* might promise, a person may keep many *vrats* throughout his or her lifetime without obtaining the anticipated boons. He or she might even experience great tragedy.

When practicing Hindus experience suffering that they feel is unjust or for which they do not believe they are responsible, they may invoke a variety of causes for that suffering, including planetary influences, witchcraft and sorcery, or the notion of an unalterable karmic destiny. Individuals are especially likely to invoke this last explanation, that of an unalterable destiny, when they make efforts to avert or to rectify misfortunes without avail, such as when one undertakes *vrats* but does not see the desired outcome (Keyes 1983: 17).[1] Hence, when *vrats* don't deliver what they promise, there are some foreseeable ways that a faithful votary might choose to explain the course of events to themselves or to others.

My interest in what happens when *vrats* fail to deliver what they promise, however, has less to do with how a votary might *explain* that failure than with how that person might seem to *experience* it emotionally in light of expectations established in popular belief and stories about the power of *vrats* to help one achieve desired objectives. Such experience is, of course, difficult to capture; ultimately, it may simply lie beyond the understanding of someone like myself who is not Hindu and not a devout keeper of *vrats*. But I am drawn to say something about this issue by events that occurred while I was conducting research in the city of Benares, north India, in 1995, 1997, and 1998,[2] and the impact of these events on a very religious elderly woman named Shyamavati.[3]

The events I observed suggest that when tragedy strikes a faithful and devoted votary, the disjunction between what is hoped for or anticipated and what actually occurs can cause great spiritual and emotional turmoil for the votary in spite of whatever explanation he or she might offer for the misfortune. In Shyamavati's case, such turmoil seems related to expectations regarding both mutual commitment between deity and devotee and karmic justice that inform *vrat* and other devotional traditions. These expectations are strongly reinforced in both narrative and popular belief, especially with respect to women's observance of *vrats* and can lead to feelings of disorientation and even betrayal when they are dramatically undermined. I would suggest, too, that such feelings might tend to be more pronounced for Hindu women than for Hindu men when *vrats* fail to deliver what they promise, given the gender-specific ways, as discussed below, that women tend to relate to *vrats*.

The Case of Shyamavati

I met Shyamavati in 1995 when I began to study Benarsi women's observances of the *vrat* associated with the month of Kartik, which usually falls in October–November.[4] Kartik is considered a sacred month, and the merits of Kartik are lauded in sections of the Skanda and Padma Puranas that both go by the name Kartik Mahatmya, "Glorification of Kartik."[5] In Benares one or the other version is recited daily during the month in both Sanskrit and Hindi translation in a number of places, including temples and homes throughout the city. Both Kartik Mahatmyas describe Kartik as especially dear to Vishnu and advocate that one honor Vishnu continually during the month. Even in Benares, widely hailed as Shiva's city, Kartik is celebrated as a month-long Vaishnava festival and marks a turn of attention throughout the city toward Vishnu and his worship.

In Benares both men and women observe the Kartik *vrat*, although the majority of Kartik votaries are women. Like other *vrats*, the Kartik *vrat* entails rules regarding abstention from certain foods, but many of the women I spoke with did not observe such rules or observed them only minimally, since they require long-term cooking arrangements that can inconvenience other family members.[6] Instead, the main observance associated with the Kartik *vrat* is daily ritual bathing in a body of water before sunrise throughout the entire month (Kartik *snan*). In Benares the Ganges River is the natural goal for observers of the Kartik *vrat*, for the sacred Ganges flows along the edge of the whole city.

After taking their ritual bath, many female votaries gather together in groups on the *ghats*, the steps and platform areas by the river's edge, to perform a collective *puja* accompanied by songs and devotional stories. Participants construct religious icons out of Ganges mud; forming a circle around the icons, they then perform *puja* to them. In Benares this form of ritual worship is per-

Figure 13.1 The Ganges River flowing at the edge of Benares (photo by William C. French)

formed daily throughout the month and is exclusively for women. Indeed, on several occasions during the three years that I joined participants in performing the *puja*, I watched women engage in gleeful verbal abuse of men who dared stray too close to the edge of the *puja* circle. Many deities are represented and honored, but several informants told me that the *puja* is dedicated largely to Krishna with other deities called to be present chiefly so that they, too, can participate as devotees.

While the Puranas emphasize worship of Vishnu during Kartik, female Kartik votaries in Benares tend to think of the month primarily as a time for worshipping Krishna, Vishnu's playful incarnation. Krishna is said to have spent his youth in Braj, an area of north India just south of Delhi, having assumed mortal form on earth in ancient times. Textual and popular traditions portray him as a frolicking youth who delights in mischief and pranks and is especially troublesome to the cowherdesses, or *gopis*, of the region. They complain endlessly about his antics to Yashoda, Krishna's foster mother, but they also find Krishna to be irresistibly adorable and take great delight in his boyish charm. When he grows into a young man, Krishna becomes a great lover of women, and the *gopis* that he torments in

Figure 13.2 Shyamavati using Ganges mud to make icons for use in Kartik *puja* (photo by Tracy Pintchman)

Figure 13.3 Women gathered in a circle ready to perform Kartik *puja* (photo by Tracy Pintchman)

childhood later fall into Krishna's arms in the isolated bowers of Vrindavan, a forest north of Mathura, eager to enjoy his passionate embrace.

During the daily Kartik *puja*, participating women assume the stance of *gopis* in relation to Krishna, whom they honor in their worship. Krishna is considered to be in child form for the first half of the month, and during this time participating women end the *puja* by singing a lullaby to Krishna and swinging the clay icons in a cotton cloth. On the fifth or eighth day of Kartik's second fortnight, however, a priest is called to the *puja* circle to perform Krishna's *janeu*, the ceremony marking his investiture with the sacred thread, which designates Krishna's transformation from child to young man. For the next several days, participants sing marriage songs in the circle before beginning the *puja* itself, marking an impending marriage, and on the appointed day, the eleventh of Kartik's bright fortnight, they celebrate Krishna's marriage to Tulsi, the Basil plant, who is also considered to be a goddess. The Puranas tend to portray this marriage as occurring between Vishnu and Tulsi, but the women clearly understand the groom to be Krishna.[7]

This daily round of women's Kartik worship includes the recitation of several stories toward the end of the *puja*. Some of these stories focus specifically on the merits obtained by observing the Kartik *vrat* or other *vrats*, but most of them speak of the merits and rewards of devotion in more general terms. Shyamavati, a high-caste, devout Vaishnava, was a long-term, regular Kartik votary and the informal leader and female elder of a *puja* group in which I participated for three cycles of Kartik *puja* from 1995 to 1998. She was also the primary storyteller in the group.

I first interviewed Shyamavati in 1995, when I went to her home to ask her about Kartik and the special women's *puja* associated with the Kartik *vrat*. She was in her late sixties at that time. Shyamavati told me that she had devoutly observed numerous *vrats* since her childhood, although she had begun observing the Kartik *vrat* only about thirty or forty years earlier, after she had married, moved to Benares, and had children. She proudly claimed that she had not missed the Kartik *vrat* for even one of those thirty or forty years. When I asked

Figure 13.4 Kartik votaries listening to a Ganesh story and offering dub grass (photo by Tracy Pintchman)

her if she had any special desire in doing the *vrat*, she said, "I just do *seva* (service)," indicating that she thought of the *vrat* mostly as a form of service to God. When pressed further, she remarked, "The only desire I have is, since God has given me children, may they remain well. That is my wish. What do women usually ask? That my husband and kids are okay. That is what they ask. . . . the Kartik *vrat* is for love (*prem*) and happiness in the family."

Shyamavati's answer points to the concern for family welfare that Susan Sered has highlighted in her work on women's rituals. Sered notes that for women, religion often has a lot to do with the well-being of family members. She observes that in many cultures women act as spiritual guardians of family members, noting that "women whose secular lives revolve around love and care" for family members "also develop kin-centered religiosity" (Sered 1992: 26–27). She calls this emphasis on familial well-being the "domestication of religion," which she describes as a process "in which people who profess their allegiance to a wider religious tradition personalize the rituals, institutions, symbols, and theology of that wider system in order to safeguard the health, happiness, and security of particular people with whom they are linked in relationships of caring and dependence" (1992: 10).

Mary McGee's work on women in Hindu *vrat* traditions highlights the domestic emphasis characteristic of such traditions.[8] McGee observes that most votaries are women, and for them the primary aim of *vrats* tends to be *saubhagya* or, in Hindi, *suhag*, that is, "good fortune" embodied in the form of a "good husband, healthy children, and a happy home life" (1987: 418). Although Shyamavati had been widowed about two years earlier, she had a large and prosperous family. Her only son had inherited and was successfully running the family's rickshaw-rental business. The family was financially comfortable and owned two houses, one of which accommodated Shyamavati, along with two of her grandsons and their wives and children. After her husband's death, Shyamavati's main desire was for the continuing welfare of her remaining family members, and it was with this abiding desire that she undertook not only the Kartik *vrat*, but other *vrats* and devotional observances as well.

When I returned to Benares in 1997 to continue working on my project, I anticipated spending a lot of time with Shyamavati asking her about various stories that she had told during the *puja* in 1995. As soon as I arrived back, however, I learned that she had had a great tragedy in her family shortly before my return. In the two years that had passed, the grandsons with whom Shyamavati lived had argued increasingly over money issues and had become estranged. When one grandson finally threatened his brother's life, the family kicked him out of the house and told him not to come back. Seeking revenge, he allegedly crept in one night about two months before I returned to Benares and shot to death his brother and his brother's wife. Their children, who had been sleeping in the same room, were also wounded but survived the attack. At the time of the shooting, Shyamavati was asleep in an upstairs room; awakened by the noise, she ran downstairs and was the first to discover the bloodied corpses. This event was deeply, deeply traumatic for her.

When I saw her again in 1997, Shyamavati was still emotionally distraught over what had happened, although she agreed to meet with me and a research assistant several times to discuss the stories she had narrated in 1995. I had strong reservations about pursuing my research agenda with her given what she had been through, but she seemed relieved to have some distraction from her grief and eager for company. So we went ahead and met together a total of six times during that autumn, usually for about an hour each time. As it turned out, our conversations flowed between discussion of the stories' teachings, Shyamavati's own beliefs, and what had transpired in her family, which was obviously still painful and difficult for her to accept. What I found particularly striking in those conversations was Shyamavati's struggle to make sense of her own family tragedy within the ethico-religious framework that she not only attributed to most of the narratives I asked her about, but that she also described as underlying the performance of *vrats*, along with other devotional observances, and that she herself seemed to believe strongly.

With respect to intention and goal, Shyamavati did not draw much distinction between *vrat* and much of the other religious activity in which she engaged. There is in fact a good measure of continuity between *vrats* and other forms of devotional observance in this regard, and the boundary between them is rather fluid: a pilgrimage or daily *puja*, for example, can be undertaken in the petitionary manner normally associated with *vrats*, just as *vrats* themselves can be undertaken without any desire whatsoever (Pearson 1996: 204). The fluidity of such boundaries was driven home to me in a conversation with a Benarsi who became exasperated at my question regarding whether a particular religious celebration was a *vrat* or a festival (*utsav*), remarking, "Nobody here makes that kind of distinction!" Hence much may be shared. The structure of a *vrat*, however, does appear to be somewhat distinctive.[9] The *vrat* context, for example, often provides an opportunity for telling and hearing a particular type of devotional story that is not generally recited at other times. *Vrat* narratives tend to be explicitly didactic and to emphasize the rewards that flow from religious devotion and steadfast faith in a deity or deities (Narayan 1997: 17).

In her analysis of several *vrat* stories (*katha*), Susan Wadley notes persistent underlying themes pertaining to transaction between humans and deities as well as issues of sin and merit. With respect to the first issue, she observes that in *vrat* narratives, gods consistently exercise compassion and provide boons in exchange for human trust, devotion, and service in the form of not only *vrats*, but other devotional activities as well (1985: 81–82). She describes this exchange as modeling "a transaction of the patron-client (*jajman-kamin*) variety" (81). Wadley does not distinguish between the portrayal of boons that flow from *vrats* and those that flow from other forms of devotion in her analysis, including *vrats* within the larger framework of devotional activity that is portrayed as reaping appropriate rewards, but she does focus on the specific narrative genre associated with *vrat*.

With respect to the second issue, sin and merit, Wadley observes that the narratives she explores tend to be quite clear about the relationship between the ethical force of an action and its result: sinful acts lead to sorrow and meritorious acts lead to happiness. In this context, the category of "good acts" encompasses the performance of votive and other devotional rites, which fall under the rubric of *dharma*. It is notable, too, that such stories may portray karmic effects—that is, the relationship between one's actions and their results—within the framework of one's present life without necessarily invoking any reference to future lives, reflecting broader popular notions of karma in Indian culture (Wadley 1985: 85; Wadley and Derr 1989). In her analysis, Wadley does not distinguish between orally transmitted vernacular stories and those that are Sanskritic and text-based. In relation to the Kartik *vrat*, however, I found that many narratives recounted in the Puranic Kartik Mahatmyas invoke actions performed in characters' past lives to explain their favorable or unfavorable situations. Orally transmitted stories that I heard women tell in the Kartik *puja* circle, on the other hand, tended to portray the relationship between action and result as occurring within one lifetime, and often with great immediacy (cf. Ramanujan 1991: 41). This understanding of karmic functioning would also encompass the relationship between devotional observances and familial well-being that women especially, including Shyamavati, tend to embrace.[10]

Of the forty different stories that I heard narrated during the daily *puja* of the Kartik *vrat* in 1995, themes of both reciprocity and karmic immediacy as Wadley describes them were echoed in twenty-four of them, or 65 percent. Such themes come to the fore, for example, in a story that Shyamavati narrated on October 25th, 1995 about an impoverished, religious old woman. This woman bathes in the Ganges River every day during the month of Kartik—presumably as part of the Kartik *vrat*, although this is not explicitly stated in the story—and then goes to worship Ganesh. In return, Ganesh plants a tree in her courtyard that rains down twenty-five cent (*paisa*) coins, telling her to take the money and do whatever she wants with it. As her riches increase, all the neighbors become jealous and conspire to have the tree taken away from her. Sending word about the tree to the king, they convince the king to seize the tree. After the tree is moved to the king's courtyard, however, it stops producing coins altogether. Realizing that divine will is at work, the king has the tree brought back to the courtyard of the old woman, where it begins to produce coins once again. When I asked Shyamavati about the story, she said, "The king did not have religious faith (*shraddha*) and devotion (*bhakti*). That is why that tree did not thrive in his courtyard. The old lady was poor and she had faith, and that is why Ganesh gave the tree to her."

In our conversations together in 1997, Shyamavati often highlighted themes of reciprocity and karmic immediacy in the stories I asked her about and then commented on their truth-value or related them to concrete situations. Shyamavati's own understanding of votive rites and the role they played in her life also appeared to be strongly informed by these same themes. In discussing the significance and power of *vrats* in both 1995 and 1997, Shyamavati described them as ethically correct actions, "good deeds" (*accha kartav*) that are woven into a broader ethic of "doing good," in exchange for which "God (Bhagavan) will be happy with you" and will reward you for your behavior with boons. Sometimes she did not differentiate between the rewards that flow from *vrats*, other devotional activities, and morally correct behavior toward other humans, including kindness in speech, truthfulness, and so forth. In other contexts, however, she spoke more of God's obligation to care for a faithful petitioner, noting that it is God's responsibility to provide for such a devotee and that through *vrat* and *puja* one's "well-being (*kalyan*) is guaranteed." Shyamavati never invoked past or future lives in these discussions, and at no point in our conversations did she ever mention the limits of divine capabilities in proffering boons. At points she summed up what she understood to be the main teachings of all the stories she had told, proclaiming, "If you are involved with God, then God will always give you good results.... Do good and you will get a good result, and God will be happy with you. If you believe in God, God will believe in you. *Bas* (That is all)."

It is precisely such convictions that appear to have been undermined by Shyamavati's family tragedy. Not only were Shyamavati's petitions for continued family well-being seemingly rebuffed, but they were seemingly rebuffed in a cruel and shocking manner, and the disjunction between belief and experience pained and bewildered her. Shyamavati herself brought up this issue when I first went to see her in 1997. She remembered me as the foreigner who had kept Kartik *vrat* and had done the *puja* in her circle some years earlier, and I remarked that I was looking forward to doing so again that year. Hearing this she began to cry, and she exclaimed, "I have done so much *vrat* and religious activity (*puja-path*) and yet I have had to live to see such a day! A person does religious acts to have a better time in life. I used to have my granddaughter-in-law to cook for me and now I have no one.... So I feel in my heart, what is the use of religious acts.... To my knowledge, I never did anything wrong. I never thought I would have to see such a day!"[11]

In our conversations together, Shyamavati tended to articulate the pain she felt over the deaths of her family members in terms of the detrimental effect of these deaths on the living. On the occasion of our first meeting, for example, Shyamavati expressed feelings of anger and frustration regarding the difficulties that the family deaths had caused her, feelings that are not unusual for those in mourning (Roach and Nieto 1997: 72–74). At other times she emphasized concern regarding the neighbors' gossip about her and her family or worries about her great-grandchildren's welfare. No matter what anxieties she raised when she brought up the murders, however, she frequently raised the question, too, of what could have *caused* the tragedy to occur. In this regard, the dismay and bafflement persisted that her lifetime of alleged ethically correct behavior, including proper and abundant devotional and votive ritual activity, had not protected her and her family from such a tragedy. She reported to me that neighbors had also communicated to her their surprise that such misfortune had befallen one so devout and ritually active. On a few occasions the stories themselves provoked Shyamavati's reflections on her own situation, inviting comparison between herself and a character in the narrative under consideration. This happened, for example, while we were discussing a story about a religious old woman who was a faithful Kartik votary. When this woman dies, no one is able to lift her body onto the funeral pyre, and everyone starts questioning the sincerity of her devotion. In the story, Vishnu ultimately intervenes, but Shyamavati stopped the story at the point where the woman's character comes under fire to compare herself with the woman, remarking, "People will say a similar thing about me, also [when I die,] about my grandson being killed. . . . I never did anything wrong knowingly. . . . I don't know why it happened."

While Shyamavati's bafflement persisted throughout our discussions, there were also occasions when Shyamavati resorted to the notion of "fate" (*bhagy*) to explain the murders. Toward the end of our first long conversation together, my assistant suggested fate as the reason for her tragedy, and she took some comfort in this idea. Two visits later, she raised it herself. On this occasion, she compared a Kartik votary in one of her stories to me, whom she also perceived to be a devout Kartik votary despite my awkward attempts to explain to her the academic motivation for my participation in her *puja* circle. Shyamavati remarked, "Faith, devotion, love (*prem*)—that is why you are doing all of this. So God will see that you are never deprived of anything. You have been doing the *puja* (of the Kartik *vrat*), so God will always be with you and will always help you. If you have devotion, God will always help you. . . . He must help you, definitely." When I asked her if this was always true in life as well as stories, she said that it was definitely true. At this point, a male visitor in the room interrupted, saying, "No it is not like that because you have been doing so much *puja*—so why were your grandchildren killed?" To this comment, Shyamavati replied, "Listen, this is all from previous births." She then began to speak of divine recording of deeds from life to life and the relationship between past and present deeds and destiny (*bhagy*) but was interrupted by the visitor, and a long argument ensued. Later, she returned to her point, noting, "It was written in my destiny (*bhagy*) that this would happen at the end of my life."

Shyamavati invoked the notion of fate or destiny (*bhagy*) here in response to an apparent logical contradiction. She invoked fate in other contexts, too, to explain the apparently undeserved suffering of her neighbor, or as a general principle that you obtain only what is "written" in your destiny (*bhagy*). The notion of an unalterable fate is clearly helpful to those like Shyamavati struggling to make sense of seemingly inexplicable crisis situations and can help preserve the faith of a religiously observant Hindu when the performance of a particular *vrat* fails to deliver what it promises. It is questionable, however, to what extent Shyamavati found the notion of a predetermined and unalterable destiny to be *emotionally* plausible or satisfying when it came to her own situation. A short time after responding to her neighbor's comment, she referred to her tragedy as a test of her faith through "trial by fire" (*agni-pariksha*). Proclaiming that she had just completed a Shiva-Parvati *vrat*, she declared that despite what had happened she would not "give up on (*tyagna*) God." Shortly thereafter, while discussing the relationship between actions and their results, she turned again to her own situation and perceived meritorious behavior and said, "No matter what I say, how many excuses I make, my heart is not satisfied." Hence the notion of an unalterable predetermined fate or destiny, while appealing as a general principle, does not seem convincing to Shyamavati when it comes to her own experience, given the expectations she holds regarding devotional and votive ritual activity.

It is notable too that *vrat* narratives tend to imply that fate can be altered through votive observances. Wadley observes that many stories portray *vrats* as powerful "transformers of destiny" that can enable a devotee to overcome an undesirable karmic legacy. The "moral" of these narratives is that doing a *vrat* destroys the ill effect of past sins, and the deity to whom one directs the *vrat* is expected to "overrule" karmic destiny to the benefit of the votary (1983: 155–56). Shyamavati was familiar with such themes, at least with respect to the Kartik *vrat*. Every day after Kartik *puja,* she would accompany other Kartik votaries to a nearby Vishnu temple to listen to the recitation and Hindi exposition of the Kartik Mahatmya of the Padma Purana. This text includes both narrative accounts and proclamations suggesting that negative karma will be thoroughly destroyed through observance of the Kartik *vrat*.[12] While such themes tend to be more characteristic of the Sanskritic Kartik Mahatmyas than the orally transmitted vernacular stories women narrate in Kartik *puja* circles, I did hear one story of this type narrated in Shyamavati's *puja* circle in 1995. It is quite possible that Shyamavati believed such teachings as much as she believed those of the stories we specifically discussed together.

Conclusion

When Keyes remarks that a votary might invoke the notion of karmic destiny when a ritual vow fails to produce a desired result, he does not account for the difference between how a person might *explain* such a situation and how he or she might *experience* it emotionally and spiritually in some contexts. For Shyamavati, the performance of *vrats* is not an isolated act, but is woven into a larger ethic whereby you trust in God, uphold ritual observances, and act kindly toward others, and in response God takes care of you. From such a perspective, *vrats* are not fully distinct from other dharmic acts or acts of devotion or human kindness but are an expression of personal virtue and religious dedication, which guarantees a favorable divine response in the present. Shyamavati's family tragedy undermines this ethic in ways that are, I believe, truly confusing and disorienting to her.

Keyes fails, too, to take gender into account when it comes to vows that fail to deliver what they promise. Shyamavati's turmoil is undoubtedly related to the extreme quality of her experience: after several decades of regular votive and devotional activity, she experienced a great personal loss in a dramatic manner. But one must consider to what extent gender plays a role in shaping the desires and expectations that Shyamavati brings to her performance of *vrats*. Here I think Shyamavati's case is more suggestive than conclusive. One must be very cautious, of course, about generalizing from a single case. But Kim Knott (1996) has argued persuasively that Hindu women tend to understand destiny in ways that are shaped somewhat by their gender, and McGee and Pearson have shown that women appropriate *vrat* traditions, too, in ways that are gender-specific. McGee notes that Sanskritic textual treatments of *vrat* traditions tend to portray them as acquisitory, involving the attainment of that which one does not yet have, including such lofty attainments as spiritual liberation. Women, however, tend to perceive *vrats* as rites of maintenance that help them preserve familial well-being on an ongoing basis (McGee 1991: 73–74). The nonfulfillment of such a desire would be readily apparent as it would entail the loss of what one already has, and such loss would probably seem quite punishing to a faithful devotee. Furthermore, women are the primary keepers of *vrat* rituals and the primary tellers of and audience for *vrat* narratives. Themes of karmic immediacy and divine commitment to sincere devotees and petitioners are inculcated in orally transmitted vernacular narratives that tend to be recounted to and by women. The teachings of these narratives are reinforced with each telling, and at least some women, like Shyamavati, take them to heart. Women therefore might well tend to experience the failure of *vrats* to deliver what they promise in gender-specific ways as well.

Notes

1. Where Keyes collapses karma and fate, others have noted distinctions between them, with karma encompassing notions of individual control and agency and fate or destiny remaining something hidden and out of one's control (e.g., Ramanujan 1991: 39–41). But Keyes's point that the idea of an unalterable destiny is a plausible explanation for the failure of *vrats* to produce results remains.

2. This research was made possible by Loyola University, which granted me a sabbatical in the fall of 1995 and allowed me to take an extended leave of absence in 1997–1998, and by grants from the American Institute of Indian Studies, the National

Institute of the Humanities, and the American Academy of Religion. I am grateful to all of these institutions for their support.

3. The name has been changed to help conceal her identity.

4. The traditional Hindu calendar consists of twelve lunar months, that is, months that are determined by lunar cycles. In Benares, these months are calculated from full moon to full moon. When measured against the solar calendar that is commonly used in the West, the first day of Kartik usually falls sometime in mid-October. I participated in Kartik *puja* in Benares three times, in 1995, 1997, and 1998.

5. The Kartik Mahatmyas can be found in Padma Purana 6.88–117 and Skanda Purana 2.4.1–36.

6. McGee observes that for any given *vrat* one (or sometimes two) of the rites associated with *vrats* is designated the principal rite, the *pradhana*, whose performance is central to the *vrat*, while the less critical elements are considered subsidiary rites of the *vrat* (1987: 124–25). The observance of food restrictions is often, but not always, the primary activity associated with *vrats*.

7. For more on Kartik and the Kartik *vrat* and *puja*, see Pintchman (1999 and 2003). Krishna is usually associated primarily with Radha, Krishna's chief consort and leader of the *gopi*s. In the context of this month-long *puja* tradition, however, Krishna's association with Tulsi comes to the fore as well, and Krishna is said to wed Tulsi on the eleventh day of the bright fortnight of Kartik. This day is known as Prabodhani Ekadashi ("waking eleventh"), for Vishnu is said to awaken from a four-month slumber on this day.

8. See also Wadley (1985: 163). In keeping with findings by McGee and Wadley, almost all of the thirty-six women whom I interviewed cited concern for the family as an important motivation for maintaining the *vrat*.

9. For a full discussion of the components and form of *vrats* by contemporary scholars, see McGee (1987) and Pearson (1996).

10. The women I interviewed generally declined to speak of these stories as "women's stories." Many of the women identified them as true accounts of past events and saw them as instructive for all persons. Shyamavati herself vehemently objected to my suggestion that they were only for women and invited me to retell them to my husband so that he, too, could learn their teachings. On the other hand, the few high-caste men that I had occasion to ask about these stories distinguished between Sanskritic textual narratives, which they saw as true, and women's folk stories, which they tended to disparage.

11. "Religious acts" here is my translation for *Puja-path*. *Puja-path*, meaning "worship and recitation of religious texts," encompasses the totality of religious and devotional activities in which one might engage, including not only *vrats*, but also daily *puja*, pilgrimage, and so forth.

12. See, for example, Padma Purana 6.106–7, 113–14, and 115.

References

Keyes, Charles F. 1983. "Introduction: The Study of Popular Ideas of Karma." In *Karma: An Anthropological Inquiry*, eds. Charles F. Keyes and E. Valentine Daniel, 1–24. Berkeley: University of California Press.

Knott, Kim. 1996. "Hindu Women, Destiny and Stridharma." *Religion* 26: 15–35.

McGee, Mary. 1987. "Feasting and Fasting: The Vrata Tradition and Its Significance for Hindu Women." Th.D. dissertation, Harvard Divinity School.

———. 1991. "Desired Fruits: Motive and Intention in the Votive Rites of Hindu Women." In *Roles and Rituals for Hindu Women,* ed. Julia Leslie, 71–88. London: Pinter Publishers.

Narayan, Kirin. 1997. *Mondays on the Dark Night of the Moon: Himalayan Foothill Folktales.* New York: Oxford University Press.

Pearson, Anne Mackenzie. 1996. *"Because It Gives Me Peace of Mind": Ritual Fasts in the Religious Lives of Hindu Women.* Albany: State University of New York Press.

Pintchman, Tracy. 2003. *"The Month of Kartik and Women's Ritual Devotions to Krishna."* In *The Blackwell Companion to Hinduism,* ed. Gavin Flood, 327–42. Oxford: Blackwell Publishers.

———. 1999. "The Month of Kartik as a Vaisnava *Mahotsav:* Mythic Themes and the Ocean of Milk." *Journal of Vaishnava Studies* 7/2 (March): 65–92.

Ramanujan, A. K. 1991. "Toward a Counter-System: Women's Tales." In *Gender, Genre, and Power in South Asian Expressive Traditions,* eds. Arjun Appadurai, Frank J. Korom, and Margaret A. Mills, 33-55. Philadephia: University of Pennsylvania Press.

Roach, Sally S. and Beatriz C. Nieto. 1997. *Healing and the Grief Process.* Albany: Delmar Publishers.

Sered, Susan. 1992. *Women as Ritual Experts: The Religious Lives of Elderly Jewish Women in Jerusalem.* New York: Oxford University Press.

Wadley, Susan Snow. 1983. "Vrats: Transformers of Destiny." In *Karma: An Anthropological Inquiry,* eds. Charles F. Keyes and E. Valentine Daniel, 147–52. Berkeley: University of California Press.

———. 1985. *Shakti: Power in the Conceptual Structure of Karimpur Religion.* New Delhi: Munshiram Manoharlal.

Wadley, Susan Snow and Bruce Derr. 1989. "Eating Sins in Karimpur." *Contributions to Indian Sociology* 23/1: 131–48.

14

Two Critiques of Women's Vows

JACK E. LLEWELLYN

When the editors told me about their collaborative study of vows in South Asian religion, I automatically found myself working backward from English to the South Asian language that I know best, Hindi, substituting *vrat*, which would be the most common translation of the word "vow." And when I thought of *vrats*, I naturally thought of the role that they play in the popular Hinduism of contemporary Indian women. This led me to read a book that I had been meaning to read for some time, Mary McGee's study of just this popular practice, "Feasting and Fasting," a book that is a veritable *vrata-vishva-kosha*, an encyclopedia of *vrats*. While McGee's dissertation is in many ways a masterful work, applying great erudition to the analysis of the religion of ordinary women, there is still something about it that bothered me. This is a chapter about two critiques of the practice of *vrats*, one provoked by my reading of McGee's important book and one that I found in the writings of Arya Samaj women. The second critique is different from the first in a way that only serves to highlight the normative questions involved.

My Critique of *Vrats*

Let me state my own prejudice as baldly as possible, just to stimulate a reaction from my reader. Aren't *vrat*s a bad thing?[1] Aren't they a part of a religion in which women are supposed to sacrifice their own needs and aspirations on the altar of their families? Aren't they a reflection of a social system where a wife's sphere of influence is limited to the home, while a man's sphere includes the home but ranges into the world beyond, in which a wife turns herself inward toward her family, while a husband faces out toward the world, turning his back on his family? Aren't *vrats* practices in which women mortify their own bodies for the good of others—a sacrifice no one is making for them?

Now, maybe things aren't all that bad. Certainly the practice of *vrats* is something that many contemporary Hindu women find liberating, not only affording them a pretext for spending time with other women, but also giving them access to some power, temporal as well as spiritual. But while I have made too strong a case against *vrats* in the preceding paragraph, I think that Mary McGee makes too strong a case for them in "Feasting and Fasting." This was brought home to me especially as I finished the book. The concluding paragraph (before the lengthy appendices) reads:

> The words of Lord Krsna, more familiar to the women than those of Manu, perhaps speak more directly to the balance between women's duties and desires as we have witnessed in our study of votive rites, when he says, "It is by taking delight in one's assigned duties that a person attains to final perfection." (McGee 1987: 608, quoting Bhagavad Gita 18.45a)

It is noteworthy that the author (or authors) of the Gita is not dealing primarily with gender in this context, but with caste. Verse 41 argues that the actions *(karma)* of each of the four castes are appropriate to it. In her translation of this verse Barbara Stoler Miller says that these actions "are apportioned by qualities born of their intrinsic being" (Miller 1986: 149). R. C. Zaehner's translation of the Gita makes the connection between caste and duty even more inexorable, saying that the deeds assigned on the basis of caste "arise from the nature of things as they are" (Zaehner 1969: 393). The three verses interposed between this one and the verse that McGee cites continue with the caste theme, with 42 and 43 spelling out the virtues of Brahmans and Kshatriyas, respectively, and 44 detailing the modes of livelihood of Vaishyas and Shudras. So, when the Gita says that "taking delight in one's assigned duties" leads to "final perfection," it is talking about the duties assigned on the basis of caste.

I would not argue that McGee can't quote the Bhagavad Gita in this way with respect to the duties of women, because what that book is talking about is really caste. Actually the Gita doesn't say much about gender one way or the other. But I tend to agree with her that the Gita's teaching on caste might be extended to gender as well. Just as there are basic differences between Brahmans and Kshatriyas, differences that are at least inborn, if not even more primeval than that, so, too, the author of the Gita might have been willing to allow that there are basic differences between men and women. Just as there is no point in a Kshatriya trying to practice a Brahman's dharma, so there is no point in a woman trying to practice a man's dharma. In this way, it might indeed be argued that the logic of Bhagavad Gita 18.45 could apply to gender as well as caste, but this is precisely the problem.

Consider the following passage from "Feasting and Fasting," in which McGee challenges the received wisdom about the subordination of Hindu wives.

> Yet despite the much-proclaimed dependence of a wife on her husband, it is hard to say whether or not a husband is actually more independent. Moving from the viewpoint of the theoretically articulated ideal to the actual functioning of this marital relationship in society, we may observe that a husband may have more mobility in the public sphere, but he is as dependent on his wife as she is on him when it comes to fulfilling his obligatory duties and responsibilities. Theirs is a relationship of interdependence in a society and culture that is based on interdependence. (McGee 1987: 343)

Perhaps my own reading of this passage when I first encountered it was idiosyncratic, or even perverse, but when I thought of the role of interdependence in Indian society, I thought of caste. It is decidedly the case that different caste groups are interdependent. The Brahman could not maintain his vaunted purity if he did not have a Bhangini to do his cleaning for him, and, by the same token, or perhaps a slightly different token, the Bhangini (or at least people of somewhat higher caste) needs the Brahman to perform her rituals. Yet though these groups are interdependent, it is also decidedly the case that they are not equal. The Brahman has higher social status, and is now, and for long has been, generally better off than the members of lower caste groups.

Again, I would argue that this is consistent with the teaching of the Bhagavad Gita. The message of 18.41–47 is that you must fulfill your caste dharma, whether you like it or not. Yet that is not to say that all caste dharmas are equally good in the eyes of the author of the Gita. On the contrary, it is my reading of the last three chapters of the Gita that the dharma of Brahmans is superior, morally better in some sense, than the dharma of other castes, especially Kshatriyas. The seventeenth chapter divides the world up into the three qualities or *gunas*. Of the three it seems that the quality of lucidity (to adopt Miller's translation for *sattva*) is predominant in the Brahman, while the quality of passion (or *rajas*) is predominant in the Kshatriya. If we back up further still to the sixteenth chapter, then we find that the world that has already been divided into four (castes) and three (qualities) is now divided into two (types of people), the divine and the demonic. It is noteworthy that several of the characteristics of the divine person here are also characteristics of the Brahman in 18.42.[2] There is obviously much more that could be said about the teaching of the Bhagavad Gita on caste, not to mention how that relates to the other great themes of selflessness and devotion to Krishna, but this is probably not the place to say it. I am also willing to allow that there are problems with reducing the last three chapters of the Gita to

Brahman = lucid = divine

and

Kshatriya = passionate = demonic.[3]

Still, I think that it is true that Brahmans are generally better than Kshatriyas in the religion of the Gita. The castes are practically interdependent, but they are also hierarchically arranged, with some castes better and purer than others. The members of a household are interdependent, too, of course, but aren't they also arranged hierarchically? Aren't husbands better than their wives? Isn't that a part of the ideology that underpins the practice of *vrats*?

I hasten to add that McGee does point out at various points in "Feasting and Fasting" that the religion and social role of women is often understood to be more limited than that of men in Indian culture. For example, she notes that liberation, or *moksha,* is said to be a goal that is appropriate for men, but beyond women (McGee 1987: 318).[4] Yet there were still times in McGee's book when I felt that the religion of women in India was being romanticized, with a little too much emphasis on interpreting things in a positive light. Consider what McGee has to say about the way that women transfer the merit of the *vrats* that they perform to the other members of their families. "The fact that many *vratas* are observed by one person for the benefit of another, and that the transfer of merit is an important motif in the *vrata* stories, gives us some idea of the importance of social and familial responsibility within Hindu society and of the genuine concern for the well-being of others" (McGee 1987: 62). Yet McGee notes that it is always women who are transferring this merit. The receivers are not always men; women also transfer the merit of their vows to their children, for instance, both girls and boys. But men are virtually never the givers. Whatever the role of "genuine concern for the well-being of others" in contemporary India, it does not extend to the concern of husbands for their wives, at least if that is measured by the practice of *vrats* for their benefit.[5]

The Arya Samaj Critique of *Vrats*

This initial reading of "Feasting and Fasting," and of the *vrat* tradition, may be too harsh. If it is, that may arise in part from the fact that I have spent years studying the Arya Samaj, and Arya Samajists are notorious for their withering critique of religious practices with which they are not in sympathy. The Arya Samaj is a Hindu revivalist movement founded in 1875 (Llewellyn 1993). It seeks to restore a kind of pristine Vedic religion at the cost of condemning much of contemporary popular Hinduism. In fact, I have encountered critiques specifically of the practice of *vrats* in Arya Samaj literature and in sermons by and discussions with members of that movement. I take as a specific example a passage in a booklet entitled *Adarsh Grhini-Grhapati,* by Swami Miran Yati. That author also takes exception to the practice of *vrats,* but her exception is not the same as my own.

Since I have written extensively about Miran Yati elsewhere, I will confine myself here to a few introductory remarks.[6] She was born in a village in Punjab in 1928. Having become more and more engrossed in religious pursuits, Miran Yati moved into the Vanprasth Ashram near Hardwar when she was in her late thirties. Though she was not initiated as a renouncer until 1979, Miran Yati had begun an active life as a public preacher years before, traveling to Arya Samaj centers around northern India. She has also been a tireless author, having published more than fifty booklets, mostly collections of her sermons. *Adarsh Grhini-Grhapati,* a booklet of some ninety-six pages published in 1995, is a series of sermons based upon Vedic mantras. As befits the title, *Ideal Wife and Husband,* four of these five mantras are recited in the Arya Samaj marriage ceremony.

It is in commenting on the fifth mantra that Swami Miran Yati mentions that she has seen many women undertaking a *vrat* that she calls the *karva chauth vrat.*[7] This is a vow that women take primarily to secure longevity for their husbands, but Miran Yati early on betrays her skepticism about this. After describing the ritual itself, she goes on to ask, "Can a husband's life be made long by giving a Brahman a jug of water or a jug of milk after dropping the five jewels into it?" (Miran Yati 1995: 85). Then Miran Yati recounts a *katha,* or story, about the power of the *karva chauth vrat* from a booklet about it that she had found in a stationery shop near her home. In "Feasting and Fasting" Mary McGee notes that such stories often include divine actors, so that the performance of the *vrat* is a kind of *imitatio dei,* and this *katha* is no exception. In fact, in it two layers of divinity are involved, with Krishna recounting to Draupadi a story that he had heard Shiva tell Parvati. The core of the tale involves a human woman, Virvati, whose husband dies because she inadvertently breaks her *karva chauth* vow, and then is brought back to life thanks to a year of fasting by his wife. Having reproduced this tale at some length, Swami Miran Yati goes on to heap scorn upon it, asking about Virvati's fast, "Have you ever heard of a person who didn't eat anything for a whole year and who survived?" This is followed by a comment about her husband's resurrection, "Then he lay dead for a year. The stench must have started the day after he died" (Miran Yati 1995: 90).

The central objection to the *karva chauth vrat* is that it is ineffective. Miran Yati compares undertaking this *vrat* to churning water. "If you churn milk, then you get butter. But go ahead and churn water all day long and you won't get anything at all" (Miran Yati 1995: 88–89). Popular Hindu practices are often disparaged as superstitious nonsense in the polemical literature of the Arya Samaj, so in this Miran Yati is following a tradition that is more than a century old.[8] Another important theme in this literature is a condemnation of the role of priestcraft in the promulgation of these superstitions, and there is an element of that here, too, for Miran Yati condemns the author of the *karva chauth katha* for his greed, "He wrote the pages of the *katha* and earned money" (Miran Yati 1995: 89). Yet a critique that is conspicuous by its absence is the one I expressed in the first part of this chapter. Nowhere does Swami Miran Yati say that this *vrat* is bad because it reflects an ideology of subordination for women. On the contrary, there is evidence even in this context that Miran Yati embraces the idea that a woman should accept a role that involves sacrificing herself for the good of her family. After her rejection of the *karva chauth vrat*, Miran Yati urges her listeners to adopt another vow in its place:

> It is my humble plea to all of you that you should take on the *vrat* of truth, you should become women who are *pativrata*s. Look upon your husband as your lord [*parameshvar*]. If he has any vices, then serve him speaking sweet words, love him, and in this way have such an influence over him that you win him over. Then your *vrat* will bear fruit. (Miran Yati 1995: 91–92)

With this passage we turn from *vrats* to *pativrata*, which is the subject of the next section of this chapter.

Vrats and Pativrata

According to Mary McGee, tied into the practice of the *vrats* by her Maharasthrian informants is the idea that a wife should be a *pativrata*. Literally, a *pativrata* is a woman whose vow (*vrat*) is her husband (*pati*). This term is not used to refer to the practice of any specific ritual, but in general commends for the wife an attitude of religious devotion to her husband. This attitude is expressed strongly in the preceding quote from Miran Yati, but in fairly typical language, in the exhortation that the wife should treat her husband like a god (as her *parameshvar*). This image of the woman devoted to her husband is the foundation of many of the specific rituals of McGee's informants, such that, "In many ways, to be a *pativrata* is the *vrata par excellence* of women" (McGee 1987: 336).

In the preceding quote, Swami Miran Yati embraces the *pativrata* as an ideal for contemporary women. This endorsement is expressed even more strongly in another one of her booklets on the *Vaidik Nari*, or *The Vedic Woman*. There Miran Yati praises Hindu women of yore such as Urmila, who allowed her husband Lakshman to abandon her in order to accompany his brother Ram into exile, and Bharati Devi, who bested Sankara in debate when her husband Mandana

Mishra seemed on the verge of defeat. These women are contrasted with the wives of today in a scathing passage in which the Hindi word *patni* is used to describe the traditional virtuous spouse, while the English word "wife" is the label for her modern, degenerate counterpart. To mark this distinction I have put the words in italics that are already in English in Miran Yati's original.

> They were true coreligionists of their husbands who helped and protected their husbands in time of crisis. How would today's *wife* compare with them? She has no leisure; she is so busy with adorning herself. Her entire attention is devoted to these things, "How should I do my hair? What jewelry should I wear?" If one has stopped wearing a scarf over her head, then a second will take off her scarf as soon as she sees her. She doesn't think that a woman's modesty is her ornament. Today's educated woman takes pride in the fact that she calls her husband by name. To the idea, "This is my husband and lord [again, *parameshvar*]," she attaches no worth or significance. She doesn't like to call her husband a husband and lord, a name full of respect. She really likes to call him her *husband*, because she is a *wife*. She won't even accept the name. Christians call women *woman*, that is, a temporary *wife*, not a *wife* who is dedicated to her husband [that is, a *pativrata*]. She is a *wife* who is ready for divorce, who is ready on the slightest pretext not just to argue with her *husband* but to divorce him. (Miran Yati 1988: 47–48)

Much might be said about the things that this paragraph attacks, but for the present purposes I only want to draw attention to one thing it commends, and that is that women should be *pativratas*.

I should add in other writings and sermons by Arya Samaj women I have encountered more ambivalence toward the *pativrata*. For example, take the book *Vaidik Sopan* by Shakuntala Arya. The author is an activist not only in the Arya Samaj, but also in the Bharatiya Janata Party, having served as the BJP mayor of Delhi. This book is about the ideal life as lived according to the Vedas, which is expressed in the metaphor of ascending a series of ten stairs, hence the title of the book, which might be translated *Vedic Stairs*. One of the chapters of the book is dedicated to five virtues that are particularly urged upon women. Four of them beginning with the letter "p" in Hindi, these virtues include 1) *pativrata*, but also 2) being a mother (*prajavati*), 3) purity (*pavitrata*), 4) skill in cooking (*pakkushalta*), and 5) general skill in knowing how to conduct oneself (*vyavaharkushalta*) (Arya 1989: 101–19).

Though this list obviously implies a gender-based role for women focused on the domestic realm, still Shakuntala Arya insists that a *pativrata*'s job is not just to be a door mat. About the received view of the *pativrata,* she writes:

> Ordinarily in our society the one devoted to her husband is taken to mean the one who acts according to his wishes, the one who is controlled by him. Just as a creeper wraps around a tree, so the devoted wife should always stay by her husband. She should be one who understands her husband's happiness to be her own, and in the exceptional case the woman devoted to her husband is burned alive along with corpse of her husband after his death.

But then Shakuntala Arya goes on to say that "This thinking is not suitable in today's healthy society" (Arya 1989: 113). On the contrary, a true *pativrata* is one who not only supports her husband when he is right, but who is also able to bring him around to reform himself when he is wrong. To accomplish this, Shakuntala Arya insists that "No woman can be a *pativrata* without an independent nature [*svadhinsvabhav*]" (Arya 1989: 114). It is interesting that this author takes Sita as an example of such an independent *pativrata*. The wife of Ram in the epic Ramayana, Sita is often upheld as a model for women because of her willingness to sacrifice herself for her husband, in accompanying him on his forest exile, for instance.[9] But in Shakuntala Arya's book, Sita was an ideal wife not because she did what her husband told her, but because she did what was right, despite what her husband told her to do.

> We learn from turning back to the pages of history that Sita became Ram's companion in the jungle during his exile *contrary to his wish* at the time that he left for the forest. When the seer Valmiki told Lord Ram that he should take Sita back, and Ram demanded a second trial by fire, then Sita's pride was injured, and she was willing to be swallowed up by the earth *rather than accept Ram's demand*. (Arya 1989: 114, emphasis added)

In *Vaidik Sopan* the work of a woman is generally limited to the domestic sphere, and there she will have to sacrifice herself for the good of her family, but she may also sometimes be called upon to stand up to her husband and others for their own good—that is part of being a *pativrata*, too.

I have not encountered Arya Samajists repudiating the *pativrata* as a model for women, but, as in the case of Shakuntala Arya, I have sometimes found them reinterpreting this model. Another example is *Urudhara Nari* by the late Arya Samaj educator Prajna Devi. Near the beginning of that book, Dr. Prajna Devi notes with disgust that traditionally "Only the woman met with preaching about the *pativrata* dharma. For the man *patnivrat* dharma [that is, the dharma of devotion to the wife, *patni*] was not thought of as at all necessary. Rather, he was given complete freedom to wander from place to place at will like a bee" (Devi 1985: x). It may be that it is exclusively wives who perform *vrats* for husbands among Mary McGee's informants, never husbands for wives. And it is certainly true that being vowed to one's spouse is virtually exclusively enjoined for women—I can never remember hearing of a husband who is a *patnivrat,* except in this passage. But Prajna Devi would like to put the shoe on the other foot, or it would be more correct to say that she wants to put the same shoe on both feet: just as wives must be devoted to their husbands, so should husbands to their wives. Even in Prajna Devi's writings, self-sacrifice is a virtue proper to women, but at least in this passage she serves up a helping of it to both genders.

The Limitations of Critique

In my book *The Legacy of Women's Uplift in India,* a problem that I found myself working on was the preaching of self-sacrifice for women, the practice of oppression against women, and the relationship between the two. By now it should be clear that this is a bone that I am still chewing on. I took this problem to Madhu Kishwar, (editor of the women's journal *Manushi* and social activist), in Delhi back in 1995, but I didn't find the support there that I was seeking. In response to my criticism of the Arya Samaj for imposing self-sacrifice upon women, Kishwar insisted that there are times when someone must be willing to give some things up. She took the family as an example, and particularly the problem of sexual infidelity. There might be some logic theoretically for a woman saying to herself, "If my husband can sleep with whomever he wants to, then I should, too." But in practice such thinking would destroy the woman's family. Under those circumstances the only responsible thing for the woman to do would be to remain faithful to her husband, and to do her best to make sure that he doesn't stray. Kishwar also said that self-sacrifice can be a source of real power for a woman in India, since through it she gains the respect of others.[10] Apparently coming to a judgment about all of this was going to prove more complicated than I first anticipated.

It might seem that I am triply disqualified from making such a judgment, since I am not an Indian, not a Hindu, and not a woman. And perhaps this is none of my business anyway. If we accept a certain methodological atheism as a prerequisite to the study of religion in the academy, particularly in a state-supported university in the United States of America, the kind of place where I work, then I should keep my mouth shut when it comes to making judgments. But then that might also require that I rigorously exclude all normative statements from my writing, which would mean not only that I couldn't say the practice of *vrats* is bad religion, but also that I couldn't say the oppression of women is bad politics, which is a kind of "neutrality" that I find problematic.

On the other hand, abandonment of neutrality is a slippery slope, I have to admit. The Arya Samaj reader of this chapter would surely have noted, though others might not have, how summarily I dealt with their central critique of *vrats,* that they are simply ineffective, relying on magical mumbo jumbo to coerce nonexistent divinities. I am certainly not prepared to enter the theological lists when it comes to the nature of God or the gods. So I would like to duck those kinds of theologically normative claims, even while taking a swing at politically normative ones. When it comes to theology, I can certainly see the utility of methodological atheism in the classroom, since it may reduce the potential for conflict if I begin my world religions survey course by saying, "We will only be talking about what the adherents of these various religions believe. We will not be trying to come to a conclusion about whether what they believe is true, or about which of them is right." There is a bit of sophistry in that, I think, which some of my students have complained about, particularly in graduate classes. Still, it generally works. Perhaps it would make sense to posit a difference between political and theological claims, taking the latter as more appropriate to public debate, but I can only see positing that difference provisionally—I can't see any strong theoretical support for it.

I started this chapter with reflections on Mary McGee's "Feasting and Fasting," so let me conclude with that as well. If we are to hold to the position that scholars of religion must eschew normative statements in their work, then that book contains a bit too much celebration of the practice of *vrats*, I think. If, on the other hand, we allow for the possibility of a judgment about whether *vrats* are a bad thing or a good thing, then the situation is complex. I do see *vrats* as an expression of an ideology that is oppressive toward women, requiring them to make sacrifices for their families that are not expected from men. Yet it is undoubtedly the case that in the contemporary Hindu world there have been women who have used *vrats* not only to train their young daughters-in-law in a wife's dharma (McGee 1987: 441), or to gain "peace of mind" (347–48), but also to acquire power in their families and communities. Any political evaluation of *vrats* would have to take these local acts of resistance into account, as well as the global gendered ideology in which they are framed. And as for whether the *vrats* are actually efficacious, whether the gods to whom they appeal even exist, that is a question that I would still prefer to duck, at least for the time being.

Notes

1. As to whether a scholar can make judgments such as this about "good" and "bad" religion, I will have more to say later.

2. Again using Miller's translation, you find "control" (*dama*), "penance" (*tapas*), "honesty" (*arjava*) in 18.42 and in 16.1. See Miller (1986: 133, 149) and, for the Sanskrit, Zaehner (1969: 369, 393).

3. One obvious problem is that both the person hearing this sermon on how great Brahmans are, and the person giving it, are in some sense Kshatriyas. And, as my students point out in my world religions class every semester, demolishing the Rube

Goldberg machine of a Gita interpretation that I have constructed, in 16.5 the author of the Gita says that Arjuna, Kshatriya though he is, was born with divine traits.

4. The context (from 316 to 319) is very interesting on this whole question of *moksha*.

5. When I presented this chapter as a paper at the meeting of the International Association for the History of the Religions in Durban, South Africa in 2000, Paul Younger spoke up from the audience, urging me to read the other major work on the *vrats* of contemporary women, Anne Mackenzie Pearson's *"Because It Gives Me Peace of Mind."* Now that I have done so, I should add that my objections to "Feasting and Fasting" don't apply to Pearson's book, since she does a better job, in my view, of foregrounding the overarching "androcentric gender ideology and patriarchal social structure" that "frame" women's practice of *vrats* (Pearson 1996: 220).

6. See "A Leading Preacher: Swami Miran Yati" in Llewellyn (1998: 98–125). I have also translated a bit of Miran Yati's autobiography in Llewellyn (1995: 462–72).

7. The *Manak Hindi Kosh* renders *karva chauth* as *Kartik krishn cathurthi*, that is, the dark fourth day in the month of Kartik. It says the name is derived from the Sanskrit *karaka cathurthi* (Varmma 1955: 464). Monier-Williams renders *karakacathurthi*, "the fourth day in the dark half of the month of Asvina" (Monier-Williams 1899: 254). So this is apparently a *vrat* that falls on the fourth day of the waning moon in either Kartik or Ashvin, that is, sometime around October or November. McGee (835) places *karva chauth* in the "Asvina (Kartika)" waning fortnight. Apparently the confusion here is because in some parts of India the month begins with the new moon, in other parts with the full moon, so what is the second half of Ashvin by the former reckoning is the first half of Kartik by the latter.

8. In an essay condemning astrology as well as women's *vrats*, Dr. Prajna Devi, another woman leader in the Arya Samaj, characterizes them as *adambar*; "hypocrisy," a term that carries a heavy load of opprobrium in Arya literature (Prajna Devi, "Patighni Panirekha," 2). I refer here to a handwritten copy of this article, which Prajna Devi was kind enough to send to me. I believe that it has appeared in print, but I am not sure where. When I asked for the publication information on this article and others she had provided, Prajna Devi replied only that they had appeared in obscure Arya Samaj journals.

9. For more on the contemporary status of Sita as a gendered role model, see Hess (1999) and Kishwar (1997) (which is also available on the Web at http://www.freespeech.org/manushi/98/sita.html). I have analyzed the Arya Samaj interpretation of the epic heroine in my paper, "The Arya Sita: Passive or Defiant?" presented at the Sita Symposium at Columbia University, New York, April and May, 1998.

10. Interview with Madhu Kishwar at the *Manushi* office, Delhi, March 9, 1995. McGee herself notes this specifically with regard to *vrats* when she writes: "we must not simply conclude that *vrata*s perpetuate and reinforce the traditional (stereotyped) roles of attitudes towards women (though to a large extent they do), but rather we must understand that they offer women an opportunity for self-reflection and change. As transformers of destiny, *vratas* are vehicles of great potential and power, and as the observers and maintainers of *vrata*s, women have the opportunity to channel that potential and power in many directions (1987: 487)."

References

Arya, Shakuntala. 1989. *Vaidik Sopan*. Delhi: privately published.

Devi, Prajna. 1985. *Urudhara Nari: Nari—Ek Cirantan Satya Svarup*. 3rd rev. ed. Varanasi: Panini Kanya Mahavidyalaya.

Hess, Linda. 1999. "Rejecting Sita: Indian Responses to the Ideal Man's Cruel Treatment of His Ideal Wife." *Journal of the American Academy of Religion* 67, 1 (March): 1–32.

Kishwar, Madhu. 1997. "Yes to Sita, No to Ram! The Continuing Popularity of Sita in India." *Manushi* 98 (January–February): 20–31.

Llewellyn, J. E. 1998. *The Legacy of Women's Uplift in India: Contemporary Women Leaders in the Arya Samaj*. Delhi: Sage Publications.

———. 1995. "The Autobiography of a Female Renouncer." In *Religions of India in Practice,* ed. Donald S. Lopez, 462–72. Princeton: Princeton University Press.

——— 1993. *The Arya Samaj as a Fundamentalist Movement: A Study in Comparative Fundamentalism*. Delhi: Manohar.

McGee, Mary. 1987. "Feasting and Fasting: The Vrata Tradition and Its Significance for Hindu Women." Ann Arbor: UMI, n. d. This is a photomechanical reproduction of a Th.D. dissertation, Harvard University.

Miller, Barbara Stoler, translator. 1986. *The Bhagavad-Gita: Krishna's Counsel in Time of War*. New York: Bantam Books.

Miran Yati, Swami. 1995. *Adarsh Grhini-Grhapati*. Jwalapur: privately published.

———. 1988. *Vaidik Nari*. Jwalapur: privately published.

Monier-Williams, Monier. 1899. *A Sanskrit-English Dictionary*. Revised edition, Oxford: Clarendon Press.

Pearson, Anne Mackenzie. 1996. *"Because It Gives Me Peace of Mind": Ritual Fasts in the Religious Lives of Hindu Women*. Albany: State University of New York Press.

Varmma, Ramcandra, chief editor. c. 1955. *Manak Hindi Kos*. Volume 1. Prayag: Hindi Sahitya Sammelan.

Zaehner, R. C. 1969. *The Bhagavad-Gita: With a Commentary Based on the Original Sources*. London: Oxford University Press.

IV

Conclusion: Some Promising Possibilities

15

Toward a Typology of South Asian Lay Vows

SELVA J. RAJ AND WILLIAM P. HARMAN

As you make your way through the final pages of this volume, you may find yourself perplexed by the breadth of traditions discussed here and by the bewildering variations that typify lay vows found in those traditions. There are the more public, temple-based vows as well as the private, domestic-based vows; the orthodox, officially sanctioned vows as well as the unorthodox, unconventional vows of the "god-intoxicated" devotees; the vows intended to amass spiritual power and eventual liberation as well as the vows that seek to garner benefits for mundane pursuits like healing, fertility, employment, and marriage; the corporate vows seeking health and prosperity for the family as well as the individual, private, unspoken vows secretly seeking personal benefits; the vows that reinforce orthodox religious boundaries as well as the vows that defy and transgress these boundaries, rendering them irrelevant; the gender-specific vows as well as the gender-neutral vows, performed in settings both private and public; the vows that create or reinforce devotees' identities as well as the vows that permit people to transcend identities of caste, religion, and gender; and—finally—the vows that marginalize the religiously privileged as well as the vows that privilege the socially and religiously marginalized.

Toward a Tentative Typology of South Asian Vows

To say that variety is the essence of lay religious life in South Asia is an understatement. Variegation permeates the religious and ritual fabric of the subcontinent. Accordingly, these essays reflect a pluralistic understanding of what a "vow" can be. It becomes useless to speak of one uniform type applicable to the whole gamut of South Asian traditions, but it may be useful to seek out a few patterns. We have not, then, opted for a chaos-induced despair. Rather, we want to suggest that there are various types or categories of vows, and within these categories there are specifiably patterned variations.

We begin by classifying South Asian lay vows into two broad currents. These currents are suggested by the first two categories under which the chapters in our table of contents are arranged. The first is "Getting What You Want," or what we would call "mundane vows," and the second category is "Getting What You Need," or what we would call "soteriological vows."

Soteriological vows are concerned with each individual's ultimate spiritual achievement, with what we all suspect we need to be concerned eventually. But that need is easier for most of us to postpone. Mundane vows, on the other hand, are concerned with achieving the good life in society, and with materialism, stability, and order. Vows taken in relation to soteriological goals are diffuse, and point toward transcendent and ultimate ends that could be described as otherworldly, thus not easily specified. Vows taken in relation to the mundane concerns are nonsoteriological, proximate rather than ultimate, and very much this-worldly. Soteriological vows pursue salvation in the world(s) to come, such as liberation from rebirth, salvation, nirvana, or heavenly bliss. Mundane vows pursue prosperity and success right now, in this world, and include vows for passing exams, healing, fertility, and prosperity. Soteriological vows are about getting "saved" eventually; mundane vows are about living well now.

Soteriological vows tend to be personal and individual, and only secondarily communal. The communal dimension is frequently subordinate to the personal spiritual quest commonly referred to as liberation or salvation. In the case of the Ramananda ascetics described by Lamb, the communal dimension plays an ancillary role. It assists, supports, and guides the individual's quest for soteriological goals. Also, the soteriological vows usually have explicit or tacit approval of the elite, textual tradition of religious orthodoxy. These may be gender-specific as in the case of Hindu women's vrats or gender-neutral, observed either in the domestic space or in the public arena.

The distinctions between these two major categories of vows are not always clear-cut. Performing a series of mundane vows may be understood as preparing the ground for greater achievements on a person's soteriological path. Any vow conscientiously performed invokes supernatural powers seen valuable for eventual soteriological gain. And yogis who perform great feats of self-sacrifice for the sake of spiritual detachment or improved rebirth may claim that these acts also invest them with valuable this-worldly talents, such as the ability to see the future or the past. It's a talent you can literally take to the bank, as the many fortune tellers of the subcontinent can attest.

Though we are dealing with the likes of "spiritual" South Asia, it should not be surprising that mundane vows are far more popular than soteriological vows: most lay folk would rather perform vows to help them gain employment at a particular business than dedicate themselves to performing a lifetime of vows that would help achieve a presumed better rebirth fifty years from now. South Asian devotees revere in principle the value of soteriological vows, and genuinely respect those who assume them, but it is the mundane vows that preoccupy their religious imagination and day-to-day ritual devotions.

Because the vast majority of vows in South Asia are performed in the mundane realm, most are concerned with achieving verifiable, identifiable, this-worldly goals. Such vows are "contracted" for a wide range of goals and involve a wide range of transcendent powers that people expect to deliver on requests made. Because the more mundane vows are by far the ones most often performed, we find greater variety in this particular category. The remaining paragraphs will discuss that variety, but it is important to point out that many of these vows are far from what we would call "mundane" in the normal sense of the term.

An Infinite Number of Mundane Vows

As a promise, a vow becomes a contract with a supernatural figure. For some, faith requires that the person entering into the contract do so with complete faith that what she or he wants will be granted in a way the deity sees fit. This sort of attitude engenders a style of vow in which a person pays "up front." You offer the deity your gift as a prepayment for a result you know will occur. We might call this a "down-payment vow." For example, a couple praying for a child might offer a small silver facsimile of a baby and promise to offer a gold facsimile of a baby when the prayer is answered. In some shrines like the shrine of Shahul Hamid in Nagore discussed in Narayanan's chapter, the down-payment vow is the principal vow undertaken by devotees.

Another, more cautious, approach is to pay only for "goods delivered." That is, you promise something to a deity and wait until you get it. Once you have received it, the time has come to pay up, to give the deity what was promised. This has to be seen as a more pragmatic, and less faith-filled, approach, and might be called a "fulfillment vow" because the vow is paid off only when it is fulfilled.

A very different variation on these themes is to offer the deity something even before you want something. Recognizing that you are dealing with a powerful force that can protect you and give you things you may eventually wish to have, you enter into a long-term "tribute" vow. With such a vow, you make it a habit to promise the deity regular gifts at calendrical intervals, knowing that, eventually, you will likely have a reason to ask even more of that deity. This resembles a spiritual insurance policy. You take out an original vow and maintain the payments on it indefinitely. These tribute vows serve also as thanksgiving offered to the saint or deity for his or her protection in the preceding year and to ensure his or her continued protection for the next year. Annual family pilgrimage to the saint's or deity's principal shrine during the shrine/temple festival and an assortment of offerings including votive offerings and animal sacrifices might constitute the actual vow ritual. Though not explicitly detailed in this volume, tribute vows are quite common in popular pilgrimage sites like the shrine of St. John de Britto, the Mariyamman temple, and the shrine of Shahul Hamid in Tamil Nadu.

Structurally similar to the tribute vow is the dedication vow. In the dedication vow, newborn children are dedicated to the family's chosen clan or patron saint or deity (*kula teiyvam*). Offering the first crop of hair of children and naming newborns after the patron saint or deity are some of the more popular expressions of dedication vows. In this instance, the vow acts as an insurance premium for the saint's or deity's protection for the child. The focus is clearly on the health and welfare of the child, and an occasional renewal of the vow is expected, usually on the anniversary of its commencement.

If we can talk about variations on mundane vows by classing them as "downpayment vows," "fulfillment vows," "tribute vows," and "dedication vows," we can also talk about additional characteristics each of these four categories will share. Specifically, each of these can be either transgressive, normative, identity-forming, gender-specific, or gender-neutral. Clearly, this is becoming complicated since we have twenty possible combinations! Briefly, here is how they work.

Transgressive vows would be those in which people make promises to supernatural figures not a part of the tradition to which they belong. Prominent in the vows discussed by Raj, Narayanan, Harman, Goonasekera, and Uddin, these vows serve as a metaphor for the liminal religious condition of the average South Asian lay devotee. They are vows that plunge the religious actor into ritual dialogue by placing that person in the midst of activities of a tradition not normally her own. These vows defy and transgress normative boundaries regarding sacred space, sacred figures, and sacred rites. The vows effect a subtle grassroots integration between institutionally disparate religious traditions. As suggested in our introduction, the transgressive vow constitutes perhaps the most singular feature of South Asian lay religion. Distinct from these are the normative vows, vows a person is expected to take within his or her own tradition. These vows renew and reinforce institutional boundaries. This is amply exemplified in the Hindu women's *vrats* discussed in Pintchman's chapter. Taking vows within your own tradition is the conventional thing to do. It reinforces identity in that tradition.

"Identity-forming vows" are similar. These vows help construct for devotees distinct, new religious and ethnic identities, often as a result of changed social, cultural, and political contexts. Baumann's chapter highlights how the vows performed in the public arena by the Sri Lankan Tamil Hindu diaspora in Germany not only help reinforce religious commitment but provide a ritual platform to display their newfound, complex identity as Tamils, Hindus, Sri Lankans, and Germans. Vows also help build a nationalist, communal identity for a minority community living in an alien context. This nationalist strand is even more pronounced in the Khalsa vows discussed in Fenech and Singh's chapter. Here vows are not merely nationalist symbols and identity markers but function as negotiation tools for minority political representation in a predominantly Hindu country.

Gender-specific vows form the cornerstone of Hindu women's devotional life, and are directed toward achieving family health, prosperity, and a spouse's longevity. But Hindu women utilize the very same devotional vows as religiously sanctioned tools for enhancing female solidarity, agency, autonomy, and prestige. While most gender-specific vows are firmly rooted in orthodox religious teaching (McGee 1987; Pearson 1996), these are equally visible in popular and folk Hinduism (Wadley 1980; McDaniel 2003). This predominance of gender-specific vows does not obliterate or exclude gender-neutral vows in popular Hinduism as Harman and Baumann suggest. Uddin's treatment of Muslim vows in Bangladesh highlights the gender specific quality of vows in that tradition. With the exception of Jainism, a gendered focus is less common in other South Asian religious traditions. Gender specific vows include fasting, abstinence, and prayers. These generally tend to be less dramatic. Gender-neutral vows exhibit a propensity for spectacular public displays and include extreme physical endurance, ascetic discipline, and religious commitment. Fire-walking, body-circumambulation, and carrying of firepots are examples popular at Mariyamman temples, the Kataragama shrine, the shrine of St. John de Britto, and Muslim *mazars*. While most gender-neutral vows are focused on realizing short-term, mundane goals, others, like the Hindu women's *vrats,* may link short-term goals to long-term ends such as better rebirth in the next life.

Concluding Reflections

Basic to the way vows operate in South Asia is their dialogical quality, and this dialogical dynamic functions in several distinct ways. First, the parties involved—human and supernatural—are engaged in mutual give-and-take transactions, and each side has an interest in profiting from the transaction. Generally, a devotee will always end up better off from transactions with supernatural figures that have large followings. This is usually true no matter how the "deal" turns out. Even when a devotee fails to keep her or his end of a bargain, and even if such failures are understood to displease a deity, the relationship generated by the process is usually evaluated as positive because it generates mutual interaction and dialogue with the deity.

When we consider what we have called "soteriological vows," we are addressing a dialogue not between a devotee and a deity so much as we are addressing a devotee's internal and personal dialogue with the conceptual apparatus of his or her tradition. Someone seeking to achieve *moksha* enters into dialogue with the teachings and prescriptions of a long and venerated tradition. The discipline of putting those teachings into practice is a form of sustained spiritual dialogue with the truths of that tradition. A Buddhist monk, for example, takes a vow to engage himself dialogically with the Noble Eightfold Path. He undertakes to pursue it as it, in turn, spiritually pursues him.

The concept "ritual dialogue" (Raj 2002, 2004) in the context of vows suggests another perspective. Adherents of different religious traditions, in performing each others' customary vows to each others' deities, are brought into a religiously communal contact—and dialogue—with each other. Muslims making offerings at Hindu shrines, Hindus performing rituals at Christian shrines, Christians taking Buddhist pilgrimages: these, and more, are examples of ritual, as opposed to theoretical dialogue (Raj 2000: 333–53). They transcend the rigid and apparently impermeable ritual boundaries of their respective traditions. This ritual activity differs significantly from traditionally conceived "religious dialogue." Conventional religious dialogue normally focuses on the cerebral rather than the physical, on discussions rather than on action, on the hope for mutual understanding rather than on performing similar acts in a similar space in honor of the same supernatural powers.

The enduring vitality and pervasiveness of lay vows in South Asia is a metatradition in its own right, organically emerging from religiously pluralistic contexts. Vows act as a corrective and complement to the conceptual, elitist, institutional religious models that can become divorced from the existential experiences of the masses. Vows provide direct ritual access to supernatural deities and goals, allowing common worshippers to extemporize for themselves and to bypass altogether the institutional formulas prescribed to them. Ritual dialogue, in each sense of the term, enables a shift in focus away from institutionally contrived, top-down dialogical experiments to bottom-up dialogue on the ground. Finally, ritual dialogue among different traditions cautions scholars against drawing sharp, rigid contrasts between coexisting religious groups and ideologies (Dempsey 2001: 4). As such, ritual dialogue calls for a shift in the academic study of religion in general and of South Asian religions in particular. This would be a shift from the traditional focus on self-contained, insular religious traditions; indeed, a change that might well entail a whole new way of dealing with deities.

References

Dempsey, Corinne G. 2001. *Kerala Christian Sainthood: Collisions of Culture and Worldview in South India.* NY: Oxford University Press.

McDaniel, June. 2003. *Making Virtuous Daughters and Wives: An Introduction to Women's Brata Rituals in Bengali Folk Religion.* Albany: State University of New York Press.

McGee, Mary. 1987. *Feasting and Fasting: The Vrata Tradition and Its Significance for Hindu Women*, Th.d. Dissertation, Harvard University.

Pearson, Anne Mackenzie. 1996. *"Because It Gives Me Peace of Mind": Ritual Fasts in the Religious Lives of Hindu Women.* Albany: State University of New York Press.

Raj, Selva J. 2004. "Dialogue 'On the Ground': The Complicated Identities and the Complex Negotiations of Catholics and Hindus in South India." *Journal of Hindu-Christian Studies* 17: 33–44.

———. 2002. "The Jordan, the Ganges, and the Mountain: The Three Strands of Santal Popular Catholicism." In *Popular Christianity in India: Riting Between the Lines,* eds. Selva J. Raj and Corinne G. Dempsey, 39–60. Albany: State University of New York Press.

———. 2000. "Adapting Hindu Imagery: A Critical Look at Ritual Experiments in an Indian Catholic Ashram." *Journal of Ecumenical Studies* 37: 333–53.

Wadley, Susan. 1980. "Hindu Women's Family and Household Rites in a North Indian Village." In *Unspoken Worlds: Women's Religious Lives in Non-Western Cultures*, eds. N. A. Falk and R. M. Gross, 94-109. San Francisco: Harper & Row.

Glossary

The words in this glossary represent a wide variety of languages found in South Asia. Because the glossary terms listed here often occur in slightly variant forms in several related languages, we indicate the language grouping (rather than the language) from which each term is derived. The three major language groupings are: 1) Indo-European (IE), a group that includes Hindi, Gujarati, Marathi, Marwari, Sanskrit, Bengali, Oriya, Rajasthani, Sinhala, Persian, and Pali, among others; 2) Dravidian (DR), a grouping that includes Tamil, Malayalam, Kannada, and Telugu; and 3) Semitic (SM), a grouping that includes Arabic and Hebrew, among others.

Abhisheka (IE)	Ritual involving the bathing or anointing the image of a deity, usually in a temple.
Adi Granth (IE)	Sikh sacred scripture. Also known as Guru Granth Sahib.
Akal Purakh (IE)	Sikh term for "God."
Akhand Path (IE)	Sikh ritual involving the continuous recitation of the Guru Granth Sahib.
Ampara (IE)	A group of Qur'anic chapters commonly recited during ritual prayer.
Amrit (IE)	"Nectar of immortality," in the Sikh tradition used in ritual contexts.
Amritdhari (IE)	A Sikh who has been initiated into the Khalsa.
Anahar (IE)	A grain diet; the basic Hindu vegetarian diet.

Ankappiratittai (IE)	Prone rolling of the body on the ground around a temple.
Anushthan (IE)	A predetermined spiritual undertaking for a specified length of time.
Arude (IE)	Literally, "occupying a seat." The term also connotes being possessed by a spirit.
Asanam (IE)	A ritual meal, or the act of offering a ritual meal.
Ashrama (IE)	The fourfold system of life stages in classical Hinduism.
Astangasilla (IE)	Sanskrit and Pali for the eight traditional precepts, used in reference to special Buddhist observance days.
Atiyen (DR)	"I am [your] servant;" a word used by poet saints in the Tamil bhakti tradition to refer to themselves in relation to Shiva.
Atme (IE)	A birth into one of the many worlds into which all living beings are serially born.
Ayambil (IE)	The vow to eat only one sitting per day of tasteless food.
Bachan (IE)	"Word," in giving one's word to do or not do something.
Bana (IE)	Khalsa Sikh attire.
Bara (IE)	A Sri Lankan Buddhist vow.
Baraka (SM)	A divine blessing in Bangladeshi Islam.
Batha (IE)	Cooked rice.
Bhakris (IE)	Term for flat cakes fried on a griddle.
Bhakta (IE)	A person devoted to a god or a goddess.
Bhakti (IE)	Love or devotion, usually for a deity.
Bhavana (IE)	A devotional mood.
Bodhisattva (IE)	Someone who has taken a vow to become a Buddha.
Brata (IE)	Linguistic variant for "vow."
Bratu nemu (IE)	Vow of truthfulness in the Sikh tradition.

Chaitra (IE) — Auspicious lunar month for summer festivals.
Dan (IE) — Offerings or gifts.
Danaya (IE) — Alms-giving.
Danrdiya (IE) — The largest sub-order of Ramanandi ascetics.
Dargah (IE) — A Muslim Shrine.
Dasasila/Dasasil (IE) — The ten (*dasa*) precepts (*sila*) observed by world renouncers who do not become a monk or a nun.
Deva sabha (IE) — An assembly of deities.
Devalaya (IE) — A temple dedicated to a deity.
Devatas (IE) — Minor Hindu deities.
Deviyo (IE) — Deity.
Dharma (IE) — Law, custom, duty, or religion.
Dhikr (IE) — Prayer of remembrance in Islam.
Dhuni (IE) — The sacred fire of an ascetic.
Digambar (IE) — "Sky-clad," the smaller of the two Jain sects whose monks go naked.
Dua (IE) — Petitionary prayer in Islam.
Dudhahar (IE) — A diet limited to milk products.
Ghat (IE) — Steps or a platform on a riverbank.
Gopuram (DR) — Entrance tower leading to a temple.
Grahayo (IE) — Astrological planets.
Guna (IE) — Quality, a characteristic.
Gurdwara (IE) — A Sikh place of worship.
Guru Granth Sahib (IE) — Sikh sacred scripture. See also Adi Granth
Guru vandan (IE) — Guru worship, the formal prayers made to living or deceased mendicants.
Hadith (SM) — In Islam, a collection of sacred stories about Muhammad.
Harimandir Sahib (IE) — A term for the Sikh Golden Temple in Amritsar.

Hundi (IE)	A receptacle for offerings in sacred shrines. Also called *untiyal*.
Imanfikan (IE)	A term used in Sikhism for those who fail to value their faith in God.
Jagara (IE)	Nightlong vigil, associated with rituals or celebrations.
Jai Kara (IE)	A slogan signifying victory, uttered in Sikh ritual contexts.
Jinas (IE)	Jain teachers of infinite wisdom who have escaped the world of karmic rebirth.
Kaba (SM)	Central religious shrine in Mecca.
Kacchahira (IE)	A pair of short breeches worn by the Sikh male.
Kangha (IE)	A wooden comb worn by Sikh males.
Kankanankattutal (DR)	Act of tying a cord around the wrist as a visible reminder of a vow taken.
Kappukkattutal (DR)	Act of tying a yellow string or amulet on the arm as a reminder of an unfulfilled vow.
Kapurala (IE)	Priest in a temple.
Kara (IE)	A steel wrist ring worn by Sikh males.
Karamah (IE)	Acts of generosity from a deity.
Karamat (IE)	A religious miracle in Islam.
Karaniyametta (IE)	A Buddhist non-canonical text addressing compassion.
Karma (IE)	Actions and their results. In Jain contexts, the material substance which, as a result of an act, binds to a soul leading to that soul's rebirth.
Karmayoga (IE)	Disciplined, unselfish action that leads to freedom from rebirth.
Kartik vrat (IE)	A vow performed in the 8th lunar month of Kartik, usually October/November.
Karva chauth vrat (IE)	Ritual performed by women, especially for their husbands' longevity.
Katampattal (DR)	Offering a gift of fruit to a temple deity as a vow.

Katha (IE)	A story, often illustrating the application of a social or religious rule.
Kavati (DR)	A ritual arch that devotees carry on their shoulders to fulfill vows. Also refers to the event of spirit possession which the act induces.
Kavi (IE)	Saffron clothing worn by renouncers.
Kavya (IE)	Stylized, epic poetry.
Kes (IE)	Unshorn hair of the Sikh male.
Ketu (IE)	The name of an astrological position, the south node of the moon.
Khadim (SM)	Caretaker of a Muslim shrine.
Khalsa (IE)	Order of Sikh initiates founded by Guru Gobind Singh in 1699. Also meaning, fully initiated Sikh.
Khande di pahul (IE)	Initiation ritual into Khalsa Sikhism.
Kula teiyvam (IE)	Family deity, one that insures protection for the family.
Kurukkal (IE)	Temple priest.
Kurusadi (DR)	A Christian wayside shrine.
Kuttiyaattam (DR)	A vow to dance publicly while circumambulating a shrine with steel rods embedded in one's flesh.
Kutumivankutal (DR)	A ritual in which a deity receives the offering of a devotee's hair which has been shaved off.
Langoti (IE)	Loincloth
Lungi (IE)	An unsewn piece of cloth worn from the waist down.
MahaShivaratri (IE)	"The great night of Shiva," a major festival to the Hindu god Shiva.
Mahatyagi (IE)	The most ascetic suborder of Ramanandis.
Maitri (IE)	Compassion.
Manat (IE)	Popular vows made in Islamic shrines of Bangladesh.
Mangala (IE)	Auspiciousness, that which bodes well for the future.

Mannat manani (IE)	Vows taken secretly by Sikh women in expectation of a boon. See also *suh sukhani*.
Mantra (IE)	A short phrase understood to have its own power and recited in order to harness that power.
Matam (IE)	A religious educational institution in Hinduism.
Maun (IE)	Silence.
Mawlid (SM)	Celebration of a Muslim's saint's birth anniversary.
Maya (IE)	Classical philosophical term for worldly illusion.
Maynasundari (IE)	The mythological queen of King Shripal, and the paradigmatic performer of siddhacakra worship and its attendant vows.
Mazar (SM)	A Muslim shrine, often containing the burial remains of a revered Islamic figure.
Moksha (IE)	Ultimate spiritual liberation.
Mughal (IE)	Turkish, Islamic empire or ruler in India.
Munajat (SM)	Devotional prayer in Islam.
Muri (DR)	Promissory note in Christian vow rituals.
Murtipujak (IE)	"Image worshippers," the largest subsect of the Shvetambar Jains.
Muruten (IE)	A kitchen in a temple.
Nadhr (SM)	A term for "vow," literally meaning "promise."
Nagaswaram (DR)	Traditional horn instrument in Tamil music.
Navakkirakam or **Navagraha** (IE)	Nine planets, venerated with puja in the temple.
Navkar mantra (IE)	The most important Jain mantra which venerates the five highest beings.
Nerttikkatan (DR)	The process of entering into a contractual agreement with a deity or saint, often accompanied by an offering from the devotee. Variant constructions of the term include *Nerccai* and *Nertti*.
Nirahar (IE)	No food; a fast consisting of only water consumption.

Nishacara (IE)	"Nightgoer," a description of the Hindu god Shiva.
Nonpu (DR)	A vow by women to perform early morning rituals, usually for the acquisition or the health of a husband.
Oli (IE)	"Line," a series of fasts in a particular pattern, often refers to the autumnal and vernal festivals in which Jains perform the ayambil fast.
Oppu (IE)	Proof or fulfillment of a vow.
Otuvar (DR)	A professional singer of hymns in the Tamil bhakti tradition.
Pacckkhan (IE)	A statement of intention to perform a fast, which is required for a Jain fast to be efficacious.
Paimashikan (IE)	A term used in Sikhism for "oath-breakers."
Pakkacedil (DR)	A vow to allow oneself to be lifted into the air by a series of ropes and hooks embedded in a person's flesh.
Pan (DR)	An established tune in Tamil classical music.
Panj banis (IE)	Liturgical prayers in Sikhism.
Pansil (IE)	The five vows for the Buddhist lay person.
Panth (IE)	The proper religious path as understood among Sikhs.
Paryusan (IE)	An eight-day Jain festival in early autumn marked by a dramatic increase in vow-taking.
Pativrata (IE)	Sanskrit, literally a woman whose vow (*vrat*) is her husband (*pati*), that is, a woman who is religiously devoted to her husband.
Patnivrata (IE)	A husband dedicated to the welfare of his wife.
Peni (IE)	Sinhala for treacle or edible syrup from a plant.
Phalahar (IE)	Fruit diet; a diet of only fruit, along with certain vegetables and other foods.
Pihita (IE)	Sinhala for support or help.
Pir (SM)	Muslim saint.
Pirattinai (DR)	see *vrat*.
Poruttanai (DR)	see *vrat*.

Poya (IE)	Holy days in the lunar calendar which are auspicious for Buddhist religious activities.
Prane (IE)	Life as it exists in a living being.
Pratigya (IE)	Promise.
Pratikraman (IE)	A Jain ritual recitation which recognizes and expiates sins or errors. A form of confession.
Promesa (IE)	Traditional vows made by Catholic women in Spain.
Puja (IE)	Act of Hindu worship in home or temple.
Puja vattiya (IE)	A ritual offering tray.
Pujari (IE)	Hindu ritual administrant.
Punyanumodana (IE)	Transfer of auspicious cosmic results of ethical deeds to another person.
Purana (IE)	Classical mythic and wondrous story in Hinduism.
Raga (IE)	An established tune in Carnatic music.
Rahit (IE)	Code of conduct in the Sikh tradition.
Rahu (IE)	A mythical planet in Indian astrology.
Ramanandi (IE)	An order of Hindu ascetics.
Rashi (IE)	An astrological sector (house) in a horoscope.
Ratana (IE)	A precious jewel.
Rudraksha (IE)	A seed sacred to Shiva, often used to make a necklace.
Rupe (IE)	Image, appearance, figure, diagram, picture.
Sadhana (IE)	Any form of religious practice.
Sadhu (IE)	Ascetic religious leader in Hinduism.
Salah (SM)	Daily performance of ritual prayer in Islam.
Samadhi (IE)	A term describing a burial site of a great religious figure or the state of passing beyond death.
Sampraday (IE)	Religious sect or group.
Sankalp (IE)	Statement of intention to complete a vow.
Sankara (IE)	A name for the Hindu deity Shiva.

Sannyasin (IE)	An ascetic who has renounced social life to pursue spiritual goals.
Sejda (SM)	Prostration in Islam in which the head touches the ground.
Shaiva (IE)	Relating to devotion to Shiva.
Shaiva Siddhanta (IE)	A classical philosophical school in Hinduism.
Shakti (IE)	A term for female power, often personified as a goddess.
Shapath (IE)	Oath, promise, such as that taken by an elected official.
Shivaratri (IE)	"The night of Shiva," occurring each month on the last day of the moon's waning cycle. See also *MahaShivaratri*.
Shripal (IE)	A mythological king associated with the worship of the siddhacakra.
Shvetambar (IE)	"White clad," the larger of the two major Jain sects.
Siddhacakra (IE)	A Jain yantra representing the Navkar Mantra.
Siddhi (IE)	Powers believed to be attained through the successful completion of various austerities, vows, and yogic practices.
Sikh Rahit Maryada (IE)	A text explicating the Khalsa Sikh code for conduct.
Sil (IE)	Precept.
Stupa (IE)	Buddhist hemispherical monument containing sacred objects. Vehera in colloquial Sinhala.
Suhag (IE)	Good fortune, prosperity.
Sukh sukhani (IE)	Vows taken secretly by Sikh women in expectation of a boon. See also *mannat manani*.
Sunna (SM)	"Tradition" in Islam, based on the actions of Muhammad.
Sura (SM)	A chapter of the Qur'an.
Sutra/Suttare (IE)	Formula, text, or sermon containing theory.
Swami (IE)	Title of a religious leader in Hinduism. A variant is *sami*.

Tali (DR)	Medallion worn by women given on the day of marriage and signifying a woman's marriage status.
Tap, tapas, tapasya (IE)	Austerities and/or their practice.
Teemiti (DR)	See *Tikkulipayatal*
Tevaram (IE)	The collection of hymns by the three classical major poet saints in the Tamil bhakti tradition.
Tikkulipayatal (DR)	Walking on burning coals of fire as a vow. See also *teemiti*.
Tiraya (IE)	Curtain.
Tithi (IE)	Lunar day.
Tri Tap (IE)	The three-fold austerity vow of the Tyagi and Mahatyagi sub-orders.
Tyagi (IE)	A sub-order of Ramanandi ascetics.
Ulama (SM)	Scholarly tradition in Islam.
Upavasa (IE)	Fasting.
Updhan (IE)	A complex vow to live like a Jain mendicant for forty-five days.
Urs (SM)	Celebration of a Muslim saint's wedding anniversary.
Utsava murti (IE)	Image of a deity used in processions.
Vahana (IE)	Vehicle of a god or goddess.
Vahiguru (IE)	Sikh term for God.
Vairagi (IE)	The name generally applied to members of the Danrdiya sub-order of Ramanandi ascetics.
Vairagya (IE)	Non-attachment.
Vaishnava (IE)	A devotee of Vishnu or of a deity closely associated with Vishnu.
Varaprasadi (IE)	"Likely to grant wishes," a term describing a deity likely to grant wishes.
Vattiya (IE)	Tray made by weaving strands of bark or leaf.
Vimana (IE)	Smaller tower above the main shrine of a temple.

Virakt (IE)	One who keeps nothing; a renunciant.
Vrat (IE)	"Vow," "fast," "promise" or their enactment. Variants include *vrata*, brata, and *vratu*.
Wali (SM)	Muslim saint.
Yal (IE)	Traditional stringed instrument in Tamil music.
Yantra (IE)	An abstract geometric design serving as a visual manifestation of a mantra.
Yatikava (IE)	Ritual pleading or prayer.
Ziyarat (SM)	A pilgrimage to the shrine of a Muslim saint.

Contributors

MARTIN BAUMANN is Professor of History of Religions at the University of Lucerne (Switzerland) and research fellow at the University of Hannover (Germany). His teaching and research focus includes diaspora studies, Buddhism in the West, and Hindu traditions in Europe and the Caribbean. He has published on these topics in both German and English. His most recent book is *Migration, Religion, Integration* (2000).

LOU FENECH is Associate Professor of South Asian History at the University of Northern Iowa. His areas of expertise are Sikh history, religion, and culture. His more recent publications include *Martyrdom in the Sikh Tradition: Playing the "Game of Love"* and "Contested Nationalisms; Negotiated Terrains: The Way Sikhs Remember Udham Singh 'Shahid' (1899–1941)," in *Modern Asian Studies*.

SUNIL GOONASEKERA is Senior Lecturer in Sociology at the University of Peradeniya, Sri Lanka. He has conducted field research in Rajasthan, India, on Jain monasticism. His publications include a monograph, entitled "George Keyt: Interpretations," on the life and works of the Sri Lankan artist George Keyt. Goonasekera's areas of research specialization include anthropology of religion, law, art, and music.

WILLIAM P. HARMAN is Head of the Department of Philosophy and Religion at the University of Tennessee at Chattanooga. A former president of the Midwest American Academy of Religion and former chair of the Department of Religion at DePauw University, he has written *The Sacred Marriage of a Hindu Goddess* (Indiana and Motilal) and over thirty articles or book chapters in English or French on Hinduism, ritual, and the study of religion.

M. WHITNEY KELTING is Assistant Professor of Religious Studies at Northeastern University. Her recent book, *Singing to the Jinas*, focuses on devotional singing among Gujarati Jain women in Maharashtra. Her latest project examines narratives associated with Jain women's fasting and ritual practice.

RAMDAS LAMB is Associate Professor of Religion at the University of Hawai'i, Manoa. He was a sadhu in the Ramananda Sampraday in north India for nine years. His research interests include South Asian asceticism, devotionalism, and low-caste religion, and his most recent publication is *Wrapt in the Name: The Ramnamis, Ramnam, and Untouchable Religion in Central India* (2002).

JACK E. LLEWELLYN is Professor in the Department of Religious Studies at Southwest Missouri State University. He has written two books about the Arya Samaj, a modern Hindu revivalist movement. Recently he has been working on pilgrimage, especially the Kumbha Mela, the world's largest pilgrimage festival.

VASUDHA NARAYANAN is Professor of Religion at the University of Florida. She is a former president of the American Academy of Religion and the past president of the Society for Hindu-Christian Studies. She has written and edited five books including *The Vernacular Veda: Revelation, Recitation and Ritual* (1994) and numerous articles.

KAREN PECHILIS teaches Asian and Comparative Religions and is Associate Professor of Religious Studies as well as NEH Distinguished Teaching Professor and Director of the Humanities at Drew University. She is the author of *The Embodiment of Bhakti* (2000), editor of *The Graceful Guru* (2004), and has written several articles on Hindu devotionalism.

TRACY PINTCHMAN is Professor of Religious Studies and Hindu Studies at Loyola University, Chicago. Her publications include *The Rise of the Goddess in the Hindu Tradition* (1994), *Guests at God's Wedding: Celebrating Kartik Among the Women of Benares* (2005), and she edited *Seeking Mahadevi: Constructing the Identities of the Hindu Great Goddess* (2001), in addition to publishing several articles.

SELVA J. RAJ is Stanley S. Kresge Professor and Chair of Religious Studies at Albion College. He is a former president of the Midwest American Academy of Religion and the past-president of the Society for Hindu-Christian Studies. He is a co-editor with Corinne Dempsey of *Popular Christianity in India: Riting between the Lines* (2002) and author of several articles on Hindu-Christian ritual exchange.

PASHAURA SINGH is Assistant Professor of Sikh Studies and Punjabi Language in the Department of Asian Languages and Cultures at the University of Michigan, Ann Arbor. His speciality includes Sikh Studies and Religion in Modern India, with emphasis on textual studies and hermeneutics. He is the author of *The Guru Granth Sahib: Canon, Meaning, and Authority* (Oxford University Press, 2000).

SUFIA UDDIN is Associate Professor in the Department of Religion at the University of Vermont. She has conducted field research in Bangladesh and Calcutta, India. Her research focuses on construction and transformation of Bengali–Muslim identity and popular piety in Bangladesh.

Appendix

Essays Arranged According to Tradition

I. Hinduism
- Chapter 2   "The Vow": A Short Story
- Chapter 3   Negotiating Relationships with the Goddess
- Chapter 8   Performing Vows in Diasporic Contexts: Tamil Hindus, Temples, and Goddesses in Germany
- Chapter 9   Devoting Oneself to Shiva through Song
- Chapter 10   Monastic Vows and the Ramananda Sampraday
- Chapter 13   When Vows Fail to Deliver What They Promise: The Case of Shyamavati
- Chapter 14   Two Critiques of Women's Vows

II. Islam
- Chapter 5   Religious Vows at the Shrine of Shahul Hamid
- Chapter 6   In the Company of *Pirs*: Making Vows, Receiving Favors at Bangladeshi Sufi Shrines

III. Christianity
- Chapter 4   Shared Vows, Shared Space, and Shared Deities: Vow Rituals among Tamil Catholics in South India

IV. Jainism
- Chapter 11   Negotiating Karma, Merit, and Liberation: Vow-taking in the Jain Tradition

V. Sikhism
- Chapter 12   Vows in the Sikh Tradition

VI. Buddhism
- Chapter 7   *Bara*: Buddhist Vows at Kataragama

Index

abhisheka, 140; defined, 257
Achutappa Naiker, 69, 70, 73
Adam and Eve, 69–70
Adarsh Grhini-Grhapati (Miran Yati), 239
Adi Granth, 201, 202–203, 204, 213; defined, 257
Africa, 83
Ajmeer Sharif, 94
Akali Sikhs, 211–12
Akal Purakh, 206, 207, 208; defined, 257
Akal Takhat, 211, 212–13
akhand path, 209, 213; defined, 257
Alutnuwara Deviyo, 110
Alvar, Tirumangai, 66
Ampara, 92; defined, 257
amrit, 205, 206, 210; defined, 257
Amritdhari, 205; defined, 257
amrit-vela, 204
anahar, 173; defined, 257
anand karaj, 205
Anand marriage ceremony, 205, 208–209
Anandpur, 203
animals, 96, 97, 116; and saints, 91
animal sacrifices, 4, 5, 77, 252; and healing, 64n17; and *nerccais*, 45, 49, 51, 57; and Shahul Hamid, 72
ankappiratatcinam, 33

ankappiratittai, 135–36; defined, 258. See also circumambulation
Annandurai, 157
Anne, St., 1, 47, 49; and baby auctioning rite, 53–56
Anthony, St., 1, 47–49, 52; and healing, 57–60; and shared deities, 61
Anthony of Padua, St., 48
anushthans, 168–74, 178; defined, 258
Appar, 149, 150–51, 158, 159, 160
Aptul Kaatiru Nayinar Leppai Alim,Ceyk (Sheikh), 67
arahaths, 125
Ardas, 209, 213
Arjuna, 148
arude, 117, 118, 119; defined, 258
Arulanandapuram, xvii, 47, 49, 54
Arulanandasamy, 45
Arya, Shakuntala, 241–42
Arya Samaj, 235, 238–40
asanam, 57–59; defined, 258; ill., 58
asceticism: and Jains, 188, 190, 192; and Sikhs, 201
ascetics, 4, 6, 8–9, 10, 147, 148, 250; Buddhist, 167; Jain, 167
ashrama, 191; defined, 258
astangasilla, 107; defined, 258
astrology, 12, 110–11, 116, 245n8
asylum, 131, 132

275

atasil, 107
atiyen, 155–56; defined, 258
Atman, 167
atme, 112; defined, 258
Aurangzeb, 203
Awami League, 87
ayambil, 192–95; defined, 258
Ayambil Oli, 187, 192, 193, 194
Ayodhya, xvii

Baba Buddha, 209
Baba Dip Singh, 210–11, 213
baby auction rite, 4, 43, 53–56; ill., 54, 55
bachan, 168, 170–71; defined, 258
Badar, Pir, 94
Badone, Ellen, 8
Badr, Battle of, 90, 102
Bagerhat, 88, 90
bana, 207; defined, 258
Bangladesh, 1, 3, 7, 87–105
Bangladesh National Party (BNP), 87
bani, 207
bara, 107–28; defined, 258
Bara Bazar, 90
baraka, 90; defined, 258
barakat, 76, 77, 79
batha, 117; defined, 258
baths, 57, 59, 65, 221
Baumann, Martin, 129–44
"Because It Gives Me Peace of Mind": Ritual Fasts in the Religious Lives of Hindu Women (Pearson), 29
Benares, xvii, 220, 221–22
Bengal, 91, 95, 100, 101–102
Besant Nagar, 154
bhagy, 229–30
Bhai Gurdas Bhalla, 204
Bhai Taru Singh, 210
bhakris, 17, 18, 20, 21; defined, 258
bhaktas, 8, 131, 140, 142; defined, 258
bhakti, 6, 10, 148–49, 166, 167, 171, 227; defined, 258; hymns, 151–60; poetry, 149–51; as vow, 160
bhaktiya, 119
Bhanginis, 237

Bharati Devi, 240
Bharatiya Janata Party, 241
bhavana, 119; defined, 258
Bhindranwale, Sant Jarnail Singh, 212–13
Bistam (city), 88
Bistami, Bayazid, 87, 88
blood sacrifices, 29, 30, 31, 33, 36
bodhisattva, 122, 123, 182; defined, 258
Bodhisattva, Maitri, 109–10
body position restrictions, 176–77
Brahmans, 29, 236, 237, 238
Braj, 222
bratas, 5; defined, 258
bratu, 214n3
bratu nemu, 201; defined, 258
bricolage, 80–84
Britto, John de. *See* John de Britto, St.
Buddha Maitri, 123
Buddhas, 125, 127n20
Buddhism, 2, 107, 167, 182
Buddhists, 95, 107–28
Budha (Mercury), 111

Cakkeshvari, 193
Cakul Amitu Nayakar, 67
Calixtus, George, 81
Campantar, 149, 154–55, 158
Canada, 130
Candeshvara, 135
caste identities, 45–46
castes, 48, 49, 58, 77; and the Bhagavad Gita, 236–38; Hindu, 80; interdependence of, 237; and Ramananda, 168
Catholicism, 8, 12n4
Catholics, 4, 11, 126n4; and *asanam,* 58; in Spain, 8, 12n4, 62; Tamil, 43–64, 131
Cekuna Pulavar, 67
celibacy, 172, 174, 201
Chaitra, 16; defined, 259
Chennai, xvii, 152, 154
Chittagong, xvii, 1, 88
Christian, William A., 8
Christianity, 2, 7, 83, 92, 161n2
Christians, 95

Chutalaimadan, 48, 60
Ciombatore, 84
Cira Puranam, 82
circumambulation, 32, 51, 52, 59, 253; in *asanam,* 5; in cradle rite, 56; at Ganesha temple, 141; in German Tamil temples, 134–36; ill., 135; Sikh, 208, 209. *See also ankappiratatcinam*
Civacaryar, Umapati, 161n6
civilization building, 90–91
clothing, 35, 60, 174, 178
coconuts, 5, 19, 71, 114, 118–19; ill., 120, 121
coconut sapling, 52–53, 126n13; ill., 53
coins, 112, 227; ill., 113
confession, 192, 193, 195, 196, 198
Cort, John E., 187, 190, 196
cosmology, 110–11, 125
cradle rite, 56
crocodiles, 90
culture, 2–3, 82, 83, 101
Cuntarar, 149, 158
Cutler, Norman, 156

dama, 166
dan, 219; defined, 259
danaya, 117; defined, 259
dances, 117, 119, 137, 139–40; ill., 38, 137
Dandapani, Sami, 153, 154–57, 160, 161n7
Danrdiya, 177–78; defined, 259
Darbar Sahib, 213
dargahs, 7, 65, 82, 83–84; in Bangladesh, 88; defined, 259; Kovalam, 75; Madurai, 75; Malaysian, 77
dasasila, 107; defined, 259
debt, 8, 32–33, 44
debt payment, 44, 53, 56, 60
dedication rites, 49, 52, 252
Dedimunda, 109, 110
demonic spirits, 48
Dempsey, Corinne, 61
destiny, 229–30
devalaya, 108; defined, 259

deva sabha, 111; defined, 259
devatas, 109, 110; defined, 259
Devi, Prajna, 242, 243
devivaru, 109
deviyanta barayak venava, 109
deviyos, 109, 110, 111; defined, 259
devotion, 148–49, 152, 168, 183
devotional rites, 11, 44–45, 49–60, 72, 227. *See also nerccais*
dharma, 148, 151, 227, 237, 242, 243; defined, 259
Dharmapuram Atinam, 154
dhikr, 92, 99, 101; defined, 259
dhuni, 180; defined, 259
dhuni tap, 178; ill., 179
diaspora, 129–44, 253
Dibisch, Jill, 3
Digambar, 188; defined, 259
dining, 80. *See also* food
disciplines, 32
divine grace, 68
domains: of *baras,* 123–25
donation boxes. *See* offering boxes
down payment vows, 3, 49, 65, 73, 251
Draupadi, 239
dua, 92; defined, 259
dudhahar, 173, 174; defined, 259

economics, 97–99, 101
enlightenment, 167, 182
environment, 91, 101
Epics, 167
"Epistle of Victory," 203
equity, 123
Erasmus, 81
Ernst, Carl, 81
ethical conduct, 122, 123
exorcism, 72

failures, 31, 75, 125, 253–54; of *vrats,* 219–33
faith, 6, 62, 251
faith healing, 83
familial well-being, 10, 225, 227, 231; and Jains, 187, 190, 193, 194, 198; and Sikhs, 209

Farid, Shaikh, 100
fasting, 219, 239, 253; Ayambil, 187, 192–95; Hindu, 193; and Jains, 187, 188, 192–98; and Ramanandis, 167, 170, 173, 174; and Sikhs, 201, 212; and St. Anthony's shrine, 57, 59; Updhan, 195–98. *See also* food; *upavasa*
fate, 229–30, 231n1
Fatiha, 65
"Feasting and Fasting" (McGee), 235, 236, 237, 238, 239, 244
Fenech, Louis E., 210–16
fertility, 11, 45–49, 250
fertility rites, 49, 51–56
financial metaphors, 8, 32–33. *See also* debt
firepots, 35–36, 141, 253; ill., 34, 35, 37
fire-walking, 4, 5, 118, 119, 122, 253
Five Pillars of Islam, 96, 103n11
food, 57–58, 96, 195, 219. *See also* fasting
food offerings, 19, 117
food restrictions, 173–74, 191, 221
footwash ritual, 204
France, 8
Francis Xavier, St., 47, 63n8
Frazer, James G., 124
fulfillment vows. *See* vow fulfillment

Gandhi, Indira, 212
Ganesh, 227
Ganesha temple, 141
Ganges River, 221
garlands, 158–59, 195
Garuda, 153
gender, 29–30, 43, 231, 236–27, 250, 253. *See also* women
geography: and religious traditions, 2–3, 82
Germany, 1, 6, 129–44
ghats, 221; defined, 259
al -Ghazali, 92
gifts, 32, 33. *See also* offerings
glossolalia, 36
goats. *See* animal sacrifices

gods, 109, 111, 125
Goonasekera, Sunil, 107–28
gopuram, 132; defined, 259
Gorakhnath, 167
Govind, Raja Gaur, 90
grahayo, 109, 110–11; defined, 259
Greek Orthodox, 12n3
Grnath, 208
guardian deities, 190
Gujarat, 188
Gummersbach, 141
gunas, 237; defined, 259
Gurdwara Reform Movement, 211
gurdwaras, 209, 211, 212; defined, 259
Gur-Sobha, 208
Guru: eternal, 208, 209, 210
Guru Amar Das, 203, 204
Guru Arjan, 202
Guru Gobind Singh, 203, 207, 208
Guru Granth Sahib, 208, 209; defined, 259
Guru Nanak, 201, 202, 203, 204, 205, 207, 211, 213
Guru Ram Das, 209
gurus: Jain, 195; Ramanandi, 173, 181–82, 183, 184n9; Sikh, 201–11
guru vandan: defined, 259
guru worship, 195

hadith, 97; defined, 259
hagiography, 88–91, 101, 102
hair: and Mahatyagis, 180
hair shaving, 32, 40n8, 49–51, 57, 83; ill., 50, 51; and women, 52. *See also* tonsure
Hamid, Shahul. *See* Shahul Hamid
Hanafi, 96–97
Hannover, 141
Haque, Ennamul, 88
Hare Krishnas, 129
Harimandir Sahib, 210–11; defined, 259
Harman, William P., 1–23, 25–41, 249–55
harmonium, 158
Hazrath, 65
Hazrat Nuruddin Mupti, 68

healing, 27–28, 32, 36–38, 49, 250; and Mariyamman, 29; and Shahul Hamid, 71–72; and St. Anne, 47; and St. Anthony, 48; and St. John de Britto, 45
healing rituals, 57–60
health, 27–28; and Mariyamman, 39n5
Hinduism, 1–2, 4–5, 11, 43, 202; and Arya Samaj, 239; and ashrama, 191; gender-specific vows in, 253; Tamil, 6, 36–37, 60; Tantric traditions in, 167; and women, 6
Hindus, 6, 76; and *asanam*, 58; in Germany, 129–44, 253; and hair shaving, 50; and Jains, 199n4; and Muslims, 80–84, 95; and *nerccais*, 43, 45; and possession, 59–60; and Shahul Hamid, 65, 67, 75; and shared vows, 58, 77, 79, 101; and St. Anne, 47; and St. Anthony, 48; and suffering, 220
Hindu temples, 77; in Germany, 129–44; map, *133*
hook swinging, 4, 5; ill., 138. *See also* piercing
householders, 146, 148, 174, 176, 191, 213
hundi, 65; defined, 260. *See also* offering boxes
husbands, 194, 235–44. *See also* familial well-being
hymns. *See* songs

Ibrahim, 99
icons, 221, 222, 224; ill., 222
Ideal Wife and Husband (Miran Yati), 239
identity-forming vows, 252–53
idolatry, 3
imanfikan, 203; defined, 260
immigrants, 1, 6, 129–44
inactivity: and Jains, 190, 192
inculturation, 82–83
initiation ceremony: Sikh, 205–209
institutional boundaries, 252
institutional vows, 4
intention: and Hindus, 226; and Jains, 191–95

intentionality, 31, 170
interaction, 5
intercession, 91
interdependence, 237
International Society for Krishna Consciousness (Hare Krishnas), 129
investors, 7
Irankanatan, 27
Ireland, 8
Isakki Amman, 48, 59, 60
Islam, 2, 3, 66, 83, 84, 102; in Bangladesh, 90; global *versus* local practices, 102; and Shah Jalal, 90; women in, 6. *See also* Muslims

jagara, 153; defined, 260
jaikara, 2–7, 206–207; defined, 260
Jaini, Padmanabh S., 191
Jainism, 125nn2–3, 167, 187–200; and gender-specific vows, 253; women in, 6, 10
Jains, 7, 10, 167, 187–200
jal tap, 180
Japji, 207
Jews, 7
jihad, 90
al-Jilani Muhiyudin Abd al Qadir (Katiru), 66, 68
Jinas, 7, 10, 188, 189–90, 194, 198; defined, 260
jinn, 88
John de Britto, St., 252; and coconut sapling rite, 52–53; and cradle rite, 56; and hair shaving rite, 50; and shared deities, 61; shrine, 1, 3, 45–46
Juhara Bibi, 68

Kaba, 99; defined, 260
kacchahira, 207; defined, 260
Kadavara, 117
Kallars, 45, 46
Kamakshi Ampal, Sri, 142; temple, 132, 134–42
Kanda Kumara, 109, 110–19, 122, 124; ill., 109; shrine, 1, 113, 114; theodicy and, 122–23

Kandasami, 127n20
kangha, 207; defined, 260
Kanjul Karaamattu, 67
kankanankattutal, 32; defined, 260
Kapaleeshvara Temple, 157
kappukkattutal, 32; defined, 260
kapurala, 108, 113, 114, 118; defined, 260
kara, 207; defined, 260
karamah, 76; defined, 260
karamat, 76, 77, 79, 99; defined, 260
karaniyametta, 119; defined, 260
karma, 10, 227, 228, 230, 231; and Buddhism, 123, 124, 125; defined, 260; and Hindus, 166, 220; and Jainism, 187–200; and Ramanandis, 170; and Tamil poets, 151
karmayoga, 148; defined, 260
Kartik, 220, 245n7
Kartik Mahatmyas, 220–21, 227, 230
Kartik *puja,* 221–24, 227–30; ill., 223
Kartik *vrat,* 221–25, 227–30; defined, 260
Karunanidhi, 157
karva chauth vrat, 239–40; defined, 260. See also husbands
katampattal, 32; defined, 260
Kataragama, xvii, 1, 7, 107–28
katha, 226, 239–40; defined, 261
Katiya Baba, 174
kavati, 117, 119; defined, 261; in German Tamil Hindu temples, 134, 135, 137–40; in Sri Lanka, 137, 139
kavi, 60; defined, 261
kavya, 67; defined, 261
Kelting, M. Whitney, 187–200
kes, 207; defined, 261
Ketu, 110; defined, 261
Keyes, Charles F., 230–31
khadims, 91, 93; defined, 261
khak diksha, 178
Khalsa, 3, 9, 204–13; defined, 261
Khalsa Code of Conduct, 205, 207, 208, 213
Khalsa Panth, 207, 208
khande di pahul, 205–209; defined, 261

Khan Jahan Ali, 87, 88, 90, 91
Kharat, Shankarrao, 15–21
Khardeswari Babas, 176–77
Khulna, 88
Khwaja Moin uddin Chisti, 87, 94
Kiliru (Khazir), 68
Kirinda, 108
Kiri Vehera, 113, 114
Kishwar, Madhu, 243
Knott, Kim, 231
Krishna, 148, 222–23, 236, 237, 239
Kshatriyas, 236, 237, 238
Kuja, 110–11
Kulam Katiru Navalar, Sri la Sri, 67
kula teiyvam, 44, 46, 48, 59, 60, 61, 252; defined, 261
Kumbha Mela, 180–81
kurukkal, 141; defined, 261
kurusadi, 47; defined, 261
kuttiyaattam, 32; defined, 261. See also circumambulation
kutumivankutal, 32; defined, 261. See also hair shaving

Laidlaw, James, 194, 196
Lakshman, 240
Lamb, Ramdas, 165–85
langoti, 174, 178, 180; defined, 261
The Legacy of Women's Uplift in India (Llewellyn), 243
legality, 101; and *baras,* 123–24; of Tamils in Germany, 131–32; of vows, 96–97
liberation, 250; and Jainism, 187–200; and Sikhs, 202
lifelong vows, 171–72, 191
Llewellyn, Jack E., 235–46
lodging: and Ramanadis, 176
Loha Langari, 174
Long, J. Bruce, 152, 153
lungi, 178; defined, 261

Madurai, 47, 76
Madurai Temple, 40n11
magic, 118, 124
magical monks, 190

Mahabharata, 100
mahadevale: of Kataragama, 113, 114, 117, 118
mahants, 211–12
Maharashtra, 188
Mahashivaratri, 152–53, 154, 157, 160; defined, 261
Mahatyagis, 172, 174, 176, 177, 180–81; defined, 261
Mahavir, 188
maidan tap, 180
Maijbandar, 95, 96, 101
maintenance vows, 10–11
maitri, 119; defined, 261
maitri bhavana, 119
Maitri Bodhisattva, 109–10
majlis, 99, 101
Malaysia, 71, 77
manat, 87–105; defined, 261
Mandana Mishra, 241
mangala, 119; defined, 261
Manganur, 61
Manicandra, 193
Manikkavacakar, 8
mannat manani, 209; defined, 262
Mantralayam, 79
mantras, 118, 119, 170, 194, 195, 197; defined, 262
Manu, 236
Manushi, 243
maps, xix, 133
Maravas, 45–46, 47
Mariai, 16
Mariyamman, 3, 7, 10, 61; negotiations with, 25–41; vows to, 28–38
Mariyamman Temple, 1, 25–41, 252
marriage, 29, 80, 147, 148, 223; and Jains, 196–98; and Sikhs, 205, 208–209, 213. *See also* women
martyrdom, 211, 213
matams, 148, 152, 158; defined, 262
Maule-e-Salaam Garasiyas, 82
maun, 176; defined, 262
Mauni Babas, 169, 176
mawlids, 91, 101; defined, 262
maya, 155; defined, 262

Maynasundari, 193, 194; defined, 262
mazars, 1, 87–105, 103n12; defined, 262. *See also* shrines
McGee, Mary, 31, 147–48, 219, 225, 231, 235–40, 243, 244
Mecca, 97, 99, 102
Medina, 102
Meenakshi Amman, 76
Meeran Sahib, 65, 66
Meherats, 82
Meister, Michael, 82, 83
mendicants, 187–98
merit, 112, 113, 226–27, 238; and Jainism, 187–200
Metcalfe, Barbara, 80–81
migrants, 129–44
Miller, Barbara Stoler, 236
Mirabai, 68
miracles, 90, 99, 100; and Shahul Hamid, 66, 68, 69–71; Sufi, 91
al-Misri, Ahmad ibn Naqib, 97
moksha, 152, 159, 238, 254; defined, 262
monasticism, 165–85
monks: Jain, 188. *See also* mendicants; monasticism
morality, 3
More, J. B. P., 82
Moreno-Arcas, Manuel, 32–33
Morocco, 88
Mughals, 203; defined, 262
Muhammad, Prophet, 82, 90, 91, 92, 93, 99, 102
Muhiyudin Abd al-Qadir (Katiru) al-Jilani, 67
mukti, 171
multiculturalism, 80
munajat, 92; defined, 262
mundane vows, 250–54
Munjiya Baba, 174; ill., 175
muri, 3, 44, 52, 55; defined, 262. *See also* promissory note
murti (murtti), 142
Murtipujaks, 188; defined, 262
Murugan, 33, 79, 111, 137, 138, 139, 140, 141
Murukan, 40n11

muruten, 117; defined, 262
music, 95, 101, 117, 137, 139, 157;
 Carnatic, 151, 152, 157–58. *See also*
 songs
Muslims, 3, 11, 67, 77, 79, 80–83; and
 asanam, 58; Bengali, 102; gender-
 specific vows and, 253; journals by,
 92; and Shah Jalal, 90; at shrine of
 Shahul Hamid, 65. *See also* Islam
Muthumariamman, Sri, 141

Nadars, 46
Nadar Uvari, 63n4
nadhr, 104n22; defined, 262
Nagapattinam, 66
nagaswaram, 158; defined, 262
Nagore, xvii, 1, 63, 65, 66, 67, 251
Nagore Andavar, 65, 66
Nagore Dargah, 69
Naicker, E. V. Ramasami, 157
Naiks, 21n1
Nakur Puranam, 67, 77
nam dan ishnan, 204
Nanak Panth, 204
Nankana Sahib, 211–12
Narayanan, Vasudha, 63, 65–85
Nasirabad, 88
Natha, 109, 122, 123
nationalism, 205, 253
navagraha: defined, 262. *See also* planets
navakkirakam: defined, 262. *See also*
 planets
Navaratri, 173
"Navas," 15n
Navkar Mantra, 193, 194; defined, 262
Navpad Oli, 192
Nayakar, 65
negotiations, 10, 25–41, 253
neologism, 83
nerccais, 43, 44–45, 47, 49–60, 62, 63;
 fertility, 51–56; hair-shaving, 49–51;
 healing, 57–60. *See also* devotional
 rites
nertti, 131
nerttikkatan, 31, 32, 43, 44, 60; defined,
 262. *See also nerccais*

New Delhi, xvii, 1
Nibandha, 148
nirahar, 173, 174; defined, 262
nishacara, 152; defined, 263
nondevotional rites, 11, 44–45
nonpu, 32; defined, 263
normative vows, 252

oaths: Sikh, 201, 202, 203, 206–207,
 211, 212, 213
offering boxes, 27, 73, 96; ill., 76. *See
 also hundi; untiyal*
offerings, 5, 9, 10, 16, 43, 51, 77, 113,
 114, 117, 252; in cradle rite, 56; at
 Muslim shrines, 92; to Shahul Hamid,
 72, 73. *See also* gifts; *puja;* sacrifices
Oli, 192; defined, 263
oppression: against women, 243
oppu, 108–109; defined, 263
oppukaranna, 112
oppukeruva, 116, 122
oppukirima, 113
ordination, 198
Oriyur, xvii, 45, 46, 47, 49, 61
Osho Movement, 129
osmosis, 82, 83
otuvars, 152, 153–54, 156, 157; defined,
 263
Our Lady of Good Health, 49, 56

pacckkhan, 191; defined, 263
Padma Purana, 153, 230
Padua, 47, 48
paimashikan, 203; defined, 263
pakkacedil, 32; defined, 263
Palani Hills, 33
Palaniyanti Pillai, 71
Pallars, 45, 46
palm trees, 71
pan, 151, 156, 158; defined, 263
panchasila, 107
Panch pir, 100
Pandavas, 100
pandura, 112, 113
panj banis, 206; defined, 263
panj piare, 205

pansil, 107; defined, 263
Panth, 208; defined, 263
parameshvar, 240, 241
Paravas, 47, 48, 49
Parvati, 167, 230, 239
Paryusan, 192; defined, 263
Paskarakurukkal, Sri, 139, 141
pativratas, 240–43; defined, 263
patni, 241, 242
patnivrata, 243; defined, 263
Pattini, 109, 110, 122
Pearson, Anne, 29, 148, 153, 231
Pechilis, Karen, 147–63
Penang (Malaysia), 69
peni: defined, 263
peni batha, 117
Peterson, Indira, 156
phalahar, 173–74, 180; defined, 263
Pheruman, Jathedar Darshan Singh, 212
piercing, 30, 36, 134, 135, 137–40
piety, 202, 219
pihita, 108; defined, 263
pilgrimages, 5, 91, 96, 97, 226, 252; in Bangladesh, 93; in hymns, 158, 160; Jain, 189; to Kataragama, 113; and Shiva, 149. *See also ziyarat*
pilgrims, 61, 63, 66; to Kataragama, 111–12; and Shahul Hamid, 71
Pintchman, Tracy, 219–33
pirarttanai, 31
pirattinai, 263
Pir-narayan, 100
pirs, 11, 67, 100; at Bangladesh Sufi shrines, 87–105; defined, 263. *See also* saints
planets, 109, 110–11, 118, 220
Plutarch, 81
poets: Tamil, 149–51
politicians, 87
Portugal, 8
poruttanai, 31, 263
possession, 59–60; ill., 60
power, 79, 167; of saints, 87, 88, 99; supernatural, 4, 11, 28–29, 39nn2–3, 125, 250, 254; yogic, 167
poya, 107; defined, 264

prane, 116, 124; defined, 264
Pratap Singh, 69, 70
prathana, 76
pratigya, 168, 170–71; defined, 264
pratikraman: defined, 264. *See also* confession
prayers, 5, 79, 92, 93, 95, 97, 100, 101, 253; and Jains, 189–90, 195, 196; and Shahul Hamid, 77, 79; and Sikhs, 206, 209, 213. *See also yatikava*
preta, 112
priests, 4, 62, 139, 141–42; and animal sacrifices, 51; and baby auctioning rite, 55; and hair shaving rite, 49–50; at Kataragama, 118–19
processions, 132–42
promesas, 12n6; defined, 264
promissory note, 51, 54–55. *See also muri*
promissory rites, 49
prostitutes, 4
Protestants, 131
public displays, 3–4
puja, 113, 114, 122, 138, 153, 219, 228; defined, 264; and *vrats,* 226. *See also* Kartik *puja;* offerings; worship
puja-path, 228
pujaris, 59, 60; defined, 264
puja vattiya, 114; defined, 264; ill., 115
Pune, xviii
Punjab, 212, 213
punyanumodana, 113; defined, 264
Puranas, 148, 167, 220, 222, 223; defined, 264

Qur'an, 92, 93, 101
Qutb, 65

Radha, 232n7
ragas, 151, 158; defined, 264
Raghavendra, 79
Rahit, 205, 207, 208, 213; defined, 264
Rahu, 110; defined, 264
Raj, Selva J., 1–13, 43–64, 249–55
Rajannamalai Hall, 152
Rajasthan, 188

Ram, 168, 181, 182, 202, 240, 242
Ramachandran, M. G., 157
Ramananda Sampraday, 6, 165–85, 250; history of, 167–68; subgroups of, 177–82
Ramanandis, 168–85; defined, 264; ill., 171, 181
Ramayana, 82, 167, 242
Ramcharitmanas, 182
Ramnaumi, 173
Rangam, Sri, 27
rashi, 110; defined, 264
ratana, 119; defined, 264
Ratnagireeshwar Temple, 153
rebirth, 11, 182, 189, 250, 253
reciprocity, 228
recitation, 92, 97, 100, 101
religion, 3–4, 147; and culture, 82; and women, 225
religious affiliations, 7
religious boundaries, 9, 61–62, 63, 252, 254; between Hindus and Muslims, 80–83
religious dialogue, 254
religious identities, 83, 101, 102
religious reform, 92
religious traditions, 2–3, 6–7, 80, 81, 225, 252, 254; in the diaspora, 130; Western, 7, 8, 11
renouncers, 147–49; ill., 31
renunciants, 6, 165–85. *See also* ascetics
repayment, 32–33, 44
repentance, 153, 160
Reynolds, Holly Baker, 29
rice-flour healing ritual, 29; ill., *30*
rituals, 4, 5, 9, 112; women's, 225
ritual specialists, 4, 118
rolling ritual. *See* circumambulation
rudraksha, 158; defined, 264
rupe, 116, 124; defined, 264

sacred place: and efficacy of vows, 99–100; and Islam, 99
sacred powers, 59
sacred space, 252
sacrifices, 43; to Mariyamman, 33, 36. *See also* offerings

sadhana, 166, 170, 177; defined, 264
sadhus, 161n4; defined, 264; Ramanandi, 165–85. *See also* ascetics
saints, 61, 90, 153; in Bangladesh, 91; female, 101; power of, 87, 88, 99. *See also* pirs
Saithgumbad Masjid, 90
salah, 92, 99; defined, 264
salvation, 250
samadhi, 79, 151; defined, 264
Saman, 122
Samayapuram, xviii, 1, 25–41; and animal sacrifices, 77
Sampraday: defined, 264. *See also* Ramananda Sampraday
Sangeet Natak Academy award, 157
Sani, 111
sankalp, 168, 170–72, 173, 191, 211; Danrdiya, 178; defined, 264
Sankara, 240; defined, 264
sannyasin, 147–49; defined, 265
Sant Fateh Singh, 212
Saturn, 66
Satya, 100
saubhagya, 225
Sayid Abdul Khader, 68
Sayid Muhammad Kavud (Ghouse), 68
Scandinavia, 140
sejda, 95; defined, 265
self-sacrifice, 243, 250
Senasura, 111
sense worlds, 130–31, 142
Sered, Susan, 225
sex workers, 94, 100, 102
Shah Amanat, 94–95
Shah Badar, 100
Shah Jalal, 87, 88, 90, 91, 97, 100, 101–102
Shah Muhsin, 100
Shah Sultan Balkhi, 88
Shah Sultan Bistami, 91
Shahul Hamid, 1, 65–85, 251, 252; life of, 67–69; tomb ill., 70
Shaivas, 152, 154, 158, 159, 160; defined, 265
Shaiva Siddhanta, 154; defined, 265
Shaivite Nagas, 174

Shaivites, 178
shakti, 76, 77, 79, 142; defined, 265
Shani, 138
shapath, 168; defined, 265
shared deities, 43–64
shared space, 43–64, 80, 83
shared vows, 43–64; Hindus and, 58, 77, 79, 101
Shaw, Rosalind, 80, 81, 82
Shiva, 66, 117, 139, 147–63, 167, 221, 230, 239
Shivaratri: defined, 265. *See also* Mahashivaratri
shrines, 7; in Bangladesh, 87–105; economic viability of, 97–99; of St. Anne, 47; of St. Anthony, 47–49; of St. John de Britto, 45–46; Sufi, 87–105. *See also mazars*
Shripal, 193–94; defined, 265
Shudras, 236
Shvetambar, 188; defined, 265
siddhacakra, 193, 194; defined, 265
siddhi, 169; defined, 265
Sikh Bangla Saheb Gurdwara, 1
Sikh Panth, 204, 213
Sikh Rahit Maryada, 205, 209, 210; defined, 265
Sikhs, 2–3, 9, 201–16; Akali, 211–12; Khalsa, 204–13; nationalism of, 205
sil, 107; defined, 265
silence, 112, 169, 170, 190, 192
sin, 189, 192, 226–27, 230
Singapore, 69, 71, 77
Singh, Gian, 210
Singh, Pashaura, 210–16
Singh, Vir, 210
Singh Sabha, 205, 210
singing, 147–63. *See also* music; songs
Siromani, Vidvananda, 67
Sita, 242
Sivaratri, 152
Skanda, 111
Skanda Kumara, 127n20
songs, 190, 209, 221. *See also* music; singing
sonic theology, 156
sorcery, 112, 220

soteriological vows, 107–108, 250–54
soteriology, 5, 10–11, 107
souls, 189, 190
Spain, 8, 12n4, 62
Sri Lanka, 2, 107–28; immigrants in Germany, 1, 6, 129–44
Stewart, Charles, 80, 81, 82
Stewart, Tony, 81
stupa, 113, 114; defined, 265
Sufi shrines, 87–105
suhag, 225; defined, 265
Suhi Chhant 2, 209
Sukhmani Sahib, 202
sukh sukhani, 209; defined, 265
Sultan, Shah, 100
Suniyam, 109, 110
Sunna, 93; defined, 265
supernatural, 2, 5–6, 7, 8, 9, 253
supernatural power, 4, 11, 28–29, 125, 250, 254; in Western monotheism, 39nn2–3
suras, 92; defined, 265
sutras, 119; defined, 265
suttare: defined, 265
swami: defined, 265
Swami Miran Yati, 239–41
Swaminathan, Dharmapuram P., 153–54, 157–60, 161n7
Swaminathan, Lalgudi, 157, 161n7
Swami Ramananda, 167–68
Swami Ramanuja, 168
Switzerland, 140
Sylhet, 90
syncretism, 80–84
synergism, 83
Syria, 88

Taimiya, Ibn, 91
tali, 29; defined, 266. *See also* marriage
Talib, G. S., 211
Tamil, 8, 31–32
Tamil Catholics, 43–64, 131
Tamil Nadu, 1, 25, 66, 67
Tamils, 6; in Germany, 129–44
Tamin Ansari, 75
Tampiran, Arulnampi, 157
Tantric traditions, 167

tap, 178–80, 188, 192; defined, 266
tapas, 166, 167, 244n2; defined, 266
tapasya, 167, 169, 174, 176, 177, 178; defined, 266
Tara Singh, Master, 212
teemiti, 32, 266
temples: in Germany, 129–44; ill., 135, 137, 138
Tevaram, 151, 152, 153, 154, 157, 158; defined, 266
thanksgiving rites, 44, 49, 73, 77, 252
theodicy, 122–23
Theyagaraya Nagar, 154
tikkulipayatal, 32; defined, 266
Tillai, 158
time: and Jains, 199n3
tiraya, 116–17; defined, 266
Tiruchendur, 79
Tiruchirapalli, 47
Tirukkarana Puranam ("The Sacred Purana or Narrative of Divine Miracles"), 67
Tirumalai Chetti, 71
Tirumayilai Karaneeccaram Temple, 158
Tirumuraikantapuranam, 161n6
Tiru Nagai, 66
Tirunallaru, 66
Tirunavukkaracar, 150
Tirupati, 76
Tirupati Hills, 33
Tiru Valivalam, 155
Tissamaharama, 111, 112, 113, 114
tithi, 152; defined, 266
"To Keep the [Marriage] Tali Strong": Women's Rituals in Tamilnad, India (Reynolds), 29
tomb visitation, 91–92
tongue-piercing, 4, 5
tonsure, 72, 77, 83; ill., 52. *See also* hair shaving
tradition. *See* religious traditions
trances, 117, 139
transactions, 10, 30
Transcendental Mediation, 129
transgressive vows, 252
Tree of Life, 99–100

tribute vows, 251–52
Trinidad, 130
tri tap, 178–80; defined, 266
truthfulness, 203, 207, 228
Tulasi, 71
Tulsi, 223
turtles, 88; ill., 89
Tyagis, 178–80; defined, 266; ill., 179

Udayars, 45, 46
Uddin, Sufia, 87–105
ulama, 93; defined, 266
Umdat al-salik, 97
untiyal, 27. *See also hundi;* offering boxes
Upanishads, 166
upavasa, 153; defined, 266. *See also* fasting
Updhan, 187, 195–98; defined, 266
urdwabahu, 177
Urmila, 240
urs, 91, 95, 100; defined, 266
Urudhara Nari (Devi), 242
utsav, 226
utsava murti, 139; defined, 266
Uvari, xviii, 47–48, 61; and healing, 57

vachan, 168
vahana, 137; defined, 266
Vahiguru, 208; defined, 266
Vaidik Nari (Miran Yati), 240
Vaidik Sopan (Arya), 241, 242
Vairagis, 168–85; defined, 266
vairagya, 174, 184n7; defined, 266
Vairavan, 139
Vaishnava, 221, 224; defined, 266
Vaishyas, 236
Vaitheesvaran Koil, 77, 79
Valli, 123
Valmiki, 167, 242
varaprasadi, 76; defined, 266
variation, 83
vars, 204
vattiya, 114; defined, 266; ill., 115
Vedas, 241
The Vedic Woman (Miran Yati), 240

Velankanni, 50, 56, 65, 80
Velkanni, 61
Vellala, 46, 47
Venkateswara, 33, 76
Vertovec, Steve, 130
vimana, 132; defined, 266
Vinayakar Alayam,Sri Sithi, 141
violence, 80, 83–84
virakt, 168; defined, 267
Virgin Mary, 66, 80
Virvati, 239
Vishna, 110
Vishnu, 27, 109, 110, 114, 122, 123, 221, 222, 223, 229, 230
Vishwamitra, 167
Visishtadvaita, 168
vow classification, 147–48
vow fulfillment, 3, 4, 8, 142, 251; in Bangladesh, 95–97; and Buddhists, 108–109, 112–13, 116; in Kataragama, 116; and *nerccais,* 44, 49; and Shahul Hamid, 72–75; and Sikhs, 210–11, 213
vrata, 31–32, 76, 107, 131, 188
vrat narratives, 226–27, 230, 231
vrats, 12n6, 148, 160, 166, 171, 173, 219–20, 228; and Arya Samaj, 238–40; and celibacy, 172; Danrdiya, 178; defined, 267; failures of, 219–33; and Jains, 188, 199n5; and karma, 151; and *puja,* 226; and Ramanandis, 168, 169; and sadhus, 172; Sikh, 202, 213; structure of, 226; women and, 153, 220, 221–25, 231, 235–46. *See also* Kartik *vrat*
vratu, 214n3

Wadley, Susan, 151, 226–27, 230
al-Wakil Durubi, Sheikh Abd, 97
wali, 67; defined, 267
Western traditions, 7, 8, 11, 39nn2–3
Whitehead, Alfred North, 2

witchcraft, 39n2, 112, 220
women, 4, 6, 12n6, 28, 29–30, 32, 77, 79, 148; in Bangladesh, 93–94, 100; and the Bhagavad Gita, 236–37; in German Tamil temples, 134, 136, 140, 141; Hindu, 6, 193, 220, 231, 237; and husbands, 235–44; Jain, 6, 7, 10, 191, 192, 193, 194, 195, 196–98; and Kartik *puja,* 221–24, 227, 230; and Kartik *vrat,* 221–25; and Mariyamman, *31, 34*; medieval, 161n2; Muslim, 6; and possession, 59–60; as renunciants, 184n2; and rituals, 225; role of, 238; and Shah Jalal, 103n4; Sikh, 207, 209, 213, 214n21; singers, 152, 154; and *vrats,* 153, 220, 225, 231, 235–46. *See also* familial well-being; marriage
worship, 32, 96, 97; Jain, 189, 192, 194; and Mariyamman, 28; Sikh, 205. *See also puja*

yaka, 112
yal, 154; defined, 267
yantras, 190, 193, 194, 195, 197; defined, 267
Yashoda, 222
yatikava, 113, 119; defined, 267. *See also* prayers
yogic powers, 167
yogic traditions, 167
yogis, 167, 250
Yousof, Gulam-Sarwar, 77
Yusuf (Shahul Hamid's son), 68, 69, 70, 73

Zaehner, R. C., 236
Zafar-namah, 201, 203–204
Zinda Pir, 104n23
ziyarat, 88, 91, 100, 104n20; defined, 267. *See also* pilgrimages